"A powerful testament to the faith and resilience of African American Christian women. Through deeply personal stories, these remarkable women reveal what it means to stay true to who they are as women of faith. . . . More than a collection of stories, this book is an invitation to see yourself, break through stereotypes, and live authentically."

—**Keturah Adams**, PhD, assistant professor of chemistry, Southwestern Oklahoma State University

"Listen to these voices as they clarify that our shared identity as children of God supersedes any other identity. Particularly, Dr. Victoria Carter Jones's chapter 'She Came to Slay' elucidates what it means to be a Christ follower, a slayer, for good. She gives examples from history, from Scripture, from her own personal life, and then, as a punchline at the end, she'll inspire *you* to act on 'slaying it' for the Lord by putting Him first in your life!"

—**Emily Atwood**, photographer, discipler, and stay-at-home mom of nine

"Beautiful, wise, and full of resilience, these essays invite you to gather and learn from expert women as they teach practical life lessons, navigate the intersecting struggles of racism and sexism, and empower each other as sisters in Christ."

—**Beth Allison Barr**, James Vardaman professor of history, Baylor University, and author of *The Making of Biblical Womanhood*

"This book beautifully showcases the incredible strength, wisdom, and joy that African American women bring to the table. It is a powerful read that uplifts and inspires you on your journey."

—**Delesa Franklin**, EdD, department chair and assistant professor, College of Education & Behavioral Sciences, Houston Christian University

"I was so moved by these stories of courage forged by faith under fire. These authors represent a kaleidoscope of different life situations, but a common theme runs through them all. These are women, to a one, who not only have bravely navigated their own God-stories but are stretching an arm out to help the rest of us navigate ours."

—**Christy Hurst**, Bible study teacher, Nacogdoches, Texas

"*Woman to Woman* is a collection of personal stories that touched the core of my being. The value of the writers' willingness to share a portion of their lives in order to help others is immeasurable. I highly recommend this book for women who find themselves in a season of life that is unfamiliar and in need of wisdom to navigate life's challenges."

—**Margaree King Mitchell**, author and winner of Living the Dream Award

"The voices of these multifaceted women who have navigated grief, joy, body image, and mental health stigmas are not fresh air. As someone in her mid-twenties I an

discussed openly, especially in the realm of religion. I felt seen and a sense of comradery in knowing other women have endured and pushed through similar situations I have faced."

—**Mikayla Joy Oberlton**, Miss Harris County 2024, NBCDI and the OpEd Project Public Voices Fellow 2024, Miss Prairie View 2023, Miss Georgia 2021

"Never before have I found a book that speaks to me as a Black woman holistically—mind, body, and spirit! And from such wise and accomplished scholars, professionals, and amazing mothers who are thriving in their spiritual, professional, and familial lives. This book is a literal answer to my prayers for guidance as a Black mother in the spiritual and cultural rearing of my children."

—**Michelle Elaine Ogletree**, actress, influencer, and cocreator of *Cast Me . . . !*

"I found the transparency in *Woman to Woman* refreshing. It is beautiful to witness a marginalized group such as African American women use their voices and share their firsthand experiences. I believe this book will empower more women of color to be confident in telling their stories and owning their narratives."

—**Dr. Alysn "Aly" Otinga**, educator and children's book author

"African American women have our own unique perspective of wisdom that's captured in these pages. That wisdom is powerful enough to transform the world and practical enough to guide your day-to-day life. You will reread the essays in this book again and again."

—**Kristen L. Pope**, award-winning journalist

"Sisters, this book is written for us by us. In it, African American Christian women share their stories of God's faithfulness, unfiltered and unwhitewashed. . . . These stories will encourage and inform you and remind you of God's sufficient grace toward us to become all God has called us authentically to be."

—**Jeanne Porter King**, PhD, author, pastor, and women's leadership coach

"*Woman to Woman* is a literary portrait of African American God-fearing women that captivates your attention by sharing faith, purpose, pain, joy, boldness, perseverance, and victory. A treasure for all women!"

—**Rev. Julie L. Price**, senior pastor, Northwestern Community Baptist Church, Detroit, Michigan

"A tapestry of inspiring narratives that illuminate the resilience, faith, and triumph of brilliant African American women. Each story serves as a testament to their unwavering spirit and the divine favor that guides their journeys. This compelling collection not only celebrates their unique experiences but also invites readers to reflect on the profound impact of community, courage, and divine grace."

—**Rev. Barbara D. Simon**, Power House Church of God, Metairie, Louisiana

WOMAN TO WOMAN

African American Voices on Faith, Resilience, and Joy

Norvella P. Carter, PhD, General Editor
Quinita Ogletree, PhD, Editor
Kamala V. Williams, PhD, Editor
Karon Parker, Consulting Editor
Matthew Parker, Consulting Editor

Woman to Woman: African American Voices on Faith, Resilience, and Joy
© 2025 by Institute for Black Family Development

Chapter 12 by Joyce M. Dinkins and chapter 15 by Kamala V. Williams each included with permission of the author.

All rights reserved.

Requests for permission to quote from this book should be directed to: Permissions Department, Our Daily Bread Publishing, PO Box 3566, Grand Rapids, MI 49501; or contact us by email at permissionsdept@odb.org.

Scripture quotations, unless otherwise indicated, are taken from the Holy Bible, New International Version®, NIV®. Copyright © 1973, 1978, 1984, 2011 by Biblica, Inc.™ Used by permission of Zondervan. All rights reserved worldwide. www.zondervan.com.

  Scripture quotations marked MSG are taken from *The Message*, copyright © 1993, 2002, 2018 by Eugene H. Peterson. Used by permission of NavPress. All rights reserved. Represented by Tyndale House Publishers.

  Scripture quotations marked NKJV are taken from the New King James Version®. Copyright © 1982 by Thomas Nelson. Used by permission. All rights reserved.

  Scripture quotations marked NLT are taken from the *Holy Bible*, New Living Translation, copyright © 1996, 2004, 2015 by Tyndale House Foundation. Used by permission of Tyndale House Publishers, Carol Stream, Illinois 60188. All rights reserved.

  Scripture quotations marked TLB are taken from *The Living Bible*, copyright © 1971 by Tyndale House Foundation. Used by permission of Tyndale House Publishers, Carol Stream, Illinois 60188. All rights reserved.

Interior design by Michael J. Williams

ISBN: 978-1-64070-293-6

Library of Congress Cataloging-in-Publication Data Available

Printed in the United States of America
25 26 27 28 29 30 31 32 / 8 7 6 5 4 3 2 1

Dedicated to the Institute for Black Family
Development, a powerful presence of the Lord
in the African American community

Contents

Acknowledgments, KARON PARKER   9
Introduction: Sharing Our Life-Giving Perspectives,
    NORVELLA P. CARTER   11

Part One: Knowing Who We Are: A Collective Perspective

1. Good Morning! The Shape of Things to Come: Circles of Leadership and Relationship, GEORGIA A. HILL   17
2. She Came to Slay: Warriors, Game-Changers, and Transformers in Black History and the Bible, VICTORIA CARTER JONES   33
3. Foreign Body: A Journey to Healthy Body Image and Self-Image, DEBBYE TURNER BELL   47
4. Girl, You Are Not a Black Superwoman: Dismantling Mental Health Stigmas and Barriers, SELENA D. TATE   61

Part Two: Relationships: God at the Center

5. How Single Women Thrive, DIANE PROCTOR REEDER   77
6. Marriage Built to Last: Withstanding Seasonal Challenges, MICHELLE M. OBLETON, QUINITA OGLETREE   89
7. Engaging Your Faith as African American Mothers: The Challenge of Rearing Our Sons and Daughters in a Difficult Society, DENEESE L. JONES   107

8. Mothers Loving a Different Kind of Brilliance: "You Are a Shining Star," GWENDOLYN C. WEBB, MICHELLE BRISCOE, CHINA M. JENKINS ... 121

9. When the Ties That Bind Get Tested, Torn, and Transformed, DIANA WANDIX-WHITE, ADRIA E. LUSTER ... 137

Part Three: Managing Complex Societal Challenges

10. Navigating the Digital World: Godly Practices Despite Secular Challenges, QUINITA OGLETREE, GENALYN L. JERKINS ... 153

11. Home and Career: A Balancing Act, VICKI HARRIS ... 169

12. Generational Wealth: Pursuing Wisdom and Prosperity, JOYCE M. DINKINS ... 183

13. The Church: Breaking the Unholy Triad of Sexism, Classism, and Racism, KELLIE CARTER JACKSON ... 199

Part Four: Going the Extra Mile for Self and Others

14. Discipling through Love and Relationship, ANGELA ABNEY ... 217

15. My Journey Caring for Parents with Alzheimer's: A Story of Unconditional Love, KAMALA V. WILLIAMS ... 229

16. Overcoming Grief: Sistas Sharing Journeys, Lessons, and Insights, NORVELLA P. CARTER ... 245

17. Leaving a Legacy: The Lives of Our Foremothers, African American Grandmothers, and Mothers, PATRICIA J. LARKE, ALTRICIA LARKE, MYRA HANEY-SINGLETON ... 261

Notes ... 277

About the Contributors ... 289

Acknowledgments

Books that we read and treasure don't simply happen; they start with a vision of meaningful work, and usually take a team of talented people to refine those books into beautiful works of art. *Women to Women*, the original book, started as a vision of Dr. Matthew Parker, president of the Institute for Black Family Development. He envisioned African American Christian women who could speak through their writings to impact a community of readers. He recruited talented writers, gifted editors, and capable publishers who could accomplish the task of producing an impactful Christian book. I applaud Dr. Parker, my husband, for spearheading this initiative, not once but twice, almost three decades apart. Many thanks to

> Matthew Parker, visionary of this current work titled *Woman to Woman* and the *Women to Women* book almost thirty years ago;

> Norvella P. Carter, author recruiter, general editor, and anchor for the editorial team, past and present;

> Quinita Ogletree, coeditor and technical specialist;

> Kamala V. Williams, coeditor and resource specialist;

> The contributors, whose legacy of faith in God, love for others, and persistent pursuit of *El Shaddai* (All-Sufficient One, Lord God Almighty) is positively changing lives forever;

> Joyce M. Dinkins, next-level editor, polisher, and refiner of writing, before and after retirement;

Our Daily Bread VOICES editorial team, designers, and rights team; and

Loretta Stephens and Mikayla Oberlton, readers for the project.

Much appreciation to everyone involved in the *Woman to Woman* project for their godly wisdom, for valuing the process, and for believing in this outcome equivalent to a wonderful feast. May you gain satisfaction as you read and walk the path before you with newness, trust, and hope in our Savior.

Kudos to all who read and share this work.

To God be the glory!

—Karon Parker, Consulting Editor

Introduction

Sharing Our Life-Giving Perspectives

> She is clothed with strength and dignity; she can laugh at the days to come. She speaks with wisdom, and faithful instruction is on her tongue.
> Proverbs 31:25–26

The Bible speaks to us about the power of a godly woman, painting this picture for everyone to grasp: women with God's wisdom and joy have a lasting, positive impact. You will find these types of godly women in this book, sharing strength, wisdom, and personality meant to contribute to the spiritual growth and transformation of others. These writers speak into our hearts and serve as catalysts to empower us in ways that please God.

Whether you are a new Christian believer, a seasoned prayer warrior, a Bible student—or a nonbeliever—we welcome you to read this book offered by women who are good at coming alongside. These are women who share God's truths and love for readers' encouragement and resilience. They offer a variety of experiences, lessons learned, and insights gathered on topics pertinent to us all. These women come from a diversity of backgrounds and disciplines—but all are Spirit-filled and African American.

Almost thirty years ago, I was asked to edit a similar book on the perspectives of fifteen African American Christian women, and that became a popular work. We have chosen to follow that work in this new edition, with chapters on social media, generational wealth, mental health, caregiving, overcoming grief, and other topics that researchers say are relevant.

Statistics about Black women and the entire Black population often portray dire and depressing conclusions. However, these writings, focused on God's truth, celebrate the reality of salvation offered through Jesus Christ. The illustrations here point to the redemptive, transformative power that His Spirit gives, breathing new life into our souls. We Christian African American women share *our* stories from our perspectives and analyses that provide a counternarrative to the stories others share. And it is through our lens that integrity, beauty, resilience, and positive outcomes are in view. Emerging from these contributors' hearts—contrary to the negative yet popular writings about African American women—these chapters portray joy, leadership, beauty, resilience, and the powerful impact of our history as godly women.

The joy that emanates from the pages of this book reflects the fruit of the Spirit—the joy of being who and how we are as Christians without doubts about our value and worth before God and the world.

An ongoing Harvard study begun in 1938 has been considering what makes people happy.[1] As a professor and researcher, I'm intrigued by this decades-old longitudinal study. Is it money, material things, a desired career, power, health, a mate, or exercise that brings happiness? Yet "happiness" is temporary, a fleeting feeling that does not sustain us. Only the permanent power of the Holy Spirit can give us *joy,* a gift only Christ can engender to those who belong to Him. God promised that we can have something more than brief happiness; through our relationship with Him we have a deep, lasting, permanent, abiding joy that permeates our very soul.

Joy is internal, God-given, and it impacts our attitude and perceptions about life. Unlike happiness, joy is with us during our trials, tears, pain, and suffering. Joy sustains us despite any and all circumstances. Joy represents the abundant life in Christ.

As you read the chapters in *Woman to Woman*, you will witness this theme underlying every chapter.

A team of twenty-four Christian African American women came together to produce the content of this book—to motivate, inspire, and uplift our spirits. In addition to being writers, amazingly, they are all leaders in their communities. They are pastors, consultants, a medical doctor (and former Miss America), businesswomen, teachers, professors, directors, presidents and vice presidents of institutions and corporations, editors, and educational administrators, to name some of their positions. One author has been leading a Bible study of more than nine hundred women for years. Others are on ministry boards, serve as university faculty, and are globe-trotters in their roles. Leadership is embodied in the themes of *Woman to Woman*, in the person of each author and in the principles they share. The authors are considered experts in their fields and have been God-sent to serve our souls through their writings.

This volume centers around commonalities and real-life needs for abundant living. You will find specific topics of interest to you, including challenges and lifestyles common to African American women. One section emphasizes and discusses a range of relationships because we were designed by God to need Him first and then each other. We hope that you will benefit from this text as an individual and in your contexts with others and that you will share this with many in discussion, personal time, and Bible study.

Much joy as you read and share!

—Norvella P. Carter, General Editor

PART ONE

KNOWING WHO WE ARE

A Collective Perspective

Good Morning! The Shape of Things to Come
Circles of Leadership and Relationship

GEORGIA A. HILL

His compassions never fail. They are new every morning.
Lamentations 3:22–23

Poised between midnight's darkness and the dawn's new light, we find ourselves in a tumultuous, transformative moment. As a new torch of leadership passes into the firm grasp of African American women, we contemplate the light of our faith and the words of poets speaking at the moment of presidential transfer of power. From the poet's perch on separate presidential inaugurations, Maya Angelou and Amanda Gorman summoned Americans to hope in the light of the new moment. Challenging us to be the light (Amanda Gorman, "The Hill We Climb"[1]) and to proclaim, "Good Morning!" (Maya Angelou, "On the Pulse of Morning"[2]), these two African American women encourage all of us to step into a brave new world where African American women lead in unprecedented ways. Oh, we always knew that we could lead from the front because we have been leading from all parts elsewhere. Now, however, with title, badge, license, robe, scalpel, gavel, and stripes, we as African American women have stepped into the morning and the light of history as leaders in ways that many thought impossible. And what is also true is that so many of us, pioneers and pathfinders, are inspired by our faith. One can hear it in our speeches, our poetry, our righteous indignation, and our compassion. We are women who lead from the kitchen table and from the desk, with Bible verses and babies in tow.

We daily engage the complexities of life as believers, African Americans, women, and key contributors to the development and flowering of society. We are part Deborah (Judges 4:4–14), compelled by the challenging circumstances of racism, gender bias, bigotry, and discrimination to be a prophet of hope for family, church, and culture. We are part Queen of Sheba (1 Kings 10:1–12), interacting with men from significant positions of power: vice president of the United States of America, supreme court justice, mayor, chief of police, chief executive officer, activist, and media mogul, to name a few. We are part Mary, the mother of Jesus (Luke 1:30–31), bearing the light of the Savior into the dark places of the impoverished and the privileged, the powerless and the powerful, the abused and the architects of the systems of abuse. Black Christian women are daily giving birth to dreams given by God, even as they face age-old stereotypes and denigrations still alive in the hearts and minds of the literal and emotional ancestors of the slavery empire of this country.

With the faith of our mothers and fathers, we creatively reject the ways of hierarchy and domination. We are bringing new forms of leadership into being—rooted in the experiences of the past but shaped by God in the house of the Potter (Jeremiah 18:1–6). We are braving this new day with faith at the center of our professional and family life. God has formed us into new-day leaders. Carefully shaped on the wheel by the hands of the Potter, we lift as we climb and make decisions with heads and hearts. As pioneers and trendsetters, molded by God, we speak out against evil and fight for those who cannot fight for themselves. Like Maya Angelou, African American women of faith continue to say, "Good Morning." We continue to step into the light. We still look forward to a city "whose architect and builder is God" (Hebrews 11:10).

Beautiful, Strong, Resilient

Today's African American Christian women stand squarely on the shoulders of the sisters of the past. They step into the war of this season armed with a deep and abiding prayer life, education, organizational experience, and a spirit of activism. The war for their children and for their human dignity still rages despite the fact that they sit in some of America's most hallowed halls and at some of the most influential tables. Many in their communities are still undereducated, under-resourced, and are living in poverty.

But we are heirs of a rich heritage of faith. As we look back, we see the great women who struggled against immeasurable odds, namely through slavery, Jim Crow segregation, attacks on their civil liberties, and, of course, through war. From these women, we gain a witness to the faith that has given them amazing resilience, which made it possible for these great-great-great-grandmothers of our people to withstand unimaginable suffering and yet rise to extraordinary heights. This is the history that keeps us grounded, rooted in our trust in an Almighty God. If they could make it—if they could survive the whip and the lash, the scorn and the derision—then we can somehow make it with our mustard-seed faith. These are the shoulders that support us and carry us through.

Light Carriers: Unknown Champions

I met one such woman. I heard her preach when I was in seminary in Chicago. She was wonderful, but I did not really know all that she had done. Her message was clear as crystal. She said that the word *helpmeet*—that often-repeated phrase that was used in the church to bludgeon women into submission to their husbands—did not really appear *that* way in the Bible. The word was actually *two words*, and they meant that the woman was *help*—a term that everywhere else in Scripture describes help that comes from an Almighty God—"meet" or "corresponding" to the man. In other words, men and women were created to be *companions*, serving one another in mutual love because they correspond to and with one another by the intentional design of God.

I did not find out, until many years later, the inspiration that Reverend Prathia Hall provided to one of our country's most beloved leaders, Dr. Martin Luther King Jr. She was the driver for Dr. King at a prayer vigil held in the ashes of a church burned by the KKK in 1962. Reverend Hall was a young firebrand college student and prayed to the Lord about the vision she hoped to see. As a recurring motif, she cried out to God, "I have a dream." Standing with her and others in the smoldering remains of Mount Olive Baptist Church was Dr. Martin Luther King Jr. Afterward, as Reverend Hall drove Dr. King to his next destination, he expressed his admiration for her use of the phrase and said he would use it one day.[3]

There he stood on the steps of the Lincoln Memorial declaring the speech that would inspire people of all ages and faiths. "I have a dream that one day . . ." Reverend Prathia Hall would go on fighting for the rights of the marginalized and the oppressed, eventually becoming a minister proclaiming the liberating gospel of Jesus Christ. She, too, continued to believe and fight for the dream given her by God. Reverend Hall reminds us that our prayers to God are not the isolated prayers of solitary women but are, in fact, the cries of generations yearning to be free. No wonder she would lead a vigil in the middle of ashes, just days after being grazed by Klan bullets. No wonder her prayer about her dream is still being repeated because we are still holding the vision of God as a will-be-fulfilled dream in our hearts.

The tapestry of this nation's collective life has the names of unknown champions sewn into it everywhere. Their names may not appear in history books, news articles, or on the internet, but they nonetheless carry the light for the rest of us. They are the teachers who bring snacks and toilet paper or a student's freshly washed clothes to school for them. They are the pioneering, female, and skilled tradespeople, truck drivers, and fire and emergency personnel who suffered brutal gender and ethnic discrimination. They hauled essential cargo, built high-rise structures, brought light and energy to neighborhoods, and rescued folk from deep ravines and burning buildings. I was happy to meet a grandmother whose gnarled hands told the story of being the first female welder in one of my city's local auto plants. Sadly, I did not become aware of her past accomplishments until I spoke at her funeral.

Are you an unknown champion? You who belong to the Lord are, indeed, *light* carriers. Remember the smile you caused, the tears of thanksgiving in response to your actions, the look of hope that was left after you showed up. Perhaps you prefer not to brag, but your story may remind some struggling sister that the dawn still shines bright with possibility. Write it down, friend. Tell your story of pushing past barriers and bursting through glass ceilings. African American women need to remind and encourage one another. Write the story of another sister's life. Listen to the elders, and share the richness of their lives. Report what the youth are doing to brighten and improve the troubled world they have inherited. God told the children of Israel to erect a pile of stones as a memorial when they crossed the River Jordan into the promised land:

> We will use these stones to build a memorial. In the future your children will ask you, "What do these stones mean?" Then you can tell them, "They remind us that the Jordan River stopped flowing when the Ark of the Lord's Covenant went across." These stones will stand as a memorial among the people of Israel forever." (Joshua 4:6–7 NLT)

If rocks, pebbles, and boulders can tell a story, how much more can the adventurous words about our lives?

Living an Authentic Faith

In seminary, I did not know then what I know now. I had encountered a civil rights icon whose words inspired yet another civil rights icon, whose message then and now inspires generations! This knowledge has reminded me that there are many victories in the struggle to live an authentic faith. During the world's global pandemic, African Americans looked increasingly to their past for hope and inspiration and, in so doing, have reopened a treasure chest of historical miracles! These are stories of Black women and men who overcame despite incredible odds. Virtual resources, such as documentaries, theatrical productions, music, art, and book discussions became more readily available to viewers during that incredible season, compelling us to look and learn again. Fresh from the historical review, we rediscovered ourselves, the shoulders we stand on, and the blood that still cries from the ground.

Looking back makes it possible to better understand the life we now live. For African American women of Christian faith, a self-examination reveals not only how we live but how we lead and how we thrive in a world undergoing dramatic shifts in demographics, values, climate, technology, and power.

Keeping it real, we must acknowledge that greater secularism, increased violence, political turmoil, and the emotional distancing of technological advancement have created great challenges to healthy societal growth and development. A growing reliance on the computer and the cell phone has created a society where people can communicate instantaneously across international borders, though they prefer texting across the dinner table instead of speaking face-to-face. The African American Christian woman, likewise, experiences this fracturing of society. She must grapple with the resulting realities, namely, the decline of Christian culture, the renewed insistence on anachronistic and hierarchical leadership frameworks, and the challenges to one's faith presented by an increasingly hostile world. As women live and lead in this strange and rapidly changing future, they engage the battle by keeping the faith, keeping the light, and keeping the joy.

Keeping the Faith: Among the Nones

Millennials (born 1981–1996) and Generation Z folks (born 1997–2012) present a sharp and perhaps well-deserved critique of church hypocrisy and inactivity and constitute generations of people who have pulled away from Christianity. The declining numbers of confessing Christians are not limited to the younger generations. Beginning in the early 2000s, the number of Americans who self-identify as "Christian" seems to drop each year. In addition to the segment of people who have apparently turned away from the faith, Pew Research has identified another segment of the US population that has no religious affiliation at all. While those who have maintained their Christian faith have declined, the "Nones," those who identify as atheist or agnostic, are on the rise. At the end of 2021, Pew Research Center found that Christians outnumbered Nones by roughly two to one, but in 2007 Christians outnumbered Nones by a five-to-one ratio. As of 2021, Nones comprised three out of every ten adults in the US population.[4]

The number of those who are religiously unaffiliated has grown within the African American community. Today Nones represent 21 percent of the Black population, but with this striking distinction: over 90 percent of Black Nones still believe in God, though many no longer attend church or pray.[5] This religious cultural shift in the Black community is significant because it suggests that the fabric of church attendance that largely defined Black life for baby boomers and Gen X-ers is absent from millennials and Gen Z-ers. The language of faith and the customs and traditions of earlier generations have become suspect in these perilous times, and perhaps the church would do well to look in the mirror to assess the accusation. Some within the church have done exactly that and responded to the critique with an authentic faith. Resisting the tendency to pretend or to pose, women of faith on stage, in church, and in the office present unvarnished views of the unique women God calls them to be.

Through the Valley of Shadows: Pastors and Ministers Tell Their Stories

A young African American female pastor, popular in person and online, addressed the issue of teen pregnancy by sharing her personal story from the pulpit. Rather than hide her past, which has been a common approach in traditional Black churches, she has opened the discussion to thousands of women, young and old, who have been hiding in shame. Her candor strikes a decisive blow against the criticism of inauthenticity in the Black church. The true story of this young woman's struggles ministered to the hearts and minds of women who may have experienced rejection or condemnation from within the church. The groundswell of support she has garnered among faithful followers of Jesus Christ reminds us that hundreds of thousands are looking for churchwomen simply to be real.

Where are all the single ladies in the pulpit? Although we don't often hear about the challenges of singleness for women in the pulpit, there have been a few brave souls who have ventured to tell the truth. One such pastor from the South, who serves a church with a rich history, has made it clear through her thunderous sermons and thought-provoking commentary that single female pastors deal with some of the same issues confronting other single sisters of faith, but that there are some unique challenges as well.

Unlike the traditional model of male pastoral leadership that includes a spouse, a substantial number of female pastors are single. These women face additional hurdles in ministry that their male counterparts do not face. Perhaps, that pastor once told a congregation in Detroit, her unwillingness to deal with relationship drama as a pastor might compel her to rely on friends, family, and her pet dog more than on a Saturday night date. This pastor's barrier-breaking life of service has brought her to leadership in a number of previously male-dominated clergy arenas. Yet she was able to take off the mask long enough to be honest about life in the pastor's robe and collar. Her enthusiastic support for African American women leaders is enhanced by her refreshing honesty about the slings, arrows, and joys of women pastors who do not have spouses. Bringing the truth of women's lives into her sermons makes her relatable and extends the reach of the sacred desk to the pew and the front porch.

African American Christian women minister from non-church pulpits as well, including corporate arenas, media systems, and internet networks. One executive shared her story on a major social media platform, shedding the churchy mask. Exposing the truth by uncovering domestic violence and childhood rape freed her and others to speak with candor about the challenges the faithful experience when trusted hands turn abusive and violent. Since the global pandemic firmly and inexorably made digital platforms a necessity for most churches, her local story quickly became national and invited others to engage in courageous conversations about mental health and sexual violence. The minister and the manager can broadcast their life lessons to lead women along paths of healing so that they, too, can realize professional goals and personal restoration.

Today's African American Christian woman must engender a faith that is authentic and that makes a meaningful impact on the community, and she must do so amidst numbers of African Americans who have lost interest in traditional church. This challenge, of course, also presents a unique opportunity that many female Christian leaders and pastors are addressing as they serve in multigenerational, multiethnic contexts, in order to bring a fresh perspective to the activity of the body of Christ in the world. Of course, church leadership is not the only form of leadership for the African American woman of faith who lets her light shine. They can be found in the secular world as well, leading from radically new seats at the leadership table.

Keeping the Light: At the Table

With the advent of the first African American woman vice president of the United States of America and the first African American woman US Supreme Court Justice, Black women are sitting in seats that previous generations never would have imagined women would fill. Combined with congresspeople, a slew of mayors, CEOs, and a number of city chiefs of police, African American women have the unique opportunity to reshape the leadership models put into place by the White male hierarchy—and to infuse the ethics of Jesus into policies and procedures. The reality is, however, that she must also deal with that existing structure even while dismantling or, at least, revamping it.

The shape of our leadership is not necessarily rectangular. The "head" is not necessarily located at the end of the table or even at the "power middle position" halfway down the side. We often lead from a round table, from a circle of people who gain access to the table from many directions, and who collaborate and share in the distribution of power. This circular, nonlinear approach welcomes conversation and debate, theorizing and testimony.

Hearing from others and sharing in decision-making is the parallel to our foremothers' quilting bee and cooking in the kitchen, and it is also by faith. It is a God-centered approach to human interaction. It is the deconstruction of hierarchical leadership thought patterns that focus on control, command, and reconstruction to bring about respect and honor.

The ways of African American womenfolk center our living and our leadership on the God who commands us to care for the poor, defend the voiceless, and provide for the widow (Isaiah 1:17). Womanist theologian Delores Williams describes this understanding of God and practice of faith by Black women as challenging all oppressive forces that obstruct Black women's fight for survival "and for the development of a positive, productive quality of life that is conductive to the woman's and the family's freedom and well-being."[6]

We act out the love of God from the perspective of a mother; our theology, our understanding of God's call to us in the world is rooted in a mother's heart and a grandmother's prayer. We see family and community, children, and the future as the mission of God. We embrace and encircle the people God has given to us and to the world, knowing that He encircles us with the fire of His love as He did in the following passage:

> When the servant of the man of God got up and went out early the next morning, an army with horses and chariots had surrounded the city. "Oh no, my lord! What shall we do?" the servant asked.
>
> "Don't be afraid," the prophet answered. "Those who are with us are more than those who are with them."
>
> And Elisha prayed, "Open his eyes, LORD, so that he may see." Then the LORD opened the servant's eyes, and he looked and saw the hills full of horses and chariots of fire all around Elisha. (2 Kings 6:15–17)

Elisha and the servant were surrounded by the enemy, but more than that, they were surrounded by God's angelic and fiery protection. What a sight it must have been to see the fire of God's holy army lighting up the hillside.

Mary McLeod Bethune, the founder of Bethune-Cookman College and the first African American female presidential cabinet member under Franklin Delano Roosevelt, also experienced the power of holy light, albeit from human hands. In the early days of Bethune Normal School, the Klan threatened to ride through the campus and made good on their threat. Bethune shocked them by having her teachers suddenly turn on every single light in the building and all outdoor floodlights. The Klan was left standing in a pool of light and soon dispersed and scattered into the night, as her girls sang spirituals.[7]

Perhaps it is respect for the circle of God's love—the "without beginning and without end" trinitarian circle of God, Jesus, and the Holy Spirit—that inspires African American women of faith to lead from a round table. Perhaps inspiration comes from kitchen-table wisdom about the circle of life shared from grandmas and big mamas: "Honey, what goes around comes around" and "Be careful how you treat people. The people you see on your way up will be the same people you see on your way down." And perhaps it is the table itself—that great symbol of egalitarianism where Jesus preached powerful sermons by His conduct—that inspires a different way of leading others.

Although we must function within the leadership ladder of capitalist society and counterfeit democracy, African American women of faith have looked to Jesus for lessons on liberation and cooperation. The table was the great equalizer in the days that the Lord walked the earth. Jesus sat at the table with the faithful, as well as sinners, hypocrites, and the outcasts.

> Later, Levi held a banquet in his home with Jesus as the guest of honor. Many of Levi's fellow tax collectors and other guests also ate with them. But the Pharisees and their teachers of religious law complained bitterly to Jesus' disciples, "Why do you eat and drink with such scum?"
>
> Jesus answered them, "Healthy people don't need a doctor—sick people do. I have come to call not those who think they are righteous, but those

who know they are sinners and need to repent." (Luke 5:29–32 NLT)

People were drawn to the table of Jesus Christ by need, not status. His love reached beyond the bounds of human decency to include those deemed indecent. The table of Jesus Christ was open to those in need and also for those who were looking for a new way of living. The desperate remind the world of the immediate need for change—change that offers meaningful life to those whom the world has crushed under the weight of political, economic, and social oppression. People of faith ought to hear the cries of the desperate seeking the genuine transformative power of Christ. Therefore, African American Christian women welcome others to the table of discourse and decision-making to equalize inequity and demolish hierarchy, to both lead and care for those whom they lead.

Keeping the Joy: The Circle of Friendship

From the easel to the dinner table and from the studio to the schoolhouse, African American Christian women have made a profound impact on American culture. Through writing, music, dance, art, education, cuisine, fashion, science, media, politics, and more, they have left an indelible mark on this nation despite the horrendousness of racism and the violence they have personally endured. Their contributions to this great nation are often not overtly Christian in their content, but a closer examination reveals a deeply rooted faith out of which springs determination, innovation, fearlessness and, yes, even joy!

Consider it pure joy. (James 1:2)

The movie *Hidden Figures* was right. This popular film exposes a fascinating truth previously hidden from history: America's first flights into outer space were enabled by mathematicians who happened to be Black and female and, in many cases, Christian. This story of three of those women is emblematic of the ways in which Black women's faith and contributions have been overlooked and underappreciated. Faith that moves in God's mysterious ways fueled a technological revolution that changed the world through the patient calculations of women of faith. However, their work had never been acknowledged or reported. The film did, however, portray something that perhaps even the factual data might not reveal: the way the friendship between the women sustained and nourished them through the challenges and obstacles they faced. Perhaps it is this gift of relationship, that comes from God, that makes it possible for faithful women to forge ahead on unknown paths and to keep joy in the presence of hate.

Pioneering African American Christian women have encountered a hostile world bent on blocking or obstructing their participation in fields previously reserved for White men. The issue for Christian sisters is not simply whether they will encounter bias and discrimination but how they will keep the faith during the challenge. Enslaved women faced this issue every day they experienced the whip and the chain. Every day, they had to care for children who would grow up to torture them in manifold ways. They were challenged to "keep their religion," to continue to believe in the God of heaven even as they experienced hell on earth. How did they make it during those long, scary nights and sometimes even scarier days? Together.

Without oversimplifying a complex equation, the circles of friendship, nurtured by sisters of faith, have for generations carried us through. The quilting bee, the sewing circle, the church choir, and the kitchen have been places for the nurture of broken hearts and fractured souls. African American Christian women have stepped into leadership positions at the front while simultaneously bringing the traditions of the past with them, traditions and customs of *togetherness* that, frankly, kept them alive.

The circle of friendship, then, is not some metaphysical totem; it is the military formation of embattled women who refuse to give up because they determined to go *together*. At the beginning of the global pandemic, when masks were scarce but the need for them was great, I traveled to Highland Park, Michigan.

Good Morning! The Shape of Things to Come 29

A church-based ministry was making masks. To me, they exemplified the women of a quilting bee. I slipped a check under the door and picked up a bag on the front porch filled with masks. I took the masks to a church with a soup kitchen that had shifted to home delivery so the meals could be delivered. The Highland Park sisters gathered fabric and elastic and fought against the scourge of a terrifying contagion with thread and needles and a faith that would not let go.

I have seen this countless times: women who stand against evil with arms locked in faith, women who combat grief and fear with hugs and prayer. A number of years ago, when I was serving a church as an associate pastor, I had the pleasure of starting a telephone prayer line. I was very pleased that three women joined on that first day, because I was prepared to pray by myself. The prayer line began more than ten years ago. The numbers have increased, and so has the faith. We have prayed through divorces, deaths, financial losses, sicknesses, births, absentee husbands, and one-is-a-whole-number singleness. I am not just a giver on this prayer line; I am also a recipient. These sisters have prayed me through personal pain and joy. The day after my father died, I was on the prayer line sharing hope as well as seeking solace. I have called into the line from Liberia and Israel. The prayer line has never missed a day.

The victory is not mine, however. The prayer line continues because others lead and others pray. While I am a leader, I am not the only leader. The prayer line flourishes because it is actually not a line at all. It is a community that stretches north, south, east, and west. It is not a linear formation; it is rooted in the ancient tradition of the quilting circle, where each woman contributes to the end product. Each woman has a gift to share: the fabric, the cutting, the piecing, or the sewing. It is an egalitarian shape where leaders and followers sit around the table.

Our twice-weekly morning prayer has sustained us because we have developed the relationships that have carried us through the lives we have lived. This is joy-keeping. It is burden-sharing that is filled with laughter and tears, arms of embrace, and shoulders to lean upon. It is the shape of things past and things to come.

Seated around Jesus

> Then he looked at those seated in a circle around him and said, "Here are my mother and my brothers!" (Mark 3:34)

African American Christian women leading is not new. We have become more visible, however, and, perhaps, more widely accepted because of the positions we hold. Then again, increased visibility, particularly the visibility that comes with challenging the status quo or forcefully opposing injustice, brings increased risk of recrimination. "In fact, everyone who wants to live a godly life in Christ Jesus will be persecuted" (2 Timothy 3:12). Yet Black women of faith repeatedly draw on that faith to face the hostility and violence of the world with their arms linked and hands clasped. Whether surrounded by a counterfeit slaveholding Christianity that lifted a Bible with liberation verses removed or surrounded by nonbelievers, the sisters have continued to look to their Lord for help and sustenance. They have kept the joy and the faith and have led from a round table—a table with Jesus at the center. Perhaps that is what sustained the quilting bee and the sewing circle, not the circle but the center. When people told Jesus that His family was looking for Him, He looked at the people seated in a circle around Him and declared that they were His family, they who followed the will of God. So, African American women with Jesus at the center of their lives still trust in morning joy and morning mercies. We still say, "Good Morning!"

2

She Came to Slay

Warriors, Game-Changers, and Transformers in Black History and the Bible

VICTORIA CARTER JONES

> The LORD's victory over Sisera will
> be at the hands of a woman.
> Judges 4:9 NLT

I was on the phone with one of my sisters, and she was elated. "What are you so excited about?" I asked. She told me her friend Erica Armstrong Dunbar had just published *She Came to Slay: The Life and Times of Harriet Tubman*, and the book had arrived in the mail. She began to tell me how Harriet Tubman had been the only woman to lead men into battle during the Civil War. Our conversation sparked my search for the story behind the provocative title of this book and served as a catalyst for studying powerful, godly women of color in Black history and the Bible.

She Came to Slay

"She came to slay" evokes visions of courage, strength, and dominance. This expression lets people know a particular person is fearless, confident, and competent in her actions. Women can be conquerors. Women, too, are equipped to, as another slang statement warns, "kick butt and take names" of evil opponents and villains who may cross their paths. Today people use *slay* as a term of empowerment. Women "slay" in various settings: in the home, church, government, business, community, the workplace, and elsewhere. When a woman comes to slay for the Lord, she has nothing to fear and everything to gain despite barriers and insurmountable obstacles.

Women in Black History

Black female standouts have a beautiful, abundant history of being warriors, game-changers, and transformers for the Lord. However, many don't yet know this history.

Harriet Tubman, the Worshiping Warrior, is one example. She was a prayer warrior who spent time on her knees before the Lord in the rugged woods of the South. During these times, Tubman received visions from Him about how to rescue her people from the ravages of slavery.[1] She was obsessed with the abolition of slavery and the horror, death, and destruction this institution had on the lives of her people. Tubman was on a mission, not just to save herself or even a handful of people. She entered her journey to abolish the system of slavery altogether. Slaying is not merely about reforming systems but eradicating evil. Over and over again, Tubman entered the slaveholding South to rescue enslaved loved ones, friends, neighbors, and strangers.

During one of the dangerous trips from slaveholding Maryland to the free state of Pennsylvania, Tubman warned her passengers on the Underground Railroad "there would be no going back." One man began to threaten that he was going to forfeit the mission and return to his master. He was terrified the group would be captured and tortured before being sent back into hard, violent labor. Unwilling to lose any member of her group and unwilling to have her route compromised, Tubman pulled out a pistol and turned it on the anxious man. "You go on or die," she said. The man complied to continue with the others, and, true to Tubman's word, everyone in her band found freedom. "Slaying" is about faith and courage. It is about getting rid of the things in this world that harm and plague people's lives. It also signals that African American Christian women who come to slay have a mission and will not stop until God is pleased.

African American Women, Slayers of Evil

I grew up in a Christian home and knew that my mother, grandmother, and aunts prayed for me. In hindsight, I have pleasant memories of these slayers of evil as they watched, chaperoned, and hovered over me like eagles with their chicks. Dr. Shirley June stated in the earlier publication of *Women to Women* in 1996,

> Many of us may have similar examples of African American women who have deeply impacted our outlook in life and direction. They are a reminder of the debt of gratitude we owe to countless others whose stamina, acts of faith, and courage inspired us in the midst of discouraging odds: the woman, the mother, the grandmother, or the aunt who always knew from conviction and experience that "the Lord will make a way"; the teachers who wanted us to do our best and insisted on excellence; those in church who urged us to take on new challenges and opportunities to grow and serve; those who modeled before us a fulfilling life in Christ. These African American women helped to fashion a girl, a woman, and a generation of African American women with faith and convictions. Those women have been able to provide hope where voices of affirmation are all too few.[2]

African American warriors, game-changers, and transformers impacted families, churches, and the communities they served. *Black Women in America*, a classic, historical encyclopedia by Darlene

Clark Hine,[3] includes biographical information and contributions of more than six hundred African American women. Hine, in her research, demonstrated the worldwide impact of these women. In 2014, a movement called "Say Her Name" was launched as a way to support the stories of Black women and girls who faced police violence[4] and, later, to remind the general public to keep alive the names of civil rights activists and other significant individuals, who could go unheard. Listed are a few who may or may not be familiar but who were dedicated to God, were slayers of evil, and were not always recognized for their faith:

Ida B. Wells-Barnett (1862–1931)[5]
Ida was deeply religious and a faithful church attendee. She was a prominent journalist, activist, and researcher. She organized support for an anti-lynching movement and was a warrior against the oppression of Black people.

Mary McLeod Bethune (1875–1955)[6]
Mary was trained to be a missionary and wanted to serve in Africa. She was best known as the founder of Bethune-Cookman College, but she was a passionate believer and dedicated Christian. She was considered an evangelist during her time as a student at Moody Bible Institute in Chicago, a powerful transformer who met with presidents, and a prayer warrior throughout her life.

Eva Roberta Coles-Boone (1880–1902)[7]
Eva was an educator but earned the rare and controversial position of becoming a missionary to what is now known as the Democratic Republic of the Congo, Central Africa. She was determined and dedicated to the Lord during a time of unprecedented missionary assignments. She was a game-changer and opened the door for others to follow in her footsteps as missionaries.

Fannie Jackson Coppin (1837–1913)[8]
Fannie was a missionary in South Africa for more than a decade and founded a Bethel Institute school there. She loved God and developed self-help programs as a part of her missionary

work. As a transformer, she is cited as our nation's first African American woman school principal.

Drusilla Dunjee Houston (1876–1941)[9]
Drusilla was a devoted warrior for the Lord, a gifted writer, an independent historian, and a classical pianist. She founded the McAlester Seminary for girls. She lived with constant threats on her life because her writings objected to racism. Drusilla was one of the earliest recognized African American females to author a study on Ethiopia and ancient Black populations in Arabia, Persia, Babylonia, and India.

Nannie Helen Burroughs (1879–1961)[10]
Nannie was a fiery, dedicated, steadfast warrior for the Lord. She was a religious leader in the National Baptist Convention and was cited as a stirring orator, not afraid to speak out against racism, speak up for women's right to vote, and decry sexism. She publicly criticized President Woodrow Wilson for not doing enough to stop lynching and for segregating federal workplaces. She founded the National Training School for Women and Girls in 1909 and did not accept support from White donors or White philanthropy for her school's survival.

Much of the work on African American women contributors is often buried in the archives of Black history. Only through diligent, intentional study can it be uncovered. Yet these contributions are worthy of our exploration and can inspire all who look for God's redemptive work in the lives of women of color in our history and in the Bible.

Beware, the Enemy Comes to Slay

Leaders have power because they lead people. Leaders with skills can positively empower others with their impact or harm people with their skills. They have two choices: use power for God, or use power for self-serving purposes that abuse and harm others. As a warrior for God, you will inevitably be engaged in spiritual warfare, but stand firm (Ephesians 6:14). Evil comes about in a range of people, circumstances, and situations. Harriet Tubman's enemy was the institution of slavery, along with the people who created, benefitted from, and supported it.

Queen Jezebel in the Bible is a perfect example of a woman who had a reputation for being one of the most vile and wicked women ever (1 Kings 18–21). In fact, her warrior mentality and threats were so horrific, even the great prophet Elijah was frightened enough to run for his life when he heard she was coming after him (19:3). Idolatry, hate, envy, and deceit infiltrated this queen's life. When plans did not go her way, she would murder whoever was in her path, destroying their family and legacy in order to see her schemes completed. Jezebel, an evil warrior, would kill aggressively, randomly, and in great numbers. She was the epitome and full embodiment of a person who came to slay—but for harmful purposes.

It takes the power of a true warrior of God to witness, pray for, and challenge the works of evil warriors. Perhaps you know some Jezebels in your environment of family, place of employment, community, or who are masquerading as saints in the church. Our role as warriors for God is to serve to lead others, even the Jezebels, out of the world of sin and into the forgiving, loving arms of our Savior and Redeemer, as Tubman did. The most aggressive Jezebel, when redeemed, can become the most aggressive warrior for the Lord through the power of the Holy Spirit.

Women of Color in the Bible

The very presence of women in the Bible should be transformational to us as descendants of those who have gone before us. Eve, the mother of all human beings, was an example of the power we have as women, the state we are in—needing a Savior and Redeemer—and the battles we face as warriors against sin.

Rahab, the Game-Changer (Joshua 2:1–24)

Everyone has a past, a present, and a future. The story of Rahab is no different than the life of anyone who has struggled. Rahab did not allow her past and present circumstances to stand in the way of her taking action to save her family. *Game-changer* refers to "an event, idea, or procedure that effects a significant shift in the current manner of doing or thinking about something."[11] Rahab's circle of people could not guess she was going to shift her thinking and actions in a way that "changed the game" and lives of everyone around her.

Some people unfamiliar with Rahab's story might be shocked to learn about her bold leadership skills that eventually gave her favor with the Lord. After all, it is believed that Rahab was either a prostitute or operating a house of prostitution in a corrupt, pagan city under God's condemnation. Of her profession, well, most would say she "came to slay" in a way that was disgraceful, scandalous, and evil. However, Rahab was smart and loved her family. Because of her ability to take action in a time of crisis, her swift negotiation skills, her entire household was saved. Her efforts aided the nation of Israel in a positive manner. She became a game-changer.

Rahab had a plan. She hid the two spies, whom Joshua, leader of the Israelites, had sent to search out the land. She told the men how the people of Jericho feared the Israelites from the time the Egyptians were defeated during the Red Sea saga. Despite the king of Jericho's demand for Rahab to relinquish the spies, she concealed them. When the soldiers arrived to look for them, she lied and said they were not there. The soldiers examined her tavern, but she had hidden the spies well. Once the soldiers left the house, Rahab requested the spies save not just her life but the lives of her entire family (Joshua 2:12–13).

Rahab's action was a game-changing intercession for her family that demonstrated her leadership skills and devotion to her family. She knew that victory over the Canaanites was inevitable, so she wisely negotiated her situation for those of her household. As a result, Joshua and his men honored their promise to her. After the city was destroyed, Rahab and her family were the only ones spared.

Rahab, a Canaanite descendent of Ham,[12] was a woman who eventually aligned herself with God's purpose for her life and essentially became worthy through God's grace to be the mother of Boaz and an ancestor in Jesus's lineage. Her life is an inspiring and powerful story that fully demonstrates how God can save a woman and ensure her life is not dictated by her past mistakes. God enabled Rahab to become a game-changer for herself, her family, and even the trajectory of Israel as a nation. Rahab slayed!

Ruth, the Transformer (Ruth 1–4)

All who read books from the Old Testament could easily fall in love with the story of Ruth, the woman who clung to her mother-in-law, Naomi, after Ruth's father-in-law, husband, and brother-in-law died. Ruth transformed the life of Naomi by staying with her during a time of grief, crisis, and uncertainty. When Naomi prepared to return to Judah, she told Ruth to return to her parents and live her life. But Ruth replied, "Don't force me to leave you; don't make me go home. Where you go, I go; and where you live, I'll live. Your people are my people, your God is my god; where you die, I'll die, and that's where I'll be buried, so help me GOD—not even death itself is going to come between us!" (Ruth 1:16–17 MSG). The book of Ruth illustrates her extraordinary love and devotion to her mother-in-law as well as their bonded friendship. The women shared the deep trauma of the death of their loved ones, and that produced deep devotion to one another. Had Ruth walked away, she would have added to her losses.

Historically, Ruth is remembered for being a destitute widow who gave up her chance to remarry when her husband died. She gave up her homeland and comforts in life, and she sacrificed everything to stay with her mother-in-law. Ruth was the epitome of a kindhearted and loyal woman. In the end, we learn that Ruth gained favor from God. He gave her love and loyalty from Boaz, her kinsman-redeemer who became her husband and who bought back land to guarantee hers and Naomi's inheritance. The presence of Ruth transformed the lives of Naomi and Boaz.

Ruth defies the degrading secular humor about wives and their relationships with their mothers-in-law. When someone mentions their mother-in-law, it is usually on the tail end of a joke or a negative statement. Comedians, in poor taste, write monologues about mothers-in-law that imply complaints fueled with disdain, ignited by jealousy. Yet wonderful Christian relationships between daughter-in-law and mother-in-law can be found and loving stories can be heard among people in homes, churches, and in the community. Terms such as *mother-in-love* or *daughter-in-love* crush negativity and promote love within the family, reflecting real endearment and affection. The book of Ruth shows that through loyalty, care, and wisdom, a mother-in-law and daughter-in-law relationship can be transformative.

Sometimes we forget that Ruth was not Jewish like Naomi and her family. Ruth was a Moabite, a gentile woman of color. This story shows how God's providence transformed the lives of Ruth and Naomi, and their future. Ruth is one of only two women (including Esther) with an entire book of the Bible named for them. Ruth and Boaz produced descendants who would provide the family line through which the Messiah came into the world. Ordinary people, women of color, and even daughters and their mothers-in-love can model to the world what is possible when we put our trust in God. Ruth, the transformer, slayed!

Other Women of Color in the Bible

The presence of women of color and the overall picture of African presence throughout the Bible is well researched by Bible scholars, including Esau McCaulley, Charles Copher, and Walter McCray. McCray presents extensive coverage on the identities of Hamitic (African) and other peoples in his work. He discusses the Black women named in the genealogy of our Lord Jesus Christ, including Tamar, Rahab, and Bathsheba, who are all people of Hamitic descent.[13]

As Dr. Shirley June stated in the earlier publication of *Women to Women*, "The study of the African presence in Scripture is needed because of the benign or purposed 'bleaching' of biblical persons and nations, resulting in people of color appearing absent or unimportant in God's dealings with people and nations."[14] Using Herbert Lockyer's work *All the Women of the Bible*, a combination of information provides character sketches and helps define what is meant by "African" in Scripture.[15] Consider the following:

Adah
One of Esau's Canaanite wives, she was an ancestor of the Edomites (Genesis 26:34; 36:2–19).

Bathsheba
Wife of Uriah the Hittite, she became the wife of King David and mother of King Solomon (2 Samuel 11:3–27).

Delilah
Samson's wife, a Philistine and descendant of Ham, conspired against him and contributed to his downfall (Judges 16).

Eve
As the mother of all human beings, she had the genetic potential to produce the full range of diverse people known today. Some scholars say the garden of Eden's description includes African land areas (Genesis 2–3).

Queen Candace
She was queen of Ethiopia during the time of the Ethiopian returning home from Jerusalem as a newly converted Christian (Acts 8:27).

Queen of Sheba
Also called Queen of the South by Jesus (Matthew 12:42), she came to Jerusalem to visit and ask King Solomon questions after she heard of his fame concerning the name of the Lord (1 Kings 10:1).

Sheerah
This daughter of Ephraim built three towns (1 Chronicles 7:22–28).

The presence of women of color in the Bible is undeniable. "Also, several portions of the Scripture were written in Africa, and Africans were acquainted with and used Scriptures prior to the writing of the New Testament. The widespread use of the Bible throughout Africa in ancient and modern times is known."[16]

Called to Slay, My Story

I never thought of myself as a woman who came to slay anything, until the Lord started putting me in leadership positions within my personal and spiritual life. By God's grace and mercy, I was trained, groomed, and polished to be an effective leader within my profession. But, honestly, when it came to my relationship with the Lord, I was not so confident in my ability to lead anything.

Every day I tried to be intentional about submitting to the Lord and obeying His commands, but did I wholeheartedly trust God with everything? No! There were moments when I would easily say, "Yes! Of course, I trust God, I'm a Christian." But there were other times (more often than not) when I would become extremely stressed and overwhelmed with the demands of life. I often thought, *I do believe, but Lord help my unbelief, especially as it relates to Your plans for my life!*

As a child, I grew up in a godly household. My parents were dedicated to teaching me the Bible and demonstrating how to live for Christ. I have a godly husband. My pastors ministered to me, godly mentors poured into me, I read my Bible often, prayed daily, attended church conferences, and participated in Bible studies until I literally became "spiritually fat!" I was far from being a babe in Christ. The problem was, I could tell the Lord wanted more from me. He was calling me to do more. But I was still not confident I could spiritually pour into anyone else.

After all, our purpose as believers is to create disciples, teaching others to obey the commands of the Lord (Matthew 28:19–20). So, what was my problem? I battled with this for months, as I felt insignificant. I felt I had failed God and my family. I knew what I had to do; I just couldn't do it. Looking back, I think the real issue was that I was not wholeheartedly submitting my life to God as my first priority. I used to pride myself on being a very flexible person with my time and able to juggle daily commitments. I was one who was clever at multitasking. Why? Because I am a strong Black woman who was trained to be a leader and take charge of my life. I could do it all! Or so I thought. Really, that "I-can-do" list was never-ending.

In time, I thought to myself, *How can I put You first, Lord?*

I don't have time! That's really what my actions demonstrated, and I remember mentally asking the Lord to help me get my life together so I could demonstrate that I was putting Him first. I was tired of the lip service, saying what I would do but not backing it up with actions.

One day, I was playing an imaginary game of "slay the dragon" with my young son. We both had swords and armor, and both of us had a "special power" to help us defeat our adversary. As we battled the dragon back and forth, my son boldly stood in front of me (to protect me) and yelled, "I am the strongest warrior with firepower; you can never beat me!" At the time, I continued to play along and called him my hero. But then, after a few days, I got to thinking about my relationship with God and how, if I wanted to make my life right for Him, I needed to do some slaying of my own. I needed to become a warrior for the Lord and help slay the enemy through the blessings of my gifts and talents.

So, that day, I took out some paper and a pen and started to write down ways I could prioritize my life. But this time, I realized the Holy Spirit was working in my life. *He* changed my mindset. Like a warrior going to battle, I could see myself winning this war of mismanaging my time and gifts. Once I started to slay for the Lord, to my surprise, the Lord called me to get more involved with ministry. Only this time I was not a spectator gobbling up knowledge—I was to take the lead. Almost instantly, the Lord allowed me to flourish in leadership positions in my church. I was thrilled and finally on the right path of putting God first. It was crazy! I actually had more time in the day for other tasks when I put Him first.

But God didn't stop there. I am also the leader and facilitator of two Christian women's book studies. One group started out very small, but within the first week, it grew to twenty-five women, and they are loving the study and growing. I have been learning so much about what it takes to slay for the Lord. I never thought I could lead a group of women within the ministry, or have the time. But the Lord has given me more time because of my surrender and obedience, and my household has been blessed by it. As a servant of God, I am called to slay.

Christian Women Called to Slay

As Christians with a purpose, we all have a divine calling from the Lord, and part of that calling includes submitting, trusting, and obeying Him. When we accept Christ into our lives, we wholeheartedly submit ourselves to Him. In this acceptance, we are saying, "Lord, I believe You saved me, and I trust You with my life." Accepting Christ into our lives is the first step and one of many important steps of our salvation journey of slaying for the Lord. Once we accept Christ into our hearts, we dedicate our lives to obeying His Word. Obedience to God is vital to slaying for the Lord, and it demonstrates to God that we love and trust Him.

Obeying the Lord is a form of worship that allows us to grow closer to Him. Furthermore, the Bible is extremely clear about the blessings that will come to those who are fully obedient to the Word of God and desire to slay evil in the name of the Lord.

Christians have a divine calling to slay for the Lord. When we accept that calling, blessings will follow.

Considering women of color anew in Black history and the Bible creates an appreciation for the diversity God designed in human beings. A diligent study can also serve as a reminder that Black history started long before slavery in America. And women of color are loved by God and have made major contributions to the world from biblical times to the present day.

The experiences and stories of Harriet Tubman, Rahab, Ruth, and countless other women of color who slay for the Lord are not an anomaly. Their lived stories are powerful and important to share because these narratives give hope and inspiration to future generations of women who are determined to take the lead and slay for the Lord.

Tubman left a slaveholding South to create a new home and a new nation for all oppressed peoples. Rahab used her home to hide the Hebrew spies. Ruth left her home to start a new one with Naomi. We need not look over mountains, valleys, or oceans; slaying for the Lord starts right where we are, and God's plan takes us where we need to be. The women—Harriet Tubman, Rahab, Ruth, and countless others in Black history and the Bible—were fearless. The Lord used these women to slay obstacles and barriers that might have seemed insurmountable. The Lord chose to use ordinary, troubled women to achieve transformational change. He used them to alter the trajectory of their families and future generations. God saw and empowered these women as leaders. Since He uses them and their stories, how much more can He use us? Here is the hard truth: Every Christian believer is equipped to accomplish the work of God. The challenge to us is, are we willing to slay for the Lord?

Foreign Body

A Journey to Healthy Body Image and Self-Image

DEBBYE TURNER BELL

I can do all things through Christ who strengthens me.
Philippians 4:13 NKJV

There are few situations more awkward than standing in front of a panel of judges—their eyes scrutinizing, pens poised to criticize—while wearing a swimsuit, high heels, and hair teased high within an inch of its life. Yet there I stood with all the other contestants in my group, each of us vying for the title of Miss Arkansas.

"Please make a quarter-turn, ladies," commanded the pageant emcee.

Dutifully, we all turned to the left, now facing stage left. After a few excruciating moments, instructions were given to turn to the left again. Now our backsides were facing the judges, and several hundred audience members. This continued until we made a full 360-degree revolution, allowing the judges and the audience to see us from all angles. To say that it felt like a cattle call would be an understatement. The judges searched for imperfections on our bodies as though we were scientific specimens. Bow legs, thick thighs, flat chests all deemed unsatisfactory.

As I stood there with my biggest smile, squared shoulders, and ramrod-straight back, I hoped the judges wouldn't notice that my hips were better suited for giving birth than competing in pageants. I hoped they would excuse the many scars on my legs from a rambunctious childhood and the thickness of my thighs and buttocks that is common in my African ancestry.

I squeezed my gluteal muscles to minimize the roundness of my fanny. I was wearing thick makeup on my legs to cover those childhood scars. Strategically placed padding in my swimsuit gave the illusion of cleavage that I did not naturally possess. All of this to fit into an impossible mold of physical beauty better suited for girls of European descent. It was a losing battle for this African American girl with wide hips, thick lips, frizzy hair, and a round nose.

I so wanted my body to look differently. I always had. I didn't have the words for it then, but now I know that what I was struggling with was a poor body image. Simply put, body image is what we think about ourselves when we look in the mirror or imagine our bodies in our minds. Often body image has nothing to do with reality. Some who suffer with eating disorders see themselves as grossly overweight when the exact opposite might be true. It can also be a fixation on one or a few body parts or a distortion of the perception of a body part.

What We Think Matters

One could easily dismiss the issue of body image as vanity or narcissism. But studies show that girls and women with negative body image have a higher risk of developing certain mental health conditions, such as eating disorders and depression.[1] Conversely, girls and women who have positive body image are more likely to have good physical and mental health.[2] So, how we perceive ourselves, our potential, our future, is closely tied to what we think about our bodies.

My earliest memories of being teased were about my body. As a young girl, I was rail thin. I had long, lanky arms and legs, a pronounced forehead, and tragically bucked teeth. Kids called me "string bean" and "skeleton." A bully would flick my ample forehead with the back of his hand and taunt me with insults like he was "blinded by the glare" off of it. And the boy for whom I had my first crush told me I would be "halfway cute" if I got braces and did something about my teeth. All of this added up to deep insecurities about my body that followed me for decades.

I am not alone. Most women who have negative perceptions of their bodies develop these inferior feelings early in life. Often their parents had negative body images as well, or they dieted frequently. While there is no evidence that negative body image is genetically inherited, there seems to be significant evidence that negative body image can be passed down from parent to child.[3]

Images Make an Impact

Also, a constant bombardment of thin, attractive, young women portrayed in mass media begins to form an unattainable, myopic view of beauty in young impressionable girls. Because of the magic of photoshopping, even the women portrayed on magazine covers can't live up to the images presented of them. Flaws are erased. Waists are made to appear smaller. Skin tone, eye color, even hair color can all be adjusted or dramatically altered. The final product is a work of art—as well as a work of fiction. The images on magazine covers and in videos bear little resemblance to the real person. They are fantastical, idealized versions. But little girls don't know that information. And when they can't make themselves look like the images they see in magazines, movies, and on television, a deep dissatisfaction with their own bodies can set in, leading to insecurities, depression, and anxiety.[4]

The standard for beauty during my preteen and teenage years was embodied by supermodels like Cheryl Tiegs, Lauren Hutton, Cindy Crawford, and Christie Brinkley. All super thin. Most blonde. And all White. The implicit message was if you didn't look like them, you were not beautiful. The images presented of African American women at that time were that of the overworked, overweight maid, the drug-addicted or otherwise down-on-her-luck angry Black woman, or the over-sexualized, objectified young Black girl.

Foreign Body

There were some women of color who were held up as beautiful, including Diahann Carroll, Diana Ross, Jayne Kennedy, and Beverly Johnson. However, my memory of them is that they possessed many of the features of White counterparts, with thinner lips, slimmer noses, and straight hair. The message was loud and clear in my young mind. If you didn't have these qualities, then you just weren't "pretty."

The cheerleaders at my high school were no different: thin, long and straight hair, and mostly White. When I was in high school in Jonesboro, Arkansas, there was never more than one African American cheerleader on the squad. And she was never the cheerleading captain. Again, reinforcing the impression that the definition of beauty was very narrow, homogeneous, and elusive for anyone who looked like me. This set me on a quest to starve, bleach, and chemically straighten my way into being considered beautiful.

A Reflection on Pageantry

Deciding to compete in pageants was the catalyst for this quest. Looking back at old photos now, I can hardly believe that I thought I needed to lose weight. While I had curves, for sure, I was not overweight—not by a long shot. Even so, I was on a perpetual diet, trying to lose that last rebellious ten pounds. I tried every fad diet that came down the pike. There was the cabbage soup diet, the bananas and milk diet, the cantaloupe diet, and the grapefruit diet. And here's the thing: they all worked. With each of them, I lost weight. The trick was keeping it off. No sooner than I hit my goal weight on one of those diets, I would celebrate by eating a whole pizza, chased down by a whole pie! And there I would go again, looking for that magic-bullet diet that would make me look like Beverly Johnson (one of the first African American supermodels in the United States).

Eating . . . Too Little

There was a brief time, while I was trying to win a state pageant that would get me to the Miss America stage, that I simply wouldn't eat. I carried a candy bar in my purse in case I began to feel faint. To keep myself from passing out onstage, I would take a bite of the candy bar—yes, one bite. Some days I would eat only an apple. I tried taking over-the-counter appetite suppressants, but they literally made me feel like alien critters were crawling on my head. I even tried binge-eating, then throwing up. That brief experiment with bulimia didn't last long. I am grateful that I didn't develop a long-lasting eating disorder. They are serious, even life-threatening, and all too common, particularly among young girls. But by the grace of God, I was able to walk away from that misguided experiment.

Exercising . . . Too Much

What I couldn't achieve with dieting while competing in pageants, I tried to make up for with insane exercise. I once read somewhere that running up the stairs burns more calories than any other physical activity, including playing a game of professional football. I have no idea if that's even remotely true, but it sounded good to me at the time. So, I would run up and down the stairs while preparing for my next pageant. I would do this for a full hour, wearing rubberized shorts. The shorts were supposed to make me sweat even more than normal and, thereby, lose more weight. The shorts did not give me thin thighs. They did give me a urinary tract infection!

Even after competing in pageants, I remained fixated on being thinner than my body wanted to be. In my twenties and thirties, I cannot remember one New Year that didn't come with a resolution to lose weight.

Three Diamonds: The "Weight" Stronghold

To look back now, the hold that my weight had on my self-image and self-esteem is mind-boggling. I had become Miss America, a doctor of veterinary medicine, a successful business owner, a homeowner, an employer, and a world-traveler. Yet, when I compared myself to other women, I felt inferior. I chastised the image that I saw in the mirror. I secretly longed to wear size-zero skinny jeans. I wanted that gap between the thighs that were so toned and small that the inner thighs couldn't touch, even when the knees and feet were together. In pageants, this is a part of what was called the "three diamonds." An elliptical-shaped space between the upper thighs, another space just below the knees, and a third space below the calves. The skinny girls always had the three diamonds. Pageant girls were supposed to have the three diamonds. I never did. The bottom two were the best I could muster.

Oh, the Hair, the Hair . . . the Loooooong, Straight Hair

In addition to the battle I was waging with my weight as a young woman, I was at war with my hair. My natural frizzy curls were a tragedy in my mind. I didn't simply want straight hair; I wanted looooong, straight hair. I longed for bone-straight, butt-length hair like Cher Bono. She and her husband, Sonny, had a hit variety show in the 1970s called *The Sonny and Cher Comedy Hour*. In addition to singing, dancing, and skits, Cher spent the hour tossing her flowing, black locks back and forth from one side to the other. As a young girl, I used to affix a bath towel to my head with hairpins so I could toss it back and forth like her. I'd play house with my friends, each of us with a towel pinned to our heads, pretending we had long, flowing manes.

I begged my mother to let me chemically straighten my hair as a little girl. She made me wait until I was thirteen or fourteen years old. When I finally got a relaxer, I couldn't stop touching my hair. It was soft and straight, and finally . . . "beautiful." It's a wonder that I didn't get whiplash from all the hair tossing I did. From that first relaxer, I religiously got my hair "touched up" to straighten the new growth. My hair remained relaxed for the next thirty-five years.

The odd thing about my fixation with straight hair is that the pressure not only came from seeing White models and actresses in magazines and on television. In my African American community, there was also a clear message that straight hair was more desirable than frizzy or kinky hair. The age of giant Afros in the 1960s and '70s gave way to "relaxed" hair in the '80s. Women in my church and community lived their lives around protecting their chemically straightened hair. Even a threat of rain would cause us to cancel outside activities for fear that the humidity would cause our hair to frizz. I knew women who refused to swim or even do strenuous workouts because they didn't want their roots to get "puffy." Sleeping in a silk scarf was a common practice for Black women to help the edges of their hair lay perfectly straight against their heads. It was common to see Black women at the grocery store or shopping mall wearing scarves because they were keeping their edges straight for some important upcoming function.

I used to be a correspondent for CBS News *The Early Show*, in New York City. Shortly after the advent of high-definition television, I got a text message from a family member after one of my segments telling me that my edges looked fuzzy and that I should get a touchup to look more professional.

As a community, and even as a nation, we've come quite a long way since she sent that text to me. We now celebrate natural hair. Black women are able to wear braids, dreadlocks, and natural hairstyles with pride today. But back then, it was frowned upon by the dominant culture. And as exemplified by my Black female relative, naturally curly, frizzy, or kinky hair of African descent was considered "unprofessional." I look back now and wonder how can anything that God made be unprofessional.

As recently as the early 2000s, most women of color on television, whether newscasters, actors, or entertainers, had straightened hair. Even White women with naturally curly hair straightened it to conform to a stubborn idea that "beautiful" hair had to be straight. It was even better if the hair was also blonde. The popularity of blonde hair goes back to Aphrodite, the Greek goddess of love and beauty. She was described as having blonde hair by Homer in *The Iliad*. Only 2 percent of the world's population are natural blondes. Perhaps the rarity of natural blondes fueled the allure of this hair color.[5] Whatever the reason for the attraction and admiration, by the turn of the twentieth century, blonde hair was a firm symbol of beauty and sex appeal. Movie star Marilyn Monroe perhaps cemented the notion that blondes have more fun. Today one in three women in the United States dye their hair blonde.[6]

Foreign Body

The "Double Bind"

All too often, girls get the message that their worth is rooted in their appearance. As a society, we comment on the looks of women in all sectors. Female politicians are criticized for not smiling enough. Female corporate executives have sometimes felt pressured to dress like men to be taken seriously. But those same female executives are criticized for being harsh, aggressive, or brittle when they don't appear "feminine enough." People rarely focus on the clothes or hairstyle of a male political candidate. We don't ask a male CEO "who they're wearing," what designer brand they've donned.

This paradox for women is known as a "double bind." Merriam-webster.com defines double binds as a psychological predicament in which a person receives from a single source conflicting messages that allow no appropriate response to be made. Plainly stated, double binds are circumstances where we are "darned if we do and darned if we don't." They are "Catch-22" situations where there are no good outcomes. Too often, women are held to a masculine standard of performance but are expected to express that performance with stereotypically feminine characteristics. For instance, when a woman shows strong, decisive leadership, she is accused of being harsh, brash, and aggressive. Conversely, if a women leads with a more nurturing, compassionate style, she is considered nice but not a strong leader. It's a frustrating lose-lose proposition for women in many sectors of society.

The False Notion of Physical Perfection

Although women have broken many corporate, political, and social barriers in the last century, this insidious notion that women somehow have to be soft, maternal, likeable, and beautiful while simultaneously being strong, effective, and invincible makes the journey for some women untenable, and seemingly impossible. Misogyny will ignore a women's skills, abilities, and competencies in favor of insisting on a false, impossible notion of physical perfection. It's infuriating.

The idiom "don't judge a book by its cover" is commonly spoken and universally accepted in American culture, but seemingly, that is exactly what society has done to women, from the beginning of time. From Cleopatra to Queen Nefertiti, Jackie Kennedy to Halle Berry, society has often reduced women to their looks.

The tragic result of this fixation on beauty sends messages to young girls that they are what they look like. It's maddening and preposterous. Our eyebrows, eyelashes, hips, thighs, lips, eyes, ears, nails, waists, or cheekbones have nothing to do with our intelligence, creativity, innovation, and inherent worth as human beings. Neither the size of our clothes, the numbers on our scales, nor the reflections in our mirrors have any impact on our ability to be effective, world-changing, dynamic people. The simple fact is, noses are for breathing, not fashion or even "flawlessness" by someone's beauty standards. Legs are for walking and eyes are for seeing, not for whatever beauty standards we come up with. If we are blessed to use our bodies for what they were created for, They. Are. Perfect. And it is far past time to start sending that message to little girls.

From Insecurity to Security

I've learned that age does not cure insecurity. Our insecurities simply shift. As I journeyed through my forties, I was no longer burdened by the all-consuming obsession of what people thought of me. I was becoming comfortable in my own skin. I no longer tried weird, wildly unhealthy methods to lose weight. I'd grown to love my curves. I secretly chuckled at the thought that some women got implants in the very spots that I was naturally endowed. I declared a truce with my hair. It was what it was. And on the days that it wasn't what I liked, I bought hair and wore that instead.

But marriage at age forty-two and giving birth at age forty-four opened a whole new path on my journey with self-image and body image. Pregnancy and giving birth so late in life was a total game-changer for my body. I am thankful that my pregnancy was uneventful, and my new baby girl was healthy and strong. But the body that this glorious rite of passage left behind was completely alien to me. I didn't recognize this "new" body. There were rolls and pooches and dimpled skin that seemed to magically appear overnight. Breastfeeding surely gave life and health to my baby, but it deflated what was once perky and proud. My flat stomach expanded to a round mound that blocked my view of my feet. And my face was different.

Facing My Identity

It's hard to describe, but I looked like a different person. My face became fuller. My eyes were smaller. My skin seemed thicker. Pores in my skin were suddenly visible. Simply put, I was aging. I vividly remember my father telling me I was no longer a "young hottie." First of all, I didn't know that I was ever a young hottie. Even so, it stung that I'd lost the designation that I didn't even know I once had.

This forced me to face (no pun intended) my identity head-on. If I was no longer the young attractive Miss America, if the heads of men no longer turned as I passed by on the street, if complete strangers were now calling me "ma'am," then who was I? I'd spent twenty years depending on my youth and, yes, my looks to make my way through the world. If those were no longer available resources, what was I going to lean on now?

Being Okay with Imperfections

The truth for many of us is that one of the blessed mercies of aging is that we stop caring as much about how we look. We become less willing to suffer for beauty. We become okay with our imperfections. Well, less obsessed with them. Aging can be a way to force some women to look deeper inside themselves for meaning and validation. And that's a good thing. Too many women overlook strengths, gifts, and talents because they focus inordinately on physical traits. Some women place so much value on the "perfect" body, great hair, radiant skin, long eyelashes, and such that they never notice their internal strengths, like being an amazing leader, visionary, coordinator, conciliator, bridge-builder, or entrepreneur.

As I aged visibly, I discovered skills, abilities, and qualities that had remained hidden, or ignored, for years. I learned that I can be a coach and encourager. I learned that I am calm and laser-focused under pressure. I learned that I am adept at navigating difficult and high-stakes conversations. I learned that what brings me true joy is not external at all. Clothes might make the woman, but fashion was no longer an expression of my identity. Please understand: I am not knocking fashion. It's great and an important part of our development as a civilization. I just no longer root my worth in what I wear. Or how I look.

True Beauty

Let me be clear: There is nothing wrong with outward beauty. I believe beauty is divinely created. Beauty is all around us: snow-capped mountains, pristine lakes, lush forests, white sands, turquoise oceans. And there are certainly beautiful people. However, I submit that there is beauty in everyone: all sizes, shapes, colors, and ages. It's the narrow views of what is or isn't considered "beautiful" where I take exception. There is beauty in imperfection. There is beauty in disability. If only the time is taken to notice.

Our inner beauty is what matters most, I believe. Inner beauty doesn't age. It doesn't fade, wrinkle, or droop. Too many, for too long, have focused so intently on outward beauty that the exquisite beauty that cannot be seen with eyes is all too often missed. Resilience, compassion, integrity, determination, intelligence, creativity, and innovation are hallmarks of beauty that cannot be traced, measured, or seen with our eyes. But we marvel at their achievements and results, if we only take the time to notice.

Knowing We Are Fearfully and Wonderfully Made

One of my favorite psalms in the sacred writings of the Holy Bible says, "I am fearfully and wonderfully made; marvelous are Your works, and that my soul knows very well" (Psalm 139:14 NKJV). The writer, King David, was expressing his gratitude and awe for being created as a literal masterpiece. He knew the truth that every human being is a miracle. In whatever state we are in, we are miraculous. King David was assured of this marvelous truth, down to his soul. And my hope is that you will know, down to your soul, that you are a masterpiece!

That "knowing" is what creates a positive self-image. Seeing ourselves in a holistic, compassionate, forgiving manner helps deconstruct the harsh lies told by self-doubt and insecurity. And giving ourselves credit for our intelligence, creativity, empathy, uniqueness, and individual style bolsters our self-image in emotionally and mentally healthy ways. That is not to say that we excuse bad behavior, bad attitudes, and unhealthy habits in the name of having a positive self-image. It is to say that we can work on those qualities, habits, and dysfunctions because we love ourselves enough to believe we deserve better. We should not allow those areas that genuinely need improvement to pull us into self-loathing and disdain.

We must strive to be healthier and have healthful habits. But the motivation for change or improvement shouldn't come from shortsighted, often biased, popular opinion. The motivation for change should come from a deep love of self that provokes a desire to be our best because we are worth it, not because someone else demands it.

Lessons Learned

I have learned the hard lessons of negative body image and self-image. I have the emotional scars to prove it. But I have also learned the pathway from negative self-image to healthy, positive self-image. First, I have learned to cut myself a break, not be so intolerant and hard on my human frailties and faults. Because my faith in Christ gives me new life and a new identity, I've stopped thinking that my whole world revolves around me. I no longer compare myself to others (this is much easier said than done!). I remain grateful for what I have and focus less on what I don't have. I don't wait on someone to affirm me. I speak positive words of affirmation to myself. Instead of focusing on how far away from a goal I am, I celebrate how far I have come. I remember a saying from the older members of my childhood church: "I may not be what I ought to be, but praise God Almighty that I am not what I used to be." I lean into my strengths and passions.

I don't allow fear to dictate anything that I do. Actually, I am okay with fear because it has no power over me. "God has not given us a spirit of fear, but of power and of love and of a sound mind" (2 Timothy 1:7 NKJV). I now know that courage is not the absence of fear. Courage is moving forward in spite of fear. This courage, combined with the unwavering faith that "I can do all things through Christ who strengthens me" (Philippians 4:13 NKJV), makes us nearly unstoppable. If we dare, we can face what terrifies us, live through what tries to break us, and come out on the other side whole and victorious.

Additional Insights

I finally developed the courage to separate my body image from my self-image. It is not an easy feat. It can take years of intention, trial and error, counseling, prayer, and plain old hard work. I had to be willing to admit my faults without letting that admission defeat me. I had to accept what is the natural reality of biology and genetics.

No, Daddy, I am not a young hottie anymore (if I ever really was), but that's okay. I am me and all the glorious implications that come with being me. Neither my shape or size diminish the foundational essence of who I am, what I am capable of, or my divinely given purpose for being on this earth.

Now, when I work out, it's because I want good muscle tone and a strong heart. I want to keep up with my daughter. I want to live to see her children. I must be healthy to make that goal. If I am healthy but still have pooches, flab, and sags . . . well, okay. Maybe I am just too tired to fight those old battles from my youth. I surrender. I accept this imperfect, aging body with gratitude. Every day when I wake up and I can lift myself out of bed under my own power, I am grateful.

I no longer wait for someone to affirm me because of my appearance. I am most gratified when someone tells me that my words or wisdom or actions helped them. As a leadership development consultant, I am fulfilled when I help a young professional become a better communicator. I am validated when a friend trusts me with their deepest secrets. I am humbled when someone asks me to pray with them about some difficulty in their life.

When a corporation contacts me to help them with their leadership development goals or diversity, equity, and inclusion efforts, my weight, dress size, or hairstyle never come up in the conversation. When the young girls I mentor ask me for advice concerning their lives and dreams, no attention is paid to my love handles or flabby arms.

Peace at Last

It took more than fifty years, but I have finally made peace with my "foreign body." So, what I see in the mirror, as I finish the last few years of my fifties, is okay with me. Do I want to be smaller? Yes, but because I will be healthier. I want less body fat because it would be less strain on my heart, liver, and joints. I don't have to be super thin anymore. More importantly, I don't want to be super thin anymore. Cheeseburgers and pie are too important to me (in moderation, of course). The best lesson of aging is, even with this old body, I have a new outlook. And the view is beautiful.

4

Girl, You Are Not a Black Superwoman

Dismantling Mental Health Stigmas and Barriers

SELENA D. TATE

> We are hard pressed on every side, but not crushed; perplexed, but not in despair; persecuted, but not abandoned; struck down, but not destroyed.
>
> 2 Corinthians 4:8–9

As a kid growing up, Wonder Woman was my favorite superheroine. The theme music from the *Wonder Woman* television series would excite me. Oh, how I especially loved to imitate the infamous Wonder Woman spin! I would place a long bath towel on my head for hair (please don't judge me), position my arms like the letter "T," spin around several times, and voila, I was Wonder Woman. I loved her so much my mother bought me a Wonder Woman underwear set—an undershirt and panty set I sometimes wore under my clothes. When watching the WW television series, I sat glued to the screen because I knew Wonder Woman would eventually show up to sort out the conundrum and apprehend the villain or villains. She wore a red, gold, and star-studded blue costume with knee-high red and white boots and a golden belt. The heroine possessed a simple arsenal of weapons: an invisible airplane for travel, a gold tiara, two silver protective bracelets used to deflect flying bullets and serve as a power source, and, my favorite, a golden lasso, aka a sophisticated lie detector.

Wonder Woman gracefully brought peace to a chaotic situation and, mind you, she never appeared disheveled or overwhelmed. She exuded strength and, in most cases, single-handedly resolved a troubling situation. In other words, Wonder Woman could do no wrong. She was always in control, poised, put together, reliable, resourceful, the perfect embodiment of strength. We love the Wonder Woman metaphor, but know there is the woman at the other end of the spectrum—let's call her the Bag Lady!

**From Wonder Woman to Bag Lady:
Keeping the Bag Lady at Bay**

Wonder Woman experienced an exciting upbringing. She grew up as Princess Diana on Paradise Island, a secluded and segregated enclave populated by women.[1] Raised by her mother, Queen Hippolyta, and two aunts, Antiope and Menalippe, Diana learned how to cultivate her unique gifts and talents with wisdom and in a nurturing environment. Everything she knew and learned came from the influence of three focal women. Diana grew to know, understand, and embrace her identity as a warrior princess. As the daughter of Queen Hippolyta, royalty was in her DNA and it was daily engrained in her actions.

So, one day when a distressed warplane carrying an American male pilot crashed on the island, Diana intervened to save his life. Over several weeks, the pilot was nursed back to health. Because men were not welcome on Paradise Island, a plan was swiftly devised to return the pilot to his native country. To determine who would escort the man home, the best-skilled women on the island participated in a strenuous athletic tournament to measure agility, physical strength, and mental capabilities (IQ, cognition, and problem-solving abilities). After winning the event, Princess Diana was awarded the mission of escorting the pilot home. I'm sure you know the rest of the story. Princess Diana elected to permanently dwell in America to help fight crime.

Because she was Wonder Woman, there was an expectation that she possessed the ability to resolve any and every crisis. Her role required her to be on call 24-7, which meant no holidays or mental health days allowed. It was an honor to be esteemed and regarded as the best. However, it is easy to admire one's exterior qualities, but what about the interior? Do not let the flashy costume and godlike abilities fool you; if you were to strip away the layers, I think you would find a lonely, possibly bitter, and fatigued woman. The expectation and pressure of "saving the day" would eventually wear anyone out. Unlike Batman and Robin, Wonder Woman did not have a best girlfriend to confide in, nor did she have family support. Instead, she moved through life assisting others while tightly guarding her secret identity.

As African American women, we sometimes function in the role of Wonder Woman. Often, we represent the superheroine in our families and external relationships. We can be the identified go-to people in friendships, the way makers during financial crises, the caregivers, counselors, reliable volunteers, stellar employees, and, let's not forget, the Proverbs 31 woman. In these situations, we take on a superwoman stance, swooping in to save the day because we believe or have been taught that we can and must effortlessly handle all situations. Sadly, such unrealistic beliefs and expectations rob us of peace and leave our physical bodies fatigued, our emotional tanks emptied, and our mental well-being exacerbated.

Some time ago, Erykah Badu penned and released a song titled "Bag Lady."[2] The soulful songstress sang about a woman burdened with numerous bags. The listener is immediately prompted to imagine an assortment of bags that vary in size, color, and functionality. Delivered throughout the melody is a repetitive message about the "bags" and their adverse impact in an unidentified woman's life. Although the contents in each of the bags are never divulged, I believe that, metaphorically, they exemplify losses, disappointments, injustices, painful experiences, and possibly unresolved issues. Furthermore, the bags caused the woman angst, eventually impeding her physical and psychological well-being.

The bags took on a life of their own. Some were attractive, expensive, while others were cheap and tattered, yet they served many purposes: a cocoon, a badge of honor, or a protective shield to ward off unpleasant memories or experiences. Eventually, the woman is cautioned against holding on to her many bags. The song concludes with a simple but prophetic recommendation: get rid of the baggage.

As you continue to read these penned words, I encourage you to think about your own emotional and psychological well-being. Are you aware of the "bags" that occupy and invade your life? Well, if the unidentified woman featured in the song does not change her situation, the bags occupying her space will ultimately alter the trajectory of her life.

SBW: Strong Black Woman

Do you know a real-life superheroine recognized (or maybe not) among African American women? She, too, has stellar qualities, leaving some to believe that she has an endless reservoir of unique superpowers. Pretty cool, huh? Scholars refer to her as a Strong Black Woman (SBW). Before you cheer in utter excitement or race to the internet to search and retrieve a photograph or written summary, take a moment to breathe. Do something for me: Find a mirror and spend a few minutes exploring the image reflected before you.

The SBW possesses features like yours. What do you see? Are you surprised at the image staring back? Can you relate to the SBW? Are you or someone in your family an SBW? This is not a ruse but an opportunity for you to self-reflect on how you perceive yourself. I am not a gambling woman, but I am almost sure that at one point in your life, you may have identified with the SBW or know of someone who fits the description, whether a close family member or a friend.

Scholars define an SBW as

- Independent
- Resilient
- Emotionally strong (does not break under pressure or show emotion publicly)

- A fierce warrior
- Persevering
- A survivor
- Resourceful

These are exceptional qualities; however, there is one problem. God never intended for us to be Super Black Women, or the Bag Lady. Instead, He wants us to draw strength from Him because our "help comes from the LORD, who made heaven and earth" (Psalm 121:2 NLT). Our identity is to be grounded in the Lord, not in our abilities or roles imposed on us. The Bible tells us that our godly identity or "superpowers" are rooted in God alone: "Yes, I am the vine; you are the branches. Those who remain in me, and I in them, will produce much fruit. For apart from me you can do nothing" (John 15:5 NLT). That's right: apart from God, we can do nothing, but with His help, we "can do everything through Christ, who gives [us] strength" (Philemon 4:13 NLT).

Personal Barriers

Barriers can be helpful or harmful. Sound barriers serve as a tool to prevent dangerous noise. Concrete barriers positioned in the center of a highway compel vehicles to stay in their assigned lanes, shielding drivers from haphazardly veering into opposing lanes. In contrast, barriers can deter access or prohibit progress. For the Bag Lady, her bags hindered the woman's physical agility. They jeopardized her identity, physical and mental health, and relationships. Other barriers that disrupt our daily functioning are *schemas*—cognitive frameworks, or core beliefs, fashioned through life experiences.[3] Frequently, they originate from an individual's family of origin and upbringing.

These core beliefs and thinking patterns are not innate but are learned behaviors passed down from generation to generation. They guide how we perceive ourselves and others, and they eventually influence how we relate to other people. Depending on our life experiences, we create either authentic, false, or skewed core beliefs. When schemas are applied to the SBW role, scholars formally define it as "an African American woman who constantly suppresses emotion in response to personal stressors to attend to the emotional needs of others and effectively manage multiple roles."[4]

Often, an SBW is revered for being emotionally strong and is expected to be a pillar of strength for others. Consider the image of a Black grandmother. In some African American families, she is affectionately referred to as "Big Mama," "Madea," or simply "Mother." She is the family matriarch—the "glue"—that holds everybody together. They all look to her to sort out family conundrums. Women who grew up in an environment with an SBW (mother, auntie, grandmother, or an influential female) were exposed to unhealthy schemas. Whether deliberately or inadvertently, those core beliefs are inscribed on the hearts and minds of its naive pupils. While the qualities of an SBW are noteworthy, there are adverse outcomes that correlate with a woman's well-being. Revisiting the song, we are privy to a vulnerable moment when a confession is made about the individual's mental and physical state.

When we adhere to false or skewed schemas, we put ourselves at risk for psychological distress (like depression, anxiety, eating disorders, substance disorders, and post-traumatic stress disorder). Mental depletion may make us susceptible to depression or the use of food as a coping mechanism. In addition, if we are sensitive to or have a family history of psychological behaviors or patterns, we may be predisposed to repeating such behaviors in our own personal lives. The Strong Black Woman syndrome may be one reason African American women opt against seeking mental health services.

Systemic Barriers

Some evidence argues that African Americans are less likely than non-Hispanic Whites to seek counseling. Two institutional barriers hinder African Americans from utilizing mental health services. One common barrier is the mistrust of healthcare providers. Historically, we have been victims of extensive medical malpractices. For instance, the origins of gynecological practices were perfected on enslaved Black women. Black women were treated for reproductive issues and used as research subjects. Sadly, these treatments, or "experiments," were performed without any form of anesthesia or the victims' consent.[5]

For this reason, we have learned to reject aid for fear of being mistreated, misdiagnosed, or butchered. Inadequate or lack of health insurance is another institutional barrier that discourages some of us from seeking mental health support. If the person needing mental care has a difficult financial situation, a one-hour weekly session could be an extreme financial burden, making counseling services cost-prohibitive.

Lastly, a persistent barrier affecting African Americans is the lack of culturally trained therapists. Often, this concern is dismissed or minimized by professionals in the field and graduate counseling programs. Unfortunately, the origins of traditional theoretical approaches used in mental health were founded by White males and were immersed in Western culture, which overlooks cultural differences. Some of these approaches proposed that the manifestation and treatment of mental distress is the same across White as well as other cultures. This assumption is problematic, as it deliberately ignores general differences and differences within cultures.

African American therapists are profoundly underrepresented in the counseling profession. Of the most practicing therapists in the United States, statistics show that White women dominate the counseling profession.[6] Other diverse populations are represented, yet, in disproportionate numbers. The dominant numbers of White women tell us the ratio of potential African American clients to African American therapists is incongruent. Sources confirm that African Americans interested in therapy prefer to work with African American therapists.[7]

Mental Health Stigmas

Mental health encompasses our emotional, psychological, and social well-being. Here are some behaviors and symptoms associated with mental distress:

- Excessive worry or fear
- Difficulty coping with and managing stress or problems

- Sleep disturbances (insomnia or hypersomnia)
- Extreme mood changes
- Increased or decreased appetite
- Extreme sadness or feeling low or down
- Loss of interest in personal hobbies or social activities
- Aggressive behaviors (anger or violence)
- Abuse of substances (alcohol or illicit, prescription, or over-the-counter drugs)
- Inability to concentrate or perform daily tasks or work duties
- False reality (delusions or hallucinations)
- Low sex drive
- Thoughts of self-harm or harm to others

False facts and information about mental health are crucial in fueling negative attitudes and beliefs about seeking help. Evidence shows that we learn about mental illness from various media sources. When horrific stories involving deadly shootings or killings are broadcasted, the responsible persons are immediately portrayed as "insane," "mentally unstable," "lunatic," or "manic." Such biased statements dissuade us from coming forth because they foster feelings of shame, inadequacy, and fear, and we do not want these labels attached to us.

Letting Go of the Baggage We Carry

During my master's program in marriage and family therapy, I was confronted with the baggage I carried. Tucked away in my collection of "bags" were neatly packed bundles of unresolved issues related to childhood experiences and unsolicited hurtful labels bequeathed to me by other people. It was a tedious assignment that involved creating a three-generation *genogram* (a visual depiction of my family) that changed the trajectory of my life. The experience allowed me to embrace the many affirmative elements of my family history, and it propelled me into counseling to discover and work through my adverse behaviors and patterns.

Genograms are used to identify and map past and current family members, family functioning, relationships, and multigenerational behaviors and patterns within the nuclear and extended family. It is a clinical assessment tool associated with Bowen Family Systems Theory and utilized by family therapists. The construction of a diagram begins with the identification of the family structure and the relationship between each family member. Specific symbols are used to indicate gender, type of relationship (relationship status), and interactions between people (hostile, close, distant, enmeshed, estranged, cut-off, conflictual).

What does a genogram have to do with mental illness? Reoccurring patterns and behaviors (physical or sexual abuse, addiction, medical and mental illnesses) require further exploration of the family of origin. This may call for the construction of a focused genogram. Focused genograms are an extension of a basic genogram; however, they contain topic-specific questions that allow for an in-depth inquiry and identification of specific themes within the family. Because genograms are a nonthreatening approach to use with individuals, I believe it is valid and valuable when investigating mental health.

The Black Church and Mental Health

Historically, Black churches have served multiple roles in Black communities. They offer spiritual guidance, advocacy for social justice, dissemination of vital information, and act as a provider of educational and other supportive programs. A topic underrepresented in the church is mental health. For years, mental health acknowledgment and acceptance have been considered taboo in Black churches. This is disheartening because some scholars argue that most Black churchgoers seek emotional support from the church. Rather than seek emotional support from a trained mental health professional, some African Americans rely solely on their spiritual leaders to help them resolve their mental distress. Scholars believe this is the preferred method because of the interrelationship between the pastor and congregants.

Pastors are known for being intentional in cultivating authentic relationships with each member regardless of age. Because therapy involves disclosing and sharing vulnerable information, potential clients desire an engagement with a safe and trustworthy person, so it is understandable for pastors to serve in this capacity. Most churches are nestled within the communities they serve, which makes scheduling meetings convenient and at no cost for congregants. A controversial issue in the Black church is that most pastors are not professionally trained or equipped to assist members with mental health issues.

In the Old Testament, we find Moses inundated with the concerns and problems of the Israelites.

> You are too great a burden for me to carry all by myself. The LORD your God has increased your population, making you as numerous as the stars! And may the LORD, the God of your ancestors, multiply you a thousand times more and bless you as he promised! But you are such a heavy load to carry! How can I deal with all your problems and bickering? Choose some well-respected men from each tribe who are known for their wisdom and understanding, and I will appoint them as your leaders. (Deuteronomy 1:9–13 NLT)

Relief from this taxing responsibility eventually resulted in the approval and appointment of wise and experienced men to assist the community. In today's society, to offer counseling services, an individual must acquire a state license to practice as a mental health professional.

Although the Bible does not directly reference mental health, Scripture passages that reference mental distress are sprinkled throughout. If you examine the Scriptures, you will find verses that explicitly acknowledge anxiety, worry, downheartedness, loneliness, discouragement, anger, sorrow, and fear. Here are a few eminent references that highlight distressed women and situations:

- Hagar and her son's banishment: "She wandered aimlessly in the wilderness of Beersheba.

   "When the water was gone, she put the boy in the shade of a bush. Then she went and sat down by herself about a

hundred yards away. 'I don't want to watch the boy die,' she said, as she burst into tears" (Genesis 21:14–16 NLT).
- The woman with the chronic medical issue: "Now a certain woman had a flow of blood for twelve years, and had suffered many things from many physicians. She had spent all that she had and was no better, but rather grew worse" (Mark 5:25–26 NKJV).
- Maratha's anxious and worried state while serving Jesus: "Martha, Martha, you are worried and troubled about many things" (Luke 10:41 NKJV).
- Hannah's barren womb: "'Why are you crying, Hannah?' Elkanah would ask. "Why aren't you eating? Why be downhearted just because you have no children? . . . Hannah was in deep anguish, crying bitterly as she prayed to the LORD" (1 Samuel 1:8, 10 NLT).
- The loss of Naomi's husband and two sons: "Things are far more bitter for me than for you, because the LORD himself has raised his fist against me" (Ruth 1:13 NLT).

God is not repulsed by our mental distresses, but understands our struggles. In the book of Matthew, Jesus said, "Healthy people don't need a doctor—sick people do" (Matthew 9:12 NLT). I believe this proclamation confirms that God is aware of the many spiritual, as well as physical and mental, illnesses we may encounter, and He is supportive of us seeking godly counsel and help.

Can I Get Some Assistance?

God gives us an unwavering promise guaranteeing His faithfulness. Deuteronomy 31:8 (NLT) declares, "Do not be afraid or discouraged, for the LORD will personally go ahead of you. He will be with you; he will neither fail you nor abandon you." Knowing that God will be with you as you take the initial steps toward emotional healing is a comfort. Seeking mental health services does not diminish your relationship with or faith in God (another barrier and mental health stigma to dismantle) but serves as a support system. If you needed a dentist to help resolve a dental issue, would you solicit assistance from a podiatrist? No, you might ask a trusted family member or friend for recommendations. If your pursuit proved fruitless, you could consider a different approach that involves using the internet to continue the search. Regardless of the method, persistence will result in finding the best dentist to assist you. The same resoluteness is required to break stigmas, barriers, and family patterns that interfere with seeking mental health services. Finding the right counselor requires some resources (see "Resources" below).

Song List

You may wonder why this chapter contains a song list. First, I love music and have always gravitated to it when I have felt distressed, craved encouragement, or sought guidance from the Lord. Second, my undergraduate education in music therapy exposed me to the benefits of using music to promote physical and psychological health, instruct, promote emotional expression, and increase creativity. Finally, I am a lyric girl. For some, the tempo and beat are the initial attraction to music. Not for me. I am intentional regarding the music I allow my heart and mind to filter. Now, I like groovy rhythms, but lyrics are the priority. Depending on my mood or situation, I crank up my music device, select one or more songs, and allow the lyrics to soothe my spirit. So, the songs I share with you are from my playlists. The messages communicated in these songs encourage and uplift you as you embark on a journey of mental wellness. Remember that God never intended you to be a Super Black Woman.

> **Song: "Bag Lady"**[8]
> Artist: Erykah Badu
> Theme: Self-awareness, inspire, encourage, promote healthy change, and mental wellness
>
> **Song: "Please Be My Strength"**[9]
> Artist: Gungor
> Theme: Encourage, instill hope, and convey truth

Song: "You Know My Name"[10]
Artist: Tasha Cobbs Leonard
Theme: Instill hope, uplift, and convey truth

Song: "Overrated"[11]
Artist: Jonathan McReynolds
Theme: Instill hope and dispel false beliefs

Song: "Lil' Too Heavy"[12]
Artist: PJ Morton
Theme: Self-awareness and mental wellness

Song: "My Peace"[13]
Artist: JoJo, PJ Morton
Theme: Encourage, self-awareness, and mental wellness

Song: "Find My Peace"[14]
Artist: Naomi Raine
Theme: Uplift, encourage, hope, and convey truth

Song: "Not Ready"[15]
Artist: Naomi Raine
Theme: Encourage, convey truth, and mental wellness

Song: "Fear Is Not Welcome"[16]
Artist: Brian Courtney Wilson
Theme: Inspire, encourage, convey truth, and mental wellness

Final Thoughts

If you feel anxious about going to therapy, please know that you are not alone. Most people are afraid, especially when it is their first time seeking help. I will be transparent with you. Therapy is hard work. At times, progress may appear slow. This, too, is typical, so do not allow this to dissuade you. Therapy is not a "quick fix," but you will reap the benefits over time. In John 5:6, Jesus encountered a man that had been ill for thirty-eight years. Upon meeting him, Jesus did not overwhelm him with a series of probing questions. Instead, He posed a straightforward question: "Would you like to get well?" Wow! What a powerful question. I will ask you, "Would you like to be healed?" If you said, "Yes," I encourage you to follow Jesus's instructions: "Stand up, pick up your mat, and walk" (John 5:8 NLT). Be encouraged and remember, "Those who look to him [God] for help will be radiant with joy; no shadow of shame will darken their faces" (Psalm 34:5 NLT).

Resources

Consider the following websites to help locate licensed mental health professionals in your area.

- American Association for Marriage and Family Therapy (AAMFT)—https://www.aamft.org/
- American Counseling Association (ACA)—https://www.counseling.org/
- Psychology Today—https://www.psychologytoday.com/
- The American Association of Christian Counselors (AACC)—https://www.aacc.net/
- Therapy for Black Girls—https://providers.therapyforblackgirls.com/
- Behavioral Health Clinics located on university campuses: Housed in graduate counseling programs, these clinics offer affordable individual, couple, or family counseling supervised by licensed faculty.

Essential things to look for when deciding on a counselor are

- Qualifications (educational background, years of practice, and credentials)
- Therapist's clinical experience (depression, anxiety, grief and loss, mood disorders, couple issues)
- Treatment Approach (theoretical model)
- Accepted insurance plans (individuals with limited or no insurance should inquire about sliding scale fees)

PART TWO

RELATIONSHIPS
God at the Center

How Single Women Thrive

DIANE PROCTOR REEDER

> "For I know the plans I have for you," declares the LORD, "plans to prosper you and not to harm you, plans to give you hope and a future."
> Jeremiah 29:11

Who I Am

As a single woman, people will try to define you. Unfortunately, they often will define you as "single," as if that is the only definition that counts. By single, they mean "without a man." It is a travesty that too many women are defined by what they do not have rather than by what they do have. And what they have is affirmation from the God of the universe that they are amazing creations, beautifully and wonderfully made by Him, and *He* knows the plans He has for them (Psalm 139:14 and Jeremiah 29:11).

The phrase "I am" connects you with your spiritual self. It is, after all, God's ultimate name for Himself (Exodus 3:14), and we were made in His image.

You are not generic. You are as individual as your own fingerprint. You have your own DNA; even if you are an identical twin, your DNA expresses itself differently than your sibling.

God made you for a reason. And since you are not generic, there is no one way for you not to be able to live joyfully and content in your singleness.

In fact, there are many ways to be single. Single, divorced, or widowed, every way of living comes with its own set of circumstances and necessary adjustments and, yes, even strategies for coping. I am going to give you some things to think about, things that the Lord has shown me over the years. Some were learned by reading His Word; others, in the crucible of experience; but all have served to pave my life with the joy that centers and strengthens me.

The Joys of Singleness

Our society is oriented toward couples. From advertising to restaurants to even Christian ministries, our focus is on the marital relationship. The images we see, the messages we hear, all seem to conspire to tell us that we are in a waiting period, just holding on until the man of our dreams finds us and whisks us away to sublime joy.

I would like for you to remember this: You do not have to be relegated to defining yourself in the context of whether or not you are connected romantically to a man. It is difficult sometimes to live in a society that seems so judgmental of single women. If you're divorced: *"What did you do wrong? Are you too flawed to connect happily with a significant other? And will you go off the 'deep end' looking for love in all the wrong places?"* If you're widowed: *"Poor you! What will you do now? Hey, do you think you'll marry again?"* Or: *"Don't worry, you'll find another that will be even better."* And God forbid if you never married, and you're approaching your forties or even your fifties: *"What's wrong? Why haven't you found someone? What can you do to be more enticing so that you can put a quick end to your 'season' of singleness?"*

However, there is so much more to you, about you, than the absence of a man in your life. And, thankfully, you have a unique opportunity to explore and embrace fully the freedom of the single life without the encumbrances—wonderful as they can be—of a relationship where you absolutely must take into consideration, day-in and day-out, the needs of another person. You can wake up and decide what you want to do with your day. You can take spontaneous trips, guilt-free. You can change your life without worrying about what that person in your life will think. You can learn to enjoy your own company and then reflect and give thanks for your well-lived life. You can open yourself up to the many surprises of joy and circumstances with which God pursues us—and know that He pursues us with such great love, sometimes more than we can comprehend. Those sweet times of fellowship with Him are priceless treasures that you can immerse yourself in and emerge with a new appreciation for His quiet, steadfast presence.

Are you divorced? Mourn the death of your marriage, but then reflect on your part in its demise—not to beat yourself up but to gain a greater understanding of who you are. Then, with God's help, begin to reinvent yourself, not so you can "catch the next bus" but so you can grow into the image of Jesus Christ in a way that only you can.

Widowed? I had a very wise elder woman in the church tell me something very simple: "Think about the good. Don't think about the bad." You have an opportunity to bask in the parts of your marriage that brought you joy and gave you hope. You can rehearse those experiences in your head whenever you like. You can allow them to make you smile.

Never married? Enjoy this time! Appreciate the fact that you are unencumbered, less burdened with cares and worries, and better positioned to make a profound impact on the world. Time is such a precious gift. Make the best use of it, using this brief span of time called life to think and serve and be grateful and draw close to God, loving every minute of the time He has given you.

Listening

I love the word *listen*. In my favorite book of the Bible, Isaiah, one of the versions translates Isaiah 55:3 in a uniquely wonderful way: "Listen, for the life of your soul is at stake" (TLB).

To have a remarkable and satisfying single life, you have to listen. If you do, God stands ready to meet those who have an "ear to hear." In fact, God underlines the critical importance of listening to Him in verses from Matthew through Revelation: "He who has an ear, let him hear . . ." appears in the books of Matthew, Mark, Luke, and Revelation. In Mark 4:24, Jesus urges His disciples, "Consider carefully what you hear." God invites His people in Isaiah, "Come now, let us settle the matter" (1:18). I invite you to do that today, right here.

Defining and Redefining

Have you ever asked the question, "Why do these things always seem to happen to me?" and then answer yourself? *I know*, your mind tells you, *I didn't get that job because I'm not tithing enough*, or *The Lord didn't give me that man of my dreams because I had sex before marriage and He's punishing me*. Fill in your own blanks—everyone has devised these uninformed narratives of their lives. I'm not berating; it's a very human, natural thing to do. But the story you tell yourself so very often misses the mark of what God is trying to do with you and what He wants to teach you.

What story are you telling yourself about your life? Is it a God-story; that is, the same story God tells about who you are, the one He expresses on every page of the Bible? At various times in my life, I have strung together all kinds of stories about how my life is going and why things happened the way they did. Girl, is that dangerous!

Do you know your story? Or do you believe the negative reports that others may give you? Have you dug into the Word to learn your true identity? Have you read what God says about you? The things that you think about yourself will determine, in fact, your relationship with the God of the universe. If you believe the lie that you are "less than" or unworthy or incapable of being loved, you will not be able to accept the free, unmerited grace that God offers to those who believe and accept His Son, Jesus Christ.

How well do you know your story? As a single woman, are you trying to complicate what God is doing in your life? Are you second-guessing yourself? Second-guessing God? Or are you, joyously and with expectation, pulling in everything that happens in your life to make all the stories part of the fabric of your life and testimony—and then using those stories to define you in the context of God's Word?

My testimony is that I have done this: my own emancipation! You know how it is. People may ask you as a single woman why you're not married, or they say, "I'm surprised you're not married," as if that should be the primary goal of every single woman. Marriage is wonderful, don't get me wrong—I loved being married to my husband! But now, with the vantage point of having been married for nearly sixteen years, falling in love again, and now being single and unattached, I can honestly say that I have a good understanding of the benefits and drawbacks of all those states of being. To borrow from Paul, I have learned how to "be abased, and I know how to abound," how to live joyfully in whatever state I find myself (Philippians 4:11–13 NKJV). That has helped me navigate the potential minefield of OPO (Other People's Opinions).

> But with me it is a very small thing that I should be judged by you or by a human court. In fact, I do not even judge myself. For I know of nothing against myself, yet I am not justified by this; but He who judges me is the Lord. (1 Corinthians 4:3–4 NKJV)

When I took hold of that passage, my load was lightened. I put myself in God's hands, and I am spiritually healthy enough not to allow OPO to weigh me down. OPO is a "small thing" now.

My own self-definition was forged in a story rich with family, friends, church, Bible study (read Genesis through Revelation three times—highly recommend that!), music, and living. I will share it with you. Here's what I wrote in my journal on March 15, 1999:

> Re-Defining Myself
> I am a widow. I am a single mother.
> These phrases are horrifying to me. (Please forgive me, young widows and single moms—all this is new for me.) Awful. I must find a new way to define myself, a way that resists statistics and stereotypes.
> *Child of God?* Too trite.

How Single Women Thrive

> *Beloved?* Not enough.
> *A participant, accepted in the Beloved.* Perfect!
> I am part of an ocean of spiritual ancestors, contemporary friends, persons known and unknown, who find themselves covered by and filled up with the Everlasting, or, as Terry loved to call Him, the Ancient of Days (that was his favorite name for God). I am running in the blessed river of the beloved, going where it takes me as I move toward eternity.
> I am accepted in the Beloved. I am hostage to no one's definition, slave to no one's restrictive, stultifying description of me (friend or foe). I will not be boxed in.
> I am Accepted in the Beloved.[1]

I want to challenge you. Make this promise to yourself: "Under no circumstances will I ever blindly accept anyone's definition of me, except God's." Then use God's Word to develop that self-definition.

Guard Your Thoughts, Guard Your Heart

There is one aspect to this human experience that is common to all, single or married: our ability to think. Your thoughts are everything. They determine your feelings because you feel "some kind of way" about those thoughts running around in your mind, whatever they may be. They determine your actions because you end up making decisions based on how you are thinking about a given situation. Ultimately, as those feelings and actions build over time, your thoughts actually have an impact on your destiny. Proverbs advises to consider your thought-life and how intrinsic it is to who you are (Proverbs 23:7). It exhorts: "Above all else, guard your heart, *for everything you do flows from it*" (4:23, emphasis added).

Everything I have and am comes from God's breathed-out Word—my Anchor and the only way I came out of that incredibly difficult and unexpectedly blessed four-year journey navigating the illness and eventual passing of my husband sane and intact. Bless

God for those four years that were part of shaping my destiny! I would not wish them on anyone, including myself, but I have seen His hand over it all.

Over this journey, I have had to learn, again and again, that the only way to cope with a thing is to think rightly about it; that is, truthfully. Isn't that, after all, what Jesus said would set us free? "If you hold to my teaching, you are really my disciples. Then you will know the truth, and the truth will set you free" (John 8:31–32).

Pastor Adrian Rogers, in his blog "How to Guard Your Heart," asks a profound, almost troubling question to challenge us:

> What lies do I believe about myself or the world around me, and how is that affecting my relationship with God?[2]

Rogers is talking about bad theology or incorrect beliefs, but he could easily be referring to how we think about the story of our lives.

Thinking rightly about Jesus and God's Word is where it all starts. There is something incredibly freeing about discovering who Jesus is, what His priorities are, and then aligning ourselves with that by digging into biblical truth. The result is what we all are ultimately looking for: peace in the deepest recesses of our hearts and minds.

When It Gets Real

How many of us can, very simply, accept the reality of our lives—especially when reality is not anything like what we expected or wished for? What if you reoriented your thinking to *absorb reality and make it part of your very interesting story?*

The Scriptures show us a multiplicity of frail humans who have unique stories tailored to God's purposes for them. Those unique stories continue even today, in myriad forms. Consider the beloved author Maya Angelou, whose story spans the depths and heights of humanity. This is a woman who was sexually abused as a young girl. She did not speak a word for five years, from ages eight to thirteen. She thought that her words—the testimony she gave against her rapist—killed that rapist after he was found dead subsequent to his inexplicable release from jail.[3] Then she grows into a charmed adulthood where she dances, acts, becomes a justice warrior, and writes beautiful autobiographical works and poetry and plays.

Wow, Maya knew how to live in the moment, every moment. Feeling her feelings. In tune. Expressive. Her books reflect the depth of her faith: *All God's Children Need Traveling Shoes, Oh Pray My Wings Are Gonna Fit Me Well, I Shall Not Be Moved*—all reflective of her deep respect for the songs and sermons she remembered in the Black Church. She is a shining example of how to think about life—honestly, fervently, fully expecting God to answer. Life may not always be what you want or expect . . . but Maya has a direct message for you, which I can see through so many of her writings: Trust me, you will never have to live life alone.

Maya's God-conscious mind gave her great comfort and joy, which she thankfully spread to those of us who have been blessed by her work.

What's Your Focus?

Do you set aside time to talk to God? Is He your focus? If so, that's great. It's even better if you talk to Him all the time. It is when you are walking with Him, in the everyday-ness of life that He speaks to you. Jesus spoke to Mary Magdalene as she was frantically looking for His body after He was taken down from the cross and put into a cave (John 20:16). God spoke to Moses as he was leading sheep "to the far side of the wilderness" (Exodus 3:1). The first case happened in the midst of stress and anxiety; the second happened to someone quietly going about his business. In both cases, they had a readiness to listen. They had the right focus.

Your ability to relate to and focus on God in everyday life is just as essential, if not more, as those times you regularly set aside to read His Word and talk to Him. You will learn who you are, and you will come to understand your boundaries.

Boundaries

Boundaries are every bit as important as the freedom you have in Jesus. God's principles remain true, no matter what the larger society (the Bible calls that "the world") says. For single women, God still expects them—no matter what the world's pressures might be—to refrain from sexual intimacy until and unless they get married! That is nonnegotiable with Him.

Look at it this way: As a woman, your sexuality is powerful. God made it that way. It is also powerful enough to keep a man and woman happily together for fifty to seventy-five years! Don't dissipate your power by giving it away indiscriminately. Harness all that power, and keep it for the spouse God may choose for you. You will not regret it.

In addition, while you are harnessing that power, set that other important boundary: to marry a believer in Jesus. How are you going to go through this life thinking this deeply about and struggling with your faith while yoked to one for whom none of this is important? It may be hard for you. You may find someone who is compatible on nearly every level, except the level of faith. But life will be so much richer, so much freer, if you make the decision to marry "only in the Lord" (1 Corinthians 7:39 NKJV). If you truly desire marriage, just think how much better it is to live out your faith with your spouse by your side, ministering and working together. Without that oneness of mind and heart, you just may find yourself living that faith by yourself, in a space that your unbelieving spouse and partner simply cannot enter. That inability to connect on a spiritual level can be lonelier than you ever experienced as a single woman. Boundaries are blessings. They are there for a reason.

Joy

Our friend Paul, who was faced with a lot more than many of us will ever experience, said this about joy:

> Actually, I don't have a sense of needing anything personally. I've learned by now to be quite content

> whatever my circumstances. I'm just as happy with little as with much, with much as with little. I've found the recipe for being happy whether full or hungry, hands full or hands empty. (Philippians 4:13 MSG)

When I read the passage about Paul, this is what came to mind: (1) Gratefulness, flowing through our hearts. (2) Riding the waves of daily living on the bedrock of God's faithfulness. (3) Jesus as my Solid Rock. (4) Not happy-giddy or ignoring the very real struggles that we go through within ourselves and with other people and in our circumstances, but knowing what we know about God, standing on what He has taught us through His Word and our experiences . . . and then keeping those thoughts at the forefront of our minds.

The research is clear, according to an article published by the Association for Psychological Science. People are happier throughout their lives if they focus on the positive. As they grow in wisdom that comes with age, they make it a point to release old hurts and disappointments and look for people who are positive and encouraging rather than negative and critical.[4]

The apostle Paul might say, "I could have told them that":

> Summing it all up, friends, I'd say you'll do best by filling your minds and meditating on things true, noble, reputable, authentic, compelling, gracious—the best, not the worst; the beautiful, not the ugly; things to praise, not things to curse. Put into practice what you learned from me, what you heard and saw and realized. Do that, and God, who makes everything work together, will work you into his most excellent harmonies. (Philippians 4:8–9 MSG)

Choose to live joyfully. Don't believe the lie that your singleness is just a holding pattern until you can experience a joy that some will tell you can only come from entering married life. Keep experiencing God in His Word and with other believers. Allow yourself to grow in grace. And knowing that you have received that gift from God, grow in how gracious you are to other people, even those irritable ones whose words or personalities or even attacks stick in your craw. As you do that, you will find the negative thoughts and worries and cares begin to melt away, revealing the reality of God's truth: His everlasting love for you and your ability to rest in that love. Eventually you will find that your attitude will be overwhelming gratefulness.

"The joy of the LORD is your strength" (Nehemiah 8:10). That's not a nebulous, fuzzy verse. It's God's truth. Nehemiah, the Israelite man of God who was compelled by Him to rebuild the broken-down walls of his beloved city, Jerusalem, encouraged his people with these words. But the real devastation, they would find, was in their hearts:

> They read from the Book of the Law of God, making it clear and giving the meaning so that the people understood what was being read. (Nehemiah 8:8)

The people wept (Nehemiah 8:9) as they realized how much of God's law they had put to the side during their captivity. They were overwhelmed. I have been too, by what I have to do on any given day, by the notion that I'm not doing enough, by troubles and circumstances. However, Nehemiah made his fellow Israelites realize that this was not a day to mourn but to rejoice:

> Nehemiah said, "Go and enjoy choice food and sweet drinks, and send some to those who have nothing prepared. This day is holy to our Lord. Do not grieve, for the joy of the LORD is your strength."
> The Levites calmed all the people, saying, "Be still, for this is a holy day. Do not grieve." (Nehemiah 8:10–11)

Are you overwhelmed as a single woman? Nehemiah teaches that there is a remedy: enjoy what God has given you. Give some to others as well. Do the things that bring you joy.

Have you forgotten what you used to do that you really enjoyed?

For instance, I love playing my piano. I can get lost in the songs, lost in the melodies and the harmonies, and lost in the praise and thanksgiving. What does that for you? Why not try making the time to go back to it again? When you find that truth, or when you rediscover it as if for the first time, you have yet another opportunity to obey and bring joy to God Himself . . . and then He will respond by sending His joy right back to you. That is when you find that *the joy of the Lord is your strength.*

> The LORD your God is with you, the Mighty Warrior who saves. He will take great delight in you; in his love he will no longer rebuke you, but will rejoice over you with singing. (Zephaniah 3:17)

Overwhelmed? Close your eyes. Imagine God literally singing over you. Find those verses where God is speaking peace and reconciliation to His people. Put your name there. Bask in His love for you. Let Him surprise you with His joy.

Final Thoughts

These are the things that God has shown *me*. When you live with Him as *your* center, He will show you things too. Not the same things as He's shown me, because, remember, He made you to be unique. He knows you inside and out, better than you know yourself. As a single woman, you are a whole person (one is a whole number!), you are loved by your Creator, and He knows exactly what experiences to entrust you with so that you can live out your purpose in Him.

That, my sisters, is how single women thrive.

6

Marriage Built to Last

Withstanding Seasonal Challenges

MICHELLE M. OBLETON, QUINITA OGLETREE

> There is a time for everything, and a season
> for every activity under the heavens.
> Ecclesiastes 3:1

A few days ago, I attended a wedding of a young couple I had watched grow up. I was excited to celebrate with them. The wedding was full of love, energy, and happiness. But the moments that stood out to me were related to the couple's parents. One set of parents had been married for over forty years when the husband had a traumatic health event that kept him in the hospital for more than six months. He was attending his child's wedding. However, he was unable to speak and was wheelchair-bound.

What stood out to me was the care from his wife as she sat next to him, watching the couple take their first dance. I believe she was telling him about what she was seeing. As she whispered to him, she rubbed his arm and hand. All I could think was, *In sickness and in health*. I was watching both in one moment. The joy of health of the newly married couple dancing and the wife's faithfulness during sickness reminded me that marriage will have hills and valleys, but we can be and need to be content in every season.

"To everything, there is a season" (Ecclesiastes 3:1). Former First Lady Michelle Obama shared how there was a ten-year period when she could not stand her husband. She did not divorce him, because she understood that they were in a season of their commitment. Their children were young, and they were trying to build their careers. Often, we don't spend the time before marriage having difficult conversations that will support our marriages through the different seasons. Marriages are based not just on love but also on a commitment to each other and a covenant with God. It is important for us to understand: God-built marriages can withstand any season and its challenges.

Before You Walk Down the Aisle

The room was filled to overflowing with guests who had come to the wedding. The church was elaborate with floral drapes and flowers everywhere. Everyone who was someone was there. Twelve men and twelve women, dressed to a tee, stood ready to march down the aisle in celebration of the affair. Finally, with the wedding song played by an orchestra, the bride appeared, strolling down the aisle wearing a celebrity gown by designer Monique Lhuillier. The groom, waiting at the altar, was wearing a Bonobos Italian tuxedo sold only at Neiman Marcus. This wedding was the social event of the season. Joe and Jovanna were getting married. Even their names sounded as one. They were in love. They glowed at each other with such promise of a lifetime of love. This marriage celebration would go down in history as one of the finest affairs ever.

Their marriage, however, would also go down in history as one of the shortest ever. Joe and Jovanna's marriage lasted only six months. The time it took to prepare for the wedding was about the same time it took to end it.

We live in a world where half of marriages end in divorce. Perhaps it is because we don't understand that they will have seasons. As authors on the topic of marriage, we have been married to our husbands for more than two and four decades, respectively. Our perspectives on marriage delve into the profound concept of the seasons of marriage and emphasize the significance of finding enduring fulfillment within the marital relationship. We acknowledge the inevitability of challenges that arise during these seasons, which have caused many couples to consider the painful decision of divorce. However, we emphasize the pivotal role of God as the foundation of a marriage, enabling couples to effectively navigate these seasonal challenges and maintain a strong and lasting bond.

Understanding that God is the bedrock of marriage provides couples with a profound perspective that goes beyond their individual struggles. By recognizing that their union is not solely based on their efforts but rather rooted in a higher purpose and divine guidance, couples can find solace and strength when faced with the inevitable difficulties of life's seasons. This awareness allows them to approach challenges with faith and resilience, knowing God's presence and wisdom will guide them through even the most trying times.

Before getting married, we must first understand our relationship with God. God uses our relationship with Him to guide and build our relationship with each other. God also uses our relationship with each other to teach us and shape our relationship with Him. In this, both relationships teach us about each other and lead to growth that allows each individual to be perfected and to become the perfect partner and covenant bearer for their spouse. We often hear the sayings, "They are perfect for each other" or, "You were made for me." This perfection can only be created and sustained by God. If not, when challenging seasons occur, the couple turns on each other instead of turning to God, who is their foundation. By placing their trust in God's wisdom and relying on His guidance, couples can find lasting fulfillment in their marriages, transcending the difficulties. They can find renewed joy and intimacy in their shared journey.

When couples embrace the belief that God is the foundation of their marriage, they are empowered to seek His guidance, support, and grace. They turn to prayer, seeking spiritual counsel, and will delve into their faith to find the necessary tools to navigate the challenges specific to each season. By nurturing their relationship with

God, couples cultivate a deeper connection with one another as they strive to align their actions and decisions with the principles and values that honor their commitment to each other and their faith.

No other relationship will be more critical in shaping your life than your relationship with your spouse. Sadly, many people make crucial decisions about marriage when their minds are clouded with such powerful emotions that they find it difficult to think straight. They are so caught up in the whirlwind of romance, the venue, the guests, the dress, and all the fanfare that they fail to work out some crucial issues before they commit their lives to each other.

Because marriage is a spiritual relationship, your spiritual compatibility comes first. Compatibility will influence the quality of your relationship more than any other factor. One critical question you should ask of yourself and your potential mate is, "Are you a Christian?" The answer to this question is the starting point of the true revelation of your marital situation. This is what the Word of God says:

> Do not be yoked together with unbelievers. For what do righteousness and wickedness have in common? Or what fellowship can light have with darkness? What harmony is there between Christ and Belial? Or what does a believer have in common with an unbeliever? (2 Corinthians 6:14–15)

It is true that some couples get married without any spiritual compatibility, or perhaps one is a believer and the other is not. As a result, they may maintain their marriage. However, their relationship will bring on many opposing values and goals. They cannot discuss the most precious intimate part of their lives with each other. They will clash over the values that they teach their children. They will have a different circle of friends. Recreational activities will be strained, to name a few situations.

Seasons in Marriage

In marriage, the term *seasons* is often used metaphorically to describe different phases or stages that couples may experience throughout their married life. These seasons represent a marital relationship's unique challenges, changes, and growth. While every marriage is unique and experiences may vary, here are some commonly recognized seasons in marriage:

1. Newlywed: This is the beginning phase of marriage, characterized by excitement, romance, and the exploration of shared goals and dreams. Couples are typically adjusting to their new roles as spouses and building a solid foundation for their future together. This season can last a year or more. There tends to be few arguments, which are over minor issues and are fixed easily. These issues include how towels are folded, dishes are washed (by hand or the dishwasher), or food is cooked. The problems are often because two people are blending two different ways of living, and now they need to create a norm that works for them both. This is why the Bible talks about the two becoming one and leaving their parents.

    Many couples struggle here because they have learned to depend on their parents for material and nonmaterial things. Typically before marriage, their parents were their most significant source of security. But just as the doctor cuts the umbilical cord from the baby, married couples must cut the umbilical cord of dependence and allegiance from parents. You should always honor your parents (Exodus 20:12), but you must leave them in the spirit of Genesis 2:24: "That is why a man leaves his father and mother and is united to his wife, and they become one flesh."

2. Settling In: As the initial excitement fades, couples enter a phase where they begin to establish routines, adjust to each other's habits and preferences, and find a sense of stability and comfort within the marriage. This season may involve balancing personal and shared responsibilities, resolving minor conflicts, and learning effective communication. This season requires consistency and effort. You must know how your spouse likes to communicate. A discussion may not be good when he or she first comes home from work.

Each needs to understand the importance of timing. Also, some people need to process their thoughts, so while you may want to discuss the issue right then, it may be better to wait so you do not say things in haste.

Different communication styles can impact how couples settle into each season. Some individuals prefer direct communication, while others lean toward more subtle or indirect forms of expression. Couples need to recognize and respect each other's communication styles, finding a balance that works for both partners. Active listening, empathy, and patience play key roles in effective communication, allowing couples to better understand and validate each other's perspectives. By fostering an open and honest communication environment, couples can promote greater intimacy, resolve conflicts, and strengthen their bond as they settle into each new season of their marriages.

3. Parenting: This season involves the significant transition of becoming parents for couples who choose to have children. It is a time of immense joy, fulfillment, and increased responsibilities and challenges. Couples must navigate the demands of raising children while maintaining their relationship and finding time for themselves as individuals. Often, couples lose their connection with each other during this season because they are so focused on being a parent that they forget to be spouses.

    Create a date night. If you have childcare issues, you can do it after they sleep and have a late dinner or picnic outside. If you are worried about the children, use a baby monitor as a resource. Also, as children grow older, they may try to divide and conquer the two of you. Remember, you are a team. Sometimes it is best not to answer children's requests immediately but let them know you need to speak with their father first. Likewise, a father should be careful to maintain parental unity.

    The struggle to become parents or the decision not to become parents during the parenting season is a deeply personal and significant matter within a marriage. From a

Christian perspective, the desire to have children and raise a family is often viewed as a natural and beautiful part of God's plan for marriage. However, the Bible acknowledges that not everyone will have the same journey or desire to become parents.

It can be an emotional and challenging season for couples struggling with infertility or facing challenges in conceiving. It is crucial for individuals to seek support, understanding, and empathy from their spouses, their faith community, and other trusted sources. Prayer, seeking God's guidance, and exploring options such as medical interventions, adoption, or fostering can provide avenues for hope and potential avenues for parenthood.

However, some couples may choose not to become parents for various reasons. This decision should be prayerfully considered, seeking God's wisdom and discernment. Couples need to have open and honest conversations about their desires, values, and future plans. It is essential to respect each other's perspectives while also aligning the decision with their faith and the values they hold.

Regardless of the path a couple takes, it is crucial to approach the matter with love, compassion, and understanding. Supporting each other, seeking God's guidance, and being open to His plan can bring clarity and peace amidst the struggle or the decision not to become parents. Ultimately, the focus for each couple should be on building a strong, loving, and purposeful marriage that honors God and fulfills His unique calling for their lives.

4. Empty Nesting: The empty nest season marks a significant transition in marriage, as children leave home to embark on their own journeys. From a Christian perspective, this season offers couples an opportunity to redefine their relationship and rediscover themselves as individuals and as a couple. It can be a time of mixed emotions, as parents may experience feelings of loss, nostalgia, and even a sense of purposelessness. However, it is also a time of freedom, growth, and renewed focus on the marital bond. Couples

can use this season to deepen their connection, pursue shared interests, and invest in their own personal and spiritual development. It is a time to reevaluate priorities, strengthen communication, and embrace new possibilities together, all while seeking God's guidance and relying on His grace.

In the empty nest season, couples can strengthen their marriage by nurturing their relationship and exploring new adventures. They can seize the opportunity to reignite the flame of romance, deepen their emotional intimacy, and cultivate a sense of companionship. Couples can create a fulfilling and purposeful empty nest season by investing time and effort into their marriage. They can also use this time to expand their horizons, pursue long-held dreams, and engage in joyful and fulfilling activities. With faith as their foundation, couples can approach this season with gratitude, recognizing it as a new chapter in their journey together and trusting in God's guidance as they navigate and embrace the blessings this season brings.

5. Midlife: As couples reach midlife, they may face unique challenges related to career changes, aging parents, and personal introspection. This season often involves reevaluating priorities, facing mortality, and exploring new avenues for individual and marital growth. Couples may need to support each other through these transitions and find renewed purpose and passion in their relationship. This season of transition may require discussion on how to care for aging parents. You may also begin new health regimens as a result of personal introspection and facing your own mortality.

6. Senior: In the later years of marriage, couples enter the senior season. Retirement, grandchildren, and a more profound reflection on the shared journey can mark this phase. Couples may focus on maintaining good health, cherishing the memories they have built together, and supporting each other in the face of potential health issues or life changes. Observations of older couples help us to realize seniors can change. For example, as a working couple, perhaps they

never traveled together, but as seniors during retirement years, they often travel together. There is a change when both spouses are home and not working. They can rediscover their love for each other and renew or find new interests together. For some, they may need to focus on what they love about their mates, not what irritates them.

It's important to note that these seasons are not rigid or mutually exclusive. Couples may experience multiple seasons simultaneously or transition through them at different paces. Every marriage is unique, and the seasons experienced can vary depending on individual circumstances and choices made by the couple. Also, the season can be navigated more easily if difficult conversations such as finances and parenting have been had earlier in the relationship. Also, couples must leave room for their spouses to change and grow. The person you married five to thirty years ago is not the same one you are married to now; you have changed too.

Challenges That Create Difficult Seasons

Several challenges can lead to difficult seasons in marriages. These challenges can lead to significant problems, frustrations, anger, disappointments, and other opposing forces. Our greatest challenge in marriage is when we try to live out our lives ignorant of God's principles or fail to develop a relationship with Him. Another challenge we face is not understanding the needs of our spouses.

Every marriage is unique. However, five major, commonly recognized causes lead to divorce: communication, addiction, money, lack of intimacy, and infidelity.

Constant Conflict and Communication Issues

Persistent conflict and poor communication patterns can create a toxic environment within a marriage. In a Christian marriage, couples are called to resolve disputes lovingly and respectfully, seeking reconciliation and understanding. When communication breaks down and conflicts are unresolved, living out the principles of forgiveness, grace, and unity becomes challenging.

Being able to communicate is foundational to having a successful marriage. It correlates with other challenges that can occur in marriage. How do you discuss issues of substance abuse and addiction, financial problems, intimacy, and infidelity if you do not know how to talk to one another? Also, you have to keep the level of conflict to a minimum in your home; who wants to come home to a war zone? Your dwelling should be a safe place for the whole family. When it isn't, people tend not to want to be there. They will begin to look for other places, people, and things to make them feel safe and loved. What counsel does Scripture provide?

> "In your anger, do not sin": Do not let the sun go down while you are still angry, and do not give the devil a foothold. (Ephesians 4:26–27)

> My dear brothers and sisters, take note of this: Everyone should be quick to listen, slow to speak and slow to become angry. (James 1:19)

> A gentle answer turns away wrath, but a harsh word stirs up anger. (Proverbs 15:1)

These Scriptures remind us of the value of open communication, active listening, humility, and our need to address conflicts in timely and constructive ways. By incorporating these principles into our marriages, we can foster healthier communication patterns and work toward resolving disputes in ways that align with biblical teachings.

Substance Abuse and Addiction

Substance abuse and addiction problems can strain Christian marriage immensely. Addiction goes against the biblical call to live a sober and self-controlled life and can lead to financial difficulties, emotional instability, and a breakdown of trust. So often, we think of substance abuse and addiction to drugs as the only dependencies that are harmful. However, a few other dependencies that can be just as harmful include overworking, hyperfocus on children, busyness, or excessive social media engagement. While Christians are called to offer support or seek healing, addiction can sometimes become an insurmountable obstacle, leading to a higher risk of divorce.

From a Christian perspective, substance abuse and addiction are harmful and destructive behaviors that go against God's design for human flourishing. The Bible teaches the importance of stewarding our bodies as temples of the Holy Spirit (1 Corinthians 6:19–20) and avoiding anything that enslaves or hinders us from living in alignment with God's will. Substance abuse harms the individual physically, mentally, and emotionally, and hurts relationships as well as the ability to fulfill one's God-given purpose. Christians are called to love and support those struggling with addiction, offering compassion, grace, and the hope of healing through the power of Jesus Christ. Healing involves seeking professional help, participating in support groups, and relying on the transforming work of the Holy Spirit to overcome addiction and restore a life fully devoted to God's purposes.

Being a workaholic or constantly preoccupied with busyness or social media can be a potential hindrance to living a balanced and spiritually fulfilling life. While work and productivity are essential, they should not become idols that take precedence over God, relationships, and personal well-being. The Bible encourages believers to prioritize rest, having a Sabbath, and being still before God. It warns against the dangers of worldly pursuits and reminds us that our true worth and identity come from being children of God, not from our achievements or busyness. Christians are called to find a healthy balance between work, rest, and service, ensuring that their work is done unto the Lord and aligned with His purposes. This includes cultivating a heart of surrender, seeking God's guidance, and stewarding time and priorities in a way that honors Him and fosters spiritual growth, relational connections, and personal well-being. The Bible counsels us:

> Do you not know that your bodies are temples of the Holy Spirit, who is in you, whom you have received from God? You are not your own; you were bought at a price. Therefore honor God with your bodies. (1 Corinthians 6:19–20)

> But the fruit of the Spirit is love, joy, peace, forbearance, kindness, goodness, faithfulness, gentleness and self-control. Against such things there is no law. (Galatians 5:22–23)

> Do not conform to the pattern of this world, but be transformed by the renewing of your mind. Then you will be able to test and approve what God's will is—his good, pleasing and perfect will. (Romans 12:2)

These Scriptures remind us of the importance of relying on God's strength, seeking His guidance, and embracing the power of the Holy Spirit in overcoming substance abuse and addiction. They offer hope, encouragement, and a foundation for finding healing, restoration, and freedom in Christ.

Financial Struggles and Disagreements

Financial struggles and disagreements about money can create significant stress in a marriage. In a Christian marriage, couples are encouraged to be good stewards of their resources, practice wise financial management, and support each other through challenging times. However, persistent financial struggles, differences in spending habits, or financial dishonesty can erode trust and cause ongoing conflict. If couples cannot find common ground and work together to address financial issues, that can contribute to the breakdown of the relationship. But the Bible advises us:

> And my God will meet all your needs according to the riches of his glory in Christ Jesus. (Philippians 4:19)

> The rich rule over the poor, and the borrower is slave to the lender. (Proverbs 22:7)

> Whoever loves money never has enough; whoever loves wealth is never satisfied with their income. This too is meaningless. (Ecclesiastes 5:10)

> Honor the LORD with your wealth, with the firstfruits of all your crops; then your barns will be filled to overflowing, and your vats will brim over with new wine. (Proverbs 3:9–10)

These Scriptures remind couples to seek God's guidance in financial decisions, prioritize wise stewardship, and trust in His provision. By aligning their values, communicating openly, and working together to manage their finances, couples can navigate financial struggles and disagreements in a way that honors God and strengthens their marriage.

Lack of Intimacy and Connection

Emotional and physical intimacy are important aspects of a marriage. Christian couples are called to love and serve each other selflessly, connect intimately, and honor the marriage bed. When couples consistently lack intimacy, connection, or sexual satisfaction, it can lead to feelings of emotional distance, resentment, and frustration. A persistent lack of intimacy can contribute to the erosion of the marital bond and increase the likelihood of divorce.

> Love is patient, love is kind. It does not envy, it does not boast, it is not proud. It does not dishonor others, it is not self-seeking, it is not easily angered, it keeps no record of wrongs. Love does not delight in evil but rejoices with the truth. It always protects, always trusts, always hopes, always perseveres. (1 Corinthians 13:4–7)

> Two are better than one, because they have a good return for their labor: If either of them falls down, one can help the other up. But pity anyone who falls and has no one to help them up. Also, if two lie down together, they will keep warm. But how can one keep warm alone? Though one may be overpowered, two can defend themselves. A cord

of three strands is not quickly broken. (Ecclesiastes 4:9–12)

His mouth is sweetness itself; he is altogether lovely. This is my beloved, this is my friend. (Song of Songs 5:16)

These Scriptures remind couples of the importance of love, patience, friendship, unity, and intentional connection in nurturing a deeper intimacy within their marriage. Couples can work toward reestablishing and strengthening their emotional and relational connection by applying these principles.

Infidelity and Betrayal

Infidelity, or any form of betrayal, significantly contributes to divorce and goes against the principles of faithfulness, commitment, and trust in a Christian marriage. It breaches the covenant between spouses and can cause deep emotional pain and brokenness within the relationship. Infidelity or betrayal can occur in several ways, including through engagement with pornography and inappropriate nonsexual relationships.

From a Christian perspective, pornography within marriage is harmful and detrimental to the sacred bond between husband and wife. The Bible teaches that marriage is a covenant relationship that includes physical, emotional, and spiritual intimacy. Pornography introduces distorted and counterfeit forms of intimacy that can lead to objectification, comparison, and unrealistic expectations. It can erode trust, diminish genuine intimacy, and create a divide between spouses. Christians are called to honor and cherish one another, seeking purity and faithfulness in their thoughts and actions. Instead of turning to pornography, couples are encouraged to cultivate open communication, trust, and a healthy, God-centered sexual relationship that fosters true intimacy and brings glory to God.

Inappropriate relationships occur when one begins giving another the time that should be spent with their spouse. We often hear of the term "work husband" or "work wife." From a

Christian perspective, inappropriate relationships such as "work husbands" or "work wives" within marriage are viewed as a breach of trust and a potential threat to the sacred marriage covenant. The Bible teaches the importance of faithfulness, purity, and commitment within the marital relationship. Inappropriate emotional connections or excessive reliance on someone other than one's spouse can lead to emotional infidelity, erosion of intimacy, and the potential for physical cheating. Christians are called to prioritize their spouses as their primary emotional support and companions, seeking to protect the boundaries of their marriages from any potential temptations or distractions. Cultivating open communication, setting healthy boundaries, and being transparent with one's spouse are essential in guarding against inappropriate relationships and fostering a strong, God-honoring marriage.

> But the man who commits adultery is an utter fool, for he destroys himself. (Proverbs 6:32 NLT)

> You must not commit adultery. (Exodus 20:14 NLT)

> Bear with each other and forgive one another if any of you has a grievance against someone. Forgive as the Lord forgave you. (Colossians 3:13)

The Scriptures remind individuals of the importance of faithfulness, purity, forgiveness, and seeking God's guidance in dealing with infidelity and betrayal within a marriage. While healing from such wounds may take time and require professional help, embracing biblical principles can provide a foundation for restoration and growth.

It's important to note that these factors are not exhaustive, and each situation is unique. Divorce is a complex and deeply personal decision influenced by many factors, including individual circumstances, values, and the overall dynamics of the relationship. Christian couples facing these challenging seasons are encouraged to seek guidance from their faith community, pastors, and Christian counselors, who can provide support and help to navigate the complexities of individual situations, with a focus on biblical principles of love, forgiveness, and restoration.

God's Love Unites Us during the Challenging Seasons

"A cord of three strands is not quickly broken" (Ecclesiastes 4:12). In Christian marriages, the bond between husband and wife is elevated by the inclusion of God as the central and integral tie of the union. Beyond the commitment between the two individuals, a Christian marriage is viewed as a sacred covenant made in the presence of God. During the Christian wedding ceremony, the officiant acknowledges the presence of God and emphasizes the divine role in the union. The declaration, "We are gathered here, in the presence of God and of this company," signifies that God is not only a witness but an active participant in the marriage.

The involvement of God in marriages serves as a unifying force, especially during challenging times. When difficulties arise, God plays a vital role in bringing the couple back together and reminding them of their promises to each other and Him. The scriptural phrase, "What therefore God hath joined together, let no man put asunder," reinforces the divine bond and highlights the enduring nature of marital commitment. It emphasizes that the union established in the presence of God is not to be easily broken or dissolved by human actions.

For Christian couples, God's presence provides a source of strength, guidance, and reconciliation. Through prayer, seeking spiritual counsel, and aligning their actions with their faith, couples can find solace and renewal in their relationships. They rely on their shared belief in God's power to heal wounds, restore harmony, and deepen their love for one another. The inclusion of God in their marriages serves as a constant reminder of their commitment to honor their vows and seek His wisdom in navigating the various seasons and challenges they may encounter.

Final Thoughts: Having a Winning Season in Your Marriage

Having a winning season in your marriage involves intentionally applying the principles and values outlined in Scripture. In addition, it requires a commitment to fostering love, trust, and communication within the marital relationship. This includes addressing and resolving the challenges discussed so far with a foundation of grace, forgiveness, and a reliance on God's guidance. You can build a solid and fulfilling marriage by prioritizing your spouse's well-being, cultivating genuine intimacy, and seeking God's wisdom in decision-making.

Furthermore, embracing a Christ-centered approach to your marriage means recognizing the potential pitfalls and temptations that can hinder your relationship. You create an environment that fosters deep connection and spiritual growth by guarding against harmful influences and actively pursuing a life of faithfulness, purity, and balance. Through prayer, seeking support from a community of believers, and continuously investing in your relationship, you can experience the joy and fulfillment that come from a winning season in your marriage. With God at the center, you can navigate through the ups and downs, overcome challenges, and experience a marriage that reflects His love, grace, and purpose for your lives.

A Prayer for Protection over Your Marriage

> But in that coming day no weapon turned against you will succeed. You will silence every voice raised up to accuse you. These benefits are enjoyed by the servants of the LORD; their vindication will come from me. I, the LORD, have spoken (Isaiah 54:17).

> *God,*
> *I ask that Your divine protection be on my marriage. May no plan of the enemy of my soul succeed in tearing apart what You have joined together. Quiet every evil thought, voice, plot, or temptation that is working to destroy the holy union of our marriage.*
> *"For our struggle is not against flesh and blood, but against the rulers, against the authorities, against the powers of this dark world and against the spiritual forces of evil in the heavenly realms" (Ephesians 6:10). God, help me to remember that*

I am not fighting against my spouse or any other person when I am fighting for my marriage, but rather this is a spiritual war. I come to You as my help in time of need.

Give us the power to overcome the struggles we are facing. Bring others alongside us who can help strengthen our relationship. May Your wisdom guide our steps and keep us away from the sin that so easily ensnares us. Amen.

7

Engaging Your Faith as African American Mothers

The Challenge of Rearing Our Sons and Daughters in a Difficult Society

DENEESE L. JONES

> Train up a child in the way he should go; and
> when he is old he will not depart from it.
> Proverbs 22:6 NKJV

I am very encouraged that we as African American women can meet the challenges of rearing children in the twenty-first century by fully engaging our faith. We can stand on our faith and the strength and legacy of our ancestors to maintain a perspective and vision for fulfilling our roles. The enemy of our success includes racist systems, or those who foster them, and fear. Fear blinds us to the truth, keeps us bitter with anger or regret, and leaves us without power and hope.

Fear distracts our focus from what we need in order to lead our families toward the abundant life Jesus Christ promises us.

Indeed, Christian mothers must realize that in Christ, we have everything we need to overcome any of life's challenges.

Personal Testimony

As the mother of two daughters, grandmother of three grandsons, and great-grandmother to one great-granddaughter, I have experienced that having strong faith means being active, not sitting back and bemoaning life while waiting for change. Faith means believing that the transforming power of God's Holy Spirit can move me and my offspring's lives forward. While we may feel the weight of life pressing in on us, we are not alone. Faith in God continues a revolution of new mercies in my life and my family's—and in yours.

Engaging Faith to Meet the Challenges of Infants to Young Adults

The key word "train" in Proverbs 22:6 is from the Hebrew reference to the palate. In Bible times, the midwife would stick her finger into a sweet substance and place her fingers into the infant's mouth, creating a suckling desire in the child. Our role is to live our lives as mothers in a way that creates a desire for Jesus in our children.

The age of the child mentioned in Proverbs can fall between a newborn and a person who is of marrying age. For African American women, the compounded pressures of working may create tensions in their ability to spend quality time with their children. But at the heart of every child is a prayer: *Please take time to know me. I am different from anyone else. My tenderness of heart, my likes, my dislikes, and my sensitivities are different from my brothers' and sisters'.*

When it comes to rearing our children, we really have no ultimate control over whether our children will choose the narrow gate that leads to life or the wide gate that leads to destruction (Matthew 7:14). That's the truth of the matter, although we like to think that we have control over our situations. Thus, we must bring every concern, dream, and desire about our children to

God in fervent, persistent prayer. Our expressions of faith will demonstrate godly examples and principles to our children, to help them achieve the goals we anticipate.

Discipline with Godly Wisdom

With the increased media attention given to child abuse, many Christian mothers have become confused or intimidated regarding corporal discipline. Thankfully, the Bible—including the book of Proverbs—contains specific verses that offer good principles for rearing children. Sometimes, in the game of tug-of-war between parent and child, it is easy to simply give up and give in. When we give up the task of gently but firmly shaping our children's will, the child may behave in ways that are disrespectful or harmful to themselves or others. In fact, a child's hidden purpose is often to verify the stability of boundaries.

Children find their greatest security in a structured environment where the rights of other people (and their own) are protected by definite boundaries. This testing by the children has much the same function as a security guard who may turn doorknobs at places of business after dark. Though they attempt to open the doors, they hope everything is locked and secure. Likewise, children who resist the loving authority of their mothers are greatly reassured when their leadership holds firm and confident, even though the children's behavior may not show evidence of that.

It takes a special kind of mother with godly wisdom to provide balanced, loving discipline. How can this be achieved?

1. *Note the difference between abuse and discipline.*
   Proverbs 13:24 tells us that if we truly love our children, we will discipline them diligently. *Abuse* is unfair, extreme, and degrading. This action does not grow out of love but from hate. Abuse leads to a poor self-image that will often last a lifetime. *Discipline*, on the other hand, is fair and fitting for the infraction and upholds the child's worth.

2. *Help the child understand the discipline.*
   When we discipline our children, we should spend some

time with them, talking about what they said or did and making sure they understand what the infraction was. The object of these discussions is aimed to make our children know the importance of immediate obedience. We must learn that each child is different, so the way we approach them will be through knowledge of that particular child. Discipline should not be in anger but always in stern, tough love. One of the main purposes of discipline is to have our children remember that they are responsible for their actions and must be accountable for their behavior.

3. *Learn to shape and not crush a child's spirit.*
   Look into the eyes of children around you, and you will see those who are being crushed and those who are being shaped. Our youngest daughter was a strong-willed, independent, and stubborn child. She knew what she wanted and did not have a problem demonstrating that desire—even if it meant hitting another child or screaming to get her wishes fulfilled. Today, as an adult, she continues in knowing what she wants, but in an assertive—not aggressive—manner. She has channeled her energies into better ways of demonstrating her desires. My goal as her mother was to build her up with solid direction and self-assurance that would see her through her lifetime. The child who is shaped will have a love for life. Again, a crushed spirit produces a child without any hope for the future.

4. *Keep a balance in your life with God as the primary focus.*
   We do not want to be so rigid that we do not allow our children to make mistakes, or become so loose that children are bouncing off the walls trying to find their boundaries. Children must know where the boundaries are and what the consequences are if they choose to go beyond these limits. Children can be selfish, willful, impatient, lazy, discontent, liars, conceited, and rebellious. They are naturally programmed that way because of sin. Jesus was the only child who never needed the loving application of corporal punishment by His parents. Without preparation, most

children only know foolish thought processes and reactions to life. If these instincts, habits, or preferences are not corrected and if children are not taught wisdom, they will pursue these ways and possibly early destruction.

Consistency in Guiding and Directing Children

Make sure that youngsters have a clear understanding of the rules. Discipline should be private; if you're in a public setting, wait until you can be alone. Be firm in your discipline, but assure your child of your genuine love and concern. As I reflect back on those early years, I am aware of the many mistakes I made. But I also remember that when mistakes were made, I was the first to admit them to my children. This did not make me lesser in the eyes of my children; admitting my mistakes became a model for what they should do. Even when you miss the mark on an occasion, remember that you are still moving in the proper direction. Be encouraged! Your children want to know their boundaries. They gain self-assurance in knowing.

These suggestions are some helpful ways to rear and nurture your young children:

- Teach them to pray from the moment they learn to speak, and set an example by praying aloud for them and with them, morning, bedtime, mealtime, and at other times.
- Read Bible stories to them daily and discuss how these stories relate to their real-life habits and experiences.
- Teach children and young people responsibility by allowing them to help with chores.
- Develop a conscience in young children by making them accountable for their actions and behaviors.
- Take them to Sunday school and church regularly, and let them see your consistent participation as well. Where in-person involvement may be an issue, use virtual opportunities to worship together at home with your family.
- Instill Black pride, self-confidence, and appropriate assertiveness by sharing traditional cultural values, Black heroes and

heroines, and techniques essential for successful adaptation in the modern world.

Children can begin to know what it means to live like a Christian through these exposures and as they see their parents reflect God's grace.

We are to prepare our children in "His way"—not our ways, our plans, or our ideas. Instead, when we rear our children according to "His way"—the way in which our children have been created by God—we approach each child differently. We do not compare them to one another. Each child is uniquely made. Mothers of infants, toddlers, young children, and teens should learn to design different approaches for each one as needed. It takes wisdom that can only come from God to understand who they are and to be an encouragement to them. We can pray, "Lord, help me to build them up to be all that You designed them to be."

Nurturing Children Who Are Digital Natives

How often have you heard these phrases or said these phrases?

"Parents don't know how to handle the technology." —man, aged 43

"Technology has taught kids instant gratification and no patience." —man, aged 49

"We have so much technology today that was not available twenty years ago. Social media, reality TV shows, video games have really changed our society and how we interact with each other." —woman, aged 49

"There's too much technology. Kids are addicted. They don't go outside, they don't hang out with friends, they are getting overweight due to lack of exercise and poor diet." —man, aged 46[1]

"Digital natives" are the generation of young people born into the digital age, while "digital immigrants" are those who have learned to use computers at some stage during their adult lives. Whereas digital natives are assumed to be inherently technology-savvy, digital immigrants are usually presumed to resist new technology and at least have some difficulty using or accepting it.

Never in the history of humankind has there been such uninhibited access to knowledge and information. With a tap or touch on a tablet or smartphone, a child can retrieve information and answers. Furthermore, in this digital era, many parents themselves have intentionally introduced gadgets to their children as early as possible. From the moment they can reach and grasp objects at hand, toddlers begin playing with their parents' smartphones or tablets. You can find more that forty thousand YouTube video uploads regarding babies and toddlers playing with those gadgets.[2] It's amazing how a two-year-old can be handed a gadget and they know how to use it, similar to how a toddler in past years knew how to use a feeding bottle. Just take a look around the next time you are in a restaurant and you will see toddlers and young children engulfed in using the mother's or father's cell phone; oftentimes, they will even use their own tablets.

The lack of face-to-face or direct interaction with parents or other persons is bound to negatively impact the spiritual, emotional, and social development of this future generation. This should be of utmost concern for us as Christian parents.

The development of technology today alongside cultural shifts cannot be avoided. So, when children growing up face many new challenges, we need to realize that we are raising a generation with different brains. The most sensible step forward is providing support and guidance that is good and accurate in the use and misuse of technology to foster the positive development and growth of curious children. Without direction, the greater usage of technology can transgress family boundaries, values, behavior, and children's well-being.

We must be aware and address our own actions when we find we are less present with our children because of excessively long work hours, other demands, and as screens command more of our time or attention, drastically diminishing interactions with our children.[3] In today's digitally connected world, we are called to manage our own relationship with the internet and mobile devices, along with managing our children's use of and exposure to the same technology.

Responding to the Challenges of Bullying and Bullies

Bullying is multilayered and complicated. As Christ followers, we must tenaciously protect not only *our* children but *all* children. We must engage our faith to impart this truth to our children, teach them empathy, and protect the weak as far as we are able. But, if our children are being bullied, we must get involved. By focusing on the positive aspects of bullying prevention, African American women can build strengths that will serve their children well, not only on the playground, but in many areas of life. African American mothers must bear this in mind: "Beloved, do not avenge yourselves, but rather give place to wrath; for it is written, 'Vengeance is Mine, I will repay,' says the Lord" (Romans 12:19 NKJV). It is important not to suggest to our children deliberately or intentionally that they can resolve a bullying issue by relying on their combative skills.[4]

Often it is difficult to get the appropriate responses from your children about what they may be experiencing in school, before school, after school, or even at the local community center. The trick is to ask about things that are specific but still open-ended. Move beyond "fine" and "nothing" by asking your kids to describe their worlds. It's also great to start a conversation with an anecdote from your own day. Try one of these conversation starters:

1. Tell me about the best part of your day.
2. What was the hardest thing you had to do today?
3. Did any of your classmates do anything funny?
4. Tell me about what you read in class.
5. Who did you play with today? What did you play?
6. Do you think math (or any subject) is too easy or too hard?
7. What's the biggest difference between this year and last year?

8. What rules are different at school than our rules at home? Do you think they're fair?
9. Who did you sit with at lunch?
10. Can you show me something you learned (or did) today?[5]

With anonymity and the creation of the internet and social media has come the ability for others to reach our children and harass them in the form of cyberbullying. At this point, I am not even going to try to quote statistics, because the incident numbers are increasing daily. But it is safe to assume that anyone on social media or using email, instant messaging, or numerous other internet platforms is at risk of being a target of cyberbullying. Children need to be made aware of the mentality of someone who is a cyberbully.

First, our children must not focus negatively on themselves. Sadly, cyberbullies are typically those who are insecure; they target others who can make them feel better about themselves. The cyberbully is usually more aggressive in how they act online, due to their ability to be anonymous. They may also target children who have qualities of which they are jealous, or perhaps their targets possess something they do not or that they find weak in some way. There are numerous other reasons people choose to become cyberbullies. It is important to help your child recognize they have done nothing wrong and do not deserve to be bullied. Here are some things that you can do to be proactive in dealing with cyberbullying.

1. *Talk to your child before it happens.*
   You should make your child aware that cyberbullies want confrontation. Tell your child that they must not engage with cyberbullies; there must be no online reactions. However, it is important for them to alert you as soon as they receive any communication from a cyberbully. You should not erase or delete the message. Your child does not have to read the messages they receive from bullies, but you need to keep these messages as evidence. It is essential to save as much information as possible when reporting cyberbullying.

The more you save, the easier it will be to track down the individuals who are bullying your child (for example, you can save the email, email address, date and time received, copies of all other relevant emails, and screenshots). Finally, use appropriate software to block bullies if they are encountered through chat tools or instant messaging; use privacy settings on social networking pages.

2. *Encourage your child to talk to you directly if anybody says or does something online that makes them feel uncomfortable or threatened.*
Do not panic or overreact. Children need to feel that they can comfortably talk to you. Report incidences to the school if the issue is school related. Report to the police if there is a threat of any serious harm and violence.

3. *Stress to your child the importance of protecting contact information online.*
Children should assume that people may use the information they post online to cause them harm. Remind your children that the people they communicate with and befriend online have open access to all of their posted content and information, and they can forward or use any of that information against them.

We must be vigilant to remove our children from harm's way while bringing those who harm them into the light. Ultimately, we are comforted and strengthened when we remember that Jesus was bullied. The Lord "works righteousness and justice for all the oppressed" (Psalm 103:6). We must commit to engaging our faith in protecting our children and asking God to redeem for good what was meant for evil (Genesis 50:20).

Being Advocates for Our African American Children in the Schooling Process

Culture plays a significant role not only in communicating and receiving information but also in shaping the thinking process of our children. In order to support equitable access and undiminished opportunities for success, it is critical that our advocacy efforts acknowledge, respond to, celebrate, and honor the cultures, experiences, and perspectives that we know exist in our Christian families.

The first step toward culturally responsive parental engagement is for educators and families to come together to acknowledge, discuss, and dispel assumptions, biases, and stereotypes. Creating such a dialogue requires immediate action to open communication channels. Culturally responsive parental engagement is not structured by the school. It does involve a more active voice in how the parent takes part in the schooling process. This difference is best understood as a means of highlighting ways of addressing the issue of racialized disproportionality in education and furthermore in acts of school discipline, particularly in urban settings.

There must be a recognition of the ways schools need to transform the often microaggressive and oppressive ways parents are disinvited into their children's educational process. In addition, it is important to understand the way educators may value or not value the lived knowledge and experiences of our own children from the most important stakeholder in the lives of the children—the parents.

When organized and united, African American parents can have a powerful voice on behalf of their children. It is important that we get to know the people who will be making decisions for them. By developing a plan with a strong message, we can create effective strategies for communication and outreach; parents can make a difference as advocates to improve the education, health, and security of their children. And this is the single most important thing that could change and improve the well-being of all children in schools.

Being an advocate is about speaking up on behalf of your child—asking questions, raising concerns, asking for help—and teaching them to speak up too. Doing those things can be uncomfortable for some parents, for many different reasons, but it must happen. Here are eight tips for being an advocate for your child:

- Understand what it means to be an advocate.
- Know it's okay to speak up *all* the time.
- Write down your thoughts when visiting the campus for meetings.
- Start by speaking with someone you trust.
- Ask as many questions as needed in order to educate yourself to the expectations and policies.
- Don't be afraid to show emotion—but be respectful.
- Ask about extra help for your child, and appropriate opportunities for their giftedness when you deem it appropriate.
- Keep speaking up.

As we love and support our precious children, there is a clear call to advocate on their behalf. As Christian African American mothers, we can choose to be godly advocates who help shape our children into the men and women God has called them to be. Our call to advocate greatly impacts their lives in the present and the future.

Allow Scripture to serve as a foundation for your advocacy: "The LORD directs the steps of the godly. He delights in every detail of their lives. Though they stumble, they will never fall, for the LORD holds them by the hand" (Psalm 37:23–24 NLT). If you advocate for your child from a place of anger, bitterness, or offensiveness, you may find that your attempts at advocacy fall short and don't bring about the fruit you want. Learn to discipline yourself to stop and consider your heart's condition and motivation before you write that email, have that conversation, or make that decision. You can always ask the Lord to help.

Whether it's a classroom teacher, an administrator, a counselor, a coach, or a Sunday school teacher, you must see yourself as an ally and not an enemy. This is made easier after you have checked your heart, collected your thoughts, and entered into these conversations with a *yielded* heart to the Lord. Choose to be engaged from the beginning. Don't let problems escalate. Ask the Lord for wisdom and perspective. A healthy part of advocacy is not just being a problem solver by focusing on the challenges but also celebrating the good that you see. Make it a point to celebrate the victories your child is experiencing. Perhaps the most important piece to your advocacy as a Christian African American mother is prayer. Choose to pray for your child each day. Commit yourself to being a praying mother, and watch your advocacy move mountains for your child.

Final Thoughts

Each day that I choose to intentionally stay in God's Word, I first better understand what the fullness of God is all about. Then I need to understand some basic principles for preparing and praying for my family. Oh, how we need families where people genuinely and authentically love each other. We see so much evil that originates from the family. We as African American women need to ask God to protect our families from the evil around them and put a hedge of protection around each member. Continually, we must be on guard for the lion that tries to enter and devour the children in our families.

Today, with a seeming general lack of commitment, lack of faith, and lack of life in relationships, we must pray that our families will begin to grasp the vastness of Christ's love for them individually and collectively. We cannot comprehend this love that goes beyond our knowledge. But with a great leap of faith, we must believe and live the gospel message for our own lives first, and then we can share this love with family members. "By wisdom a house is built, and through understanding it is established; through knowledge its rooms are filled with rare and beautiful treasures" (Proverbs 24:3–4).

I will pray for you and your family, that as an African American woman, you may grasp the biblical principles shared and that your rooms will be filled with the rare and beautiful treasures called *children*.

8

Mothers Loving a Different Kind of Brilliance

"You Are a Shining Star"

GWENDOLYN C. WEBB, MICHELLE BRISCOE, CHINA M. JENKINS

> As a prisoner for the Lord, then, I urge you to live a life worthy of the calling you have received. Be completely humble and gentle; be patient, bearing with one another in love. Make every effort to keep the unity of the Spirit through the bond of peace.
> Ephesians 4:1–3

As authors, we are sharing the perspectives and experiences of two African American mothers raising African American male children demonstrating autism and hemiplegic cerebral palsy. With a narrator (Gwendolyn), China and Michelle share their journeys and how they have learned, by the grace of God, to nurture two African American young men (one now a teenager and the other a young man) in a society that often does not understand what it means to live with special needs. The mothers share what they have learned from experiences with those people who neither understand nor honor African American males and those demonstrating exceptionalities. Further, they share their quest to grow in their own understanding and live life with a Christian foundation. Readers will witness their faith and growth over the years and a collective effort to support what their journey can mean for "woman to woman."

China

I am a mother of two sons—Donovan, age fifteen, and Trace, age eleven. Donovan, whose nickname is Dono, is my firstborn son, and he was diagnosed with Autism Spectrum Disorder (ASD). Trace is neurotypical, which means that his brain development and behaviors are considered typical in function. My husband, Frank, and I are both army veterans. Frank is a veteran who is disabled, and as a result, I went to graduate school to prepare for a career as the breadwinner of the family.

When I was pregnant with Donovan, I was in my first year of a doctoral program in Educational Human Resource Development. When Donovan was born, it was a very happy time. We enjoyed watching him grow and achieve most of his milestones in his first year of life. However, over time, we noticed that Donovan was not speaking. After eighteen months of being nonverbal, we sought services from an early childhood specialist.

By the time Dono was three, we knew that there were some challenges: He did not make eye contact and was still nonverbal, and he engaged in long repetitious behaviors and would flap his arms. This behavior, called *stimming*, was often demonstrated when he was agitated or overstimulated. When the specialists began to suggest that our son might be autistic, we denied it. The thought of having a special needs child was too hard to process. When Donovan was tested at age four, he was diagnosed with severe autism and moderate cognitive differences.

Michelle

I am also the mother of two sons: Edwin, age forty-three, and Shannon, age forty. Edwin, named after his father, is neurotypical.

His brain development and behaviors are considered typical in function. In fact, Edwin's early development followed and sometimes exceeded all the "typical" developmental milestones. Watching him grow brought so much joy to my husband, Lloyd, and me. When his younger brother was born three years later, that joy was duplicated. Then something happened. My baby went to the hospital.

My seven-week-old baby was in the hospital with a diagnosis of pneumococcal meningitis because of a severe ear infection. Lloyd and I had been married for five years. Intense grieving paralyzed me. At night, when no one was around but me, Shannon had seizures. I did not fully understand what would happen next.

I prayed and said, "God, I want to trust You, but I do not know how. Teach me how to trust You and I will do it." From that moment on, my journey with the Lord has been a faith-walk. My life Scripture has been: "My grace is sufficient for you, for my power is made perfect in weakness" (2 Corinthians 12:9). Shannon Gerard Briscoe spent the next seven weeks in Dallas's Children's Medical Center. He was treated for pneumococcal meningitis and seizures. Shannon would later be diagnosed with hemiplegic cerebral palsy, with cognitive and speech delay. Cerebral palsy is "a condition marked by impaired muscle coordination (spastic paralysis) and/or other disabilities, typically caused by damage to the brain."[1]

Our Initial Responses and Emotions

China

I was in shock about our new reality. Why did this happen to my son? How were we supposed to live? I did not allow myself to think about the future. I just knew that I wanted Donovan to be *fixed*. After spending much time in prayer and research, the Lord led us to get help through several alternative pathways. Donovan saw a naturopathic doctor, neurological chiropractor, and many other therapists.

Once we discovered that diet positively impacted Donovan's behavior, we made a lifestyle change in our food. We cut out gluten, dairy, soy, dyes, and other additives. We ate food that was as clean as possible. The learning curve was very steep. I was so absorbed in developing new routines and diets for Donovan, simultaneously raising a newborn and writing my research dissertation, that I shut down emotionally. When I did talk about my struggles with family or friends, most of them could not understand. While some gave an empathetic ear, others gave advice that was not helpful for my situation, and others dismissed my heartache and challenges. I found myself becoming more withdrawn as I learned there were only a few people I could trust to share my heart. Additionally, I encountered alienation from other parents of children with ASD because many of them also were struggling with accepting their diagnosis. They did not want my son to negatively influence their child's behavior.

My husband and I felt the need to be strong for one another, so we did not discuss our grief or console one another. A year after the diagnosis, Frank and I found ourselves on the verge of divorce. We needed and sought marriage counseling. After months of intensive biblical coaching on God's design for marriage, we reconciled and began to build anew our life together.

Frank and I spent three years in isolation, working with Donovan to develop his speech and independence. His progress was such an encouragement. Donovan was finally talking, he was potty trained, and his temper was better controlled. However, when I put him in class with his peers, I was extremely dismayed to see how far behind he was from the typical development for his age. It was at this time that I had to come to terms with the fact that I had a special needs child, and although he showed great progress, he was still a special needs child.

I saw how great the gap of development was among his classmates, and I realized that it might be our reality that Donovan would never recover completely from ASD. Additionally, as I watched my other son, Trace, achieve all his developmental markers, I began to realize how much I had missed in Donovan's life.

Until then, I had never grieved Donovan's diagnosis. I spent much time in prayer asking God to fix Donovan, fix our marriage, tell me what to do, supply our needs, help me to manage two children, help me get through graduate school, but I did not ask Him to heal my broken heart. I had avoided dealing with grief until that moment. It was a very significant understanding of my grief. I mourned the death of dreams for my child. I grieved that he might not go to college, get married, or have children. I grieved that he might never be independent. I feared for his livelihood as an African American male who would be misunderstood. I feared for Donovan's future after my husband and I pass away. I feared placing a burden of responsibility on Trace to take care of Donovan in our passing. I feared not giving Trace the attention that he needed. I faced my fears. Would Dono spend the rest of his life wishing to be "normal"? Would he be bitter about his lot in life? Even worse—would he have the capacity to understand the gospel and accept Christ?

Michelle

After the hemiplegic cerebral palsy diagnosis, we were told that Shannon would have to start all over with everything a newborn learns to do. There was no guarantee that he would lift his head, learn how to chew food, crawl, walk, run, possess fine motor and large motor skills, or expressive and receptive language skills. There was no guarantee that he would acquire daily living skills, possess a memory, or have comprehension. There was no guarantee that he would develop higher-order thinking skills, acquire socially appropriate behavior, or make appropriate choices.

What were we to do with that laundry list of no guarantees? The first thing I did on hearing the diagnosis from the doctors was to pray for God's wisdom, guidance, and direction. I prayed, Lloyd prayed. My husband believed that everything would be all right. He believed that the Lord would heal Shannon, that our son would return to developing within the realm of where he began at birth. As Shannon's mother, I wanted to know what all of this meant. I knew I was on a faith-walk, but there was so much I did not know. What was *cerebral palsy*? What were my medical, social, and financial resources? I began to do the research. As I read about some of the answers to those questions, I also wanted to know who would be in my spiritual support system. What would I put in place to stay connected to the Lord? What were my child's unique needs?

I then had to rethink and determine how our home life, daily routines, schedules, and orientation as a family should be modified. *How would we fully embrace a new lifestyle while raising an infant with special needs? How would I continue to be Mommy to an inquisitive and active three-year-old? How would we raise both our children in the Lord, with all the challenges facing us?* I also had to engineer the impact our lives would have on other family members. Shannon's brother was three years older. This new life had an impact on him as well.

I found that the hardest part of my experience was accepting the ordained appointment and assignment from the Lord. God is sovereign! He alone determines the outcome of all things. There is nothing outside of His control. No purpose of God can be thwarted.

How Our Assignments Had an Impact on Our Faith

China

Having a child with special needs has dramatically affected my faith. At a level that I could not have reached without the diagnosis, I have learned that the Lord is a provider and that He is a good, loving God. We were living on a small, fixed income. Our new lifestyle also cost us community with others because we did not have a lot of money. We could no longer afford to go out, and our new way of eating was not accommodated in most restaurants. Outside of paying our tithes and our bills, all our money went into helping Donovan get the best chance at life. We enrolled Donovan in several types of therapies and spent most of our money on his well-being.

I had to learn to trust God with providing for our needs, and He did so in a mighty way. Even on a small budget, we never missed a bill payment or a meal. We signed up for new therapies that cost thousands of dollars, not knowing how the payments were going to be made. Frank and I turned it over to God, and He made a way. God taught us how to be very resourceful and how to make our money stretch. He also sent us unexpected financial blessings in the form of gifts or random refund checks that came right on time to meet an urgent need. I learned very quickly that I could trust the Lord with meeting our physical needs.

Michelle

In addition to caring for a child or adult with special needs, life still happens. My husband of thirty-three years passed away suddenly three years ago. Shannon has had to make this adjustment to real-life realities. He continues to grow in his own walk with the Lord as he strives to grasp the reality that his dad is in heaven. He seems to understand that his father will have everlasting life because of the sacrifice of Jesus. He misses his father. Oh, but for the grace of God. "In all these things we are more than conquerors through him who loved us" (Romans 8:37).

Lessons Learned in the Sanctification Process

China

I have learned that I can trust the Lord to meet my heart needs. This took longer because the depth of hurt, confusion, and grief caused me to withhold trusting the Lord with my heart wounds. I also had to admit that I was withholding trust from God because I blamed Him for bringing hardship to my family. Over time, I realized that God had entrusted us with Donovan because He loves us.

Having a child with special needs has brought me closer to the Lord in that I have learned to depend on Him when I do not understand my child, don't know what to do, or I misunderstand how to parent. God has used Donovan to teach me to have joy in the simple things of life. The Lord gave me a Bible verse for his life:

> "For I know the plans I have for you," declares the LORD, "plans to prosper you and not to harm you, plans to give you hope and a future. Then you will call on me and come and pray to me, and I will listen to you. You will seek me and find me when you seek me with all your heart." (Jeremiah 29:11–13)

Donovan's interests and quirks have made me laugh and bring me joy. His easygoing temperament convicts me when I feel discontent with life. The Lord has been so faithful to our family. At fifteen years old, Donovan has defied his diagnosis—although many of his behaviors demonstrate he is still on the autism spectrum. He is now considered high-functioning. He loves school and nature, has a gentle heart, and loves being around people. He even dreams of cooking and working in a restaurant. I never dreamed that I would see these characteristics in his life.

Michelle

When Shannon was five years old, I made the decision to leave full-time employment. Shannon did not fit into local after-school programs, so I would have to transport him to and from school. At this time, I joined an international Bible study group and began to grow even more in my relationship with God. Bible study enabled me to see Him better, and it strengthened my faith. As I learned that God is faithful, I entrusted my challenges to Him. As I learned He is sovereign, I believed Him to be in control of my universe and situation. As I learned He is loving, I came to embrace that being a *special needs* mom is not a curse but a privilege.

As I trusted God, I grew in faith, and my commitment to Him determined the quality of life for me as a parent and, ultimately, for my special needs child. When I believed that God called me to this special assignment, I sought His wisdom, guidance, resources, strength, encouragement, and protection. When I believed that daily prayer, consistent Bible study, and participation in a spiritual community were God's substance for my journey, I was able to partake in and pursue them. When I humbly accepted my unique privilege to be called and entrusted with this special needs child, I valued my child and the spiritual experience.

How the Church Played a Role in Our Growth

China

In the early years of Donovan's diagnosis, Frank and I struggled with fully attending and participating in church. Donovan's vocal volume was powerful, and he was easily stimulated when he was frustrated. He would often kick or hit the other children during Sunday school. As a result, Frank and I pulled him from the general church service. We took turns watching him in the hallway while one of us attended the service. We would then switch duties for the second service. One of the Lord's blessings to us was when our church hired a children's director. She was a retired school principal who saw that we could not attend service and sought to find an aide who could assist Donovan during Sunday school. Donovan did well. My husband and I were able to participate in worship and serve in other capacities in our church as a result. I eventually realized that I could trust our church with my child. That brought great relief.

One of my prayers was that Donovan would understand the gospel and choose to accept Christ. My husband and I shared the gospel with him on numerous occasions, but he never seemed to really understand. This past year, however, the same children's director led Donovan to the Lord. I am blown away by the greatness of God!

Michelle

God used our loving church family to sustain us. We have belonged to a Bible-teaching, Bible-preaching church since the beginning of our marriage. There were no provisions for children with special needs, but the church responded with overwhelming support from the onset of Shannon's challenges. Lloyd and I were both church leaders and fully involved in ministry. We never stayed home from church.

Because of Shannon's delays, his placement in the church nursery always corresponded to where he was developmentally, not his age. When I accepted the position of Children's Ministry Director, overseeing the nursery and the children's church, I wanted to address the need for provisions for special needs children. At the time, parents would typically rotate staying home and attending church. I created a Special Needs Ministry. Three pastors' wives, who were educators and passionate about this need, provided the leadership. Now Shannon would be able to study God's Word in a way he could understand.

How Public Schools Impacted Our Growth

China

Frank and I have had our share of joys and challenges with schools over the years. In Donovan's early years of school, we learned we had to be an advocate for our child. If we did not ask for all the services for which we were entitled, the school would not freely offer them. My husband read the state laws on mandated services for children with special needs. We had to constantly remind school representatives of those mandated services at the parent-teacher meetings. In the fifth grade, we discovered that Donovan had fallen extremely behind in his learning, and the teachers did not inform us about his lack of progress.

We wrestled with the idea of homeschooling when we acknowledged that being in school was causing Donovan to have low self-esteem and confidence. Frank homeschooled him for two years and got him caught up to his age level. More importantly, Donovan's confidence was bolstered, and he was more than ready to return to school. At this writing, he has done well in the special education program during his first year of high school.

Michelle

Since family, the church, and God Himself had sustained me, how I wish I could say the same for his public school environment. The educational system was a challenge, inadequate, and a complete disappointment. We felt we were in a street fight, every day. His Individual Education Plan (IEP) was not followed. My child went several years without a speech therapist, even when the evaluations showed it was a priority for his plan.

There were teachers in special education who did not understand special education. How could this be? I had to fight and advocate for him the whole time he was in public school. For example, I remember asking if potty training could be one of his goals. They responded that he was not ready. So, I potty trained him myself over the summer. After all, he was seven years old and was most certainly ready. When he returned to school in the fall, the staff was amazed.

Snapshots of Their Brilliance

China

People with ASD are known for their quirks and can often become obsessive about the things that interest them. Donovan's obsessions have morphed over the years. He used to fixate on extension cords, grandfather clocks, fire hydrants, airplanes, and Angry Birds at various points in his life. One obsession that drove me crazy was the fixation he had for toilets. It lasted for years. He would study toilets, watch plumbing videos of flushing toilets on repeat, stick his head in toilets to get a close-up view of the flushing waters, and he would talk to everyone about toilets. He preferred American Standard over Koehler toilets and sometimes would not go into certain restrooms because of the brand of toilets. As a conversation starter, Donovan would ask random strangers if they preferred urinals over toilets or ask them about their favorite toilet brand. It is funny now, but at the time, I was mortified.

One day, I told him in a very harsh tone that he should stop talking about toilets because they are dirty, people think they are gross, and liking toilets is not normal. Donovan stomped up the stairs and shouted in an indignant voice that he did not care if others did not like toilets. He said it was perfectly fine that he liked toilets because toilets are great. I was instantly convicted.

Underlying my words was the insinuation that my son was wrong and abnormal for not conforming to socially accepted norms. I had never accused him of not being normal before, and I had imposed on him my embarrassment of something he held dear. I also realized that, unlike me, he did not care what others thought about him. He felt free to be himself and enjoy life without shame or compromise. To this day, I marvel at his self-assured view of himself. And I absolutely love his quirks. I had to apologize to him, and I never discouraged his passion for toilets again. I did, however, coach him on when to talk about toilets and why he would get awkward responses when people did not respond with the same passion. He knows that he is "special," but in his mind, that just means he thinks differently than others.

Michelle

As a preteen, Shannon loved pretty girls. There was nothing wrong with his eyes. I wanted to understand his standard for "pretty." So, one day at the dinner table, I asked, "Shannon, is your *mother* pretty?" He paused and responded, "You're smart, you're funny . . . pass the potatoes, please." *Did my child just call me ugly?* It was a very special moment because each of us laughed hysterically.

During the third month of the COVID-19 pandemic, Shannon's older brother, Edwin, and I went to exercise. We forgot to turn on the alarm in our home. When we returned, Shannon was gone. We had no idea of his whereabouts, and he did not have a phone on him. It was June and we searched for him six hours in the hot, Texas sun. Everywhere we went, people replied, "Oh, yes, he was here. He went that way."

We finally called the police. They could not find him either and came back to the house to get information to file a missing person's report. But shortly after, to our joy and surprise, my brother-in law came around the corner with Shannon. He was found at the car dealership asking about purchasing a used car. He decided that the pandemic was too confining. He needed a car. . . . Praise God.

Upon Shannon's arrival home with his uncle, we threw away the clothes he was wearing. We vaped him down with alcohol and placed him in the shower. And to our amazement, Shannon did not contract COVID-19. He had been gone six hours without a mask or gloves, had not had anything to eat or drink, and had likely interacted with several hundred people. God protected him. It was incomprehensible. So is God. His grace is sufficient.

Shannon's Transition from Child to Adult

My late husband and I served as co-guardians for Shannon. When a child with special needs turns eighteen, parents no longer have power of attorney, and cannot represent their child or apply for benefits without guardianship. So, as parents, we became guardians. I also serve as Shannon's foster parent. These legal processes may seem silly but are vital during the transition from childhood to adulthood. A biological parent does not have rights outside of guardianship and foster parenting.

The Person

What is Shannon like? He is musically gifted, cognitively brilliant, intuitive, curious, and social, all with high interpersonal skills. He is truly old-school. He watches episodes of *Martin*, *The Cosby Show*, *A Different World*, and most sitcoms involving African American families and friends. He loves social gatherings, pretty girls, and, most of all, God. Shannon is a joyous Christian. He participates in worship and arts ministries and wants to stay in church all day, for every and any service. None of these attributes changed as he grew into adolescence or adulthood, but the difference has been his desire (a) for more independence, (b) to make choices, (c) to be recognized as a fully developed person, and (d) to show love and appreciation for others. This continues to be a walk of patience for him and for me as his mother.

The Recipient of Services

Shannon receives Medicaid services and physical, occupational, and speech therapy twice a week. He receives financial government resources. He is eligible to participate in adult daycare facilities. In fact, he is eligible for many services. We have had to wait for years to access many of them. Families must begin early as they prepare for care in adulthood.

Shannon's brother, Edwin, has been aware and a supportive family member. My sons share a vibrant, loving, respectful relationship. They are very close. They differ in gifts, but they are equitably valued by one another. Edwin is the "succession plan" for Shannon, at the time of my death. If I die before both Edwin and Shannon, Edwin will oversee Shannon's care.

Practical and Spiritual Takeaways

Mothers need practical and spiritual insights, coupled with lessons learned from experienced moms, and wisdom. Here are some takeaways from us as moms and as educators of special needs children and adults.

A. Mothers:
1. Love, support, listen to, and pray for your spouse.
2. Pray for your child. Ask the Lord to give you a scriptural promise that is specifically for him or her.
3. Pray for your other children while keeping them close as you learn how to meet their siblings' needs. All your children need to know you are there for them. Have special "dates" with each of your children.
4. Create a "safe haven" atmosphere at home for all family members.
5. Find various forms of support from different sources, including emotional, childcare, and prayer support.
6. Create and develop behavior management and discipline and culturally responsive academic-engagement systems in multiple contexts (home, school, community, church).
7. Do not compare your child to other children, in discipline, in public, and in school. As an advocate, and as a mother, you must meet your child where he or she is and take the opportunity to guide him or her where God leads you and your child.
8. For church and school programs, do not accept what the system offers if it is from a deficit perspective. Extend grace to church and family who may not be familiar with your child's special needs. Yet be God's light to support them.
9. Advocate for your child to have their spiritual needs met. Your child's body or mind may be *different*, but their spirit is whole.

B. Church family, school, community members, daycare, school, ministries, and programs:
1. Listen empathetically to the concerns of parents of special needs children.

2. Pray for them and provide respite or childcare if needed.
3. Do not compare a child with special needs with other children who do not demonstrate special needs.
4. Create and develop a biblically based behavior management and discipline plan. Operate in that plan.

We know that God is working for our good. It has not been an easy journey, but we know that every step God orders is important, especially when it is difficult to follow those steps.

Final Thoughts

Societal and family systems are inclusive of many circles that affect an African American mother and her child with special needs. That brilliant child will not fit into mainstream society easily, but he or she fits into God's kingdom seamlessly when He leads the charge and the assignment. Donovan and Shannon will continue to need *special* attention and accommodations that society is not always prepared for or willing to provide. They will need understanding and specific immersion activities. They will need parents and guardians who understand their own unique call on many levels. They will continue to need a "tribe" or a village of people who appreciate the cultural tenets of an African American community and who follow God.

We are finding solace in our spiritual discipline. Our journey has not been easy, and the Lord never said it would be. As we reflect, we realize we were often operating in a position of selfish weakness as we learned to depend on Him. He has been righteous in His direction and in His purposes for our families and our children. Learning our purpose as mothers through the Father, the Son, and the Holy Spirit has been—and continues to be—a journey toward righteous empowerment. "Donovan, I find solace through God in your brilliance. Thank you for the blessing."

"Shannon, I find solace through God in your brilliance. Thank you for the blessing."

You are our shining stars in Him.

9

When the Ties That Bind Get Tested, Torn, and Transformed

DIANA WANDIX-WHITE, ADRIA E. LUSTER

> Give all your worries and cares to
> God, for he cares about you.
>
> 1 Peter 5:7 NLT

When we get married and say "I do" to holy matrimony "until death do us part," most of us aren't anticipating that death can part us before we've had time to grow old together. Also, while we know there's always the risk of divorce issuing the parting blow, we never think it will happen to us. But becoming a widow or a divorcee is not uncommon, and statistics show that both are more likely for African American women than women of other racial backgrounds.[1] Of course, divorce and widowhood also often result in single parenting and the potential for remarriage and blended families. The myriad of complex relationships that death, divorce, single parenting, and blended families create have an impact on those affected in countless and varying ways. As Christians, we have God's promise that no matter our situation or circumstances, He will never abandon us (Hebrews 13:5).

God ultimately turns believers' trials to triumph (James 1:2–4; Romans 5:3–5).

Nevertheless, if you are in the midst of your trial, you may not want to hear Bible verses quoted, platitudes expressed, or other words of wisdom handed to you. Sometimes you might simply want to hear the authentic voice of someone who has made it through—someone whose story makes you think, *Okay, I'll make it*, or *At least I know I'm not the only one*. This chapter includes a few brief stories and an extended narrative of African American women of faith. May their true stories encourage you.

How I Got Over

> Praise be to the God and Father of our Lord Jesus Christ, the Father of compassion and the God of all comfort, who comforts us in all our troubles, so that we can comfort those in any trouble with the comfort we ourselves receive from God (2 Corinthians 1:3–4).

Renee M.

He decided to tell me on the soccer field at the end of my oldest daughter's game. He gave me his ring and walked off the field. It felt like I had been gut-punched by a stranger. *Who does that?* Of course, I was the mom for end-of-game treats that day. I remember a blinding rage and sadness, and all I wanted to do was scream and cry out loud. Once I arrived home, I took the children to my neighbor's house and went home and did just that.

We had been married for eleven years. We had our ups and downs, but I never expected divorce because I felt the commitment went beyond ourselves when there are children involved. We had a one-year old and a seven-year old. I blamed him, myself, and God! Yes, I couldn't believe God would allow our union to dissolve.

In that moment, my faith was challenged. I'd be lying if I said the challenge was short term. I didn't want to go to church, pray, get out of bed, and more. I was *extra* angry. *Here I am with two children, by myself. Why?* I was a stay-at-home mom, had no income, and was still dependent on my soon-to-be ex.

I am so thankful for my praying mom! She remained in prayer for me and called daily to suggest that I go to church. Of course, I stopped taking her calls on Saturday and Sunday. LOL. I figured she'd get the point. Nope! She continued to call to help me through. I love her for never giving up on me.

Slowly, I started coming out of the deep depression. I started going to counseling on a regular basis, taking antidepression medicine, and going to church! I had to find myself again. The hardest thing to do is face yourself. Blaming others is easy, but looking in the mirror is the best thing you can do for yourself. I started exercising and made sure I got up and dressed every day. I had to for my children but more so for myself.

I eventually found peace in knowing God had been with me and would continue to cover me. Nothing is possible without God, and nothing is impossible with Him! He is my everything. I know He was there with me, for He knew what was going to happen. He didn't leave me, but helped to pick me up. I have learned to rely on my Father for everything and anything. My faith has been tested and tried, but I know without a doubt that it wasn't me who kept me . . . but God!

My life has changed for the better because all things truly do work for the good of those who love Him (Romans 8:28)!

Lastly, because of Matthew 6:15, I had to learn to forgive. I wasn't willing to let someone hurt me in this life *and* the next! I never thought I'd be able to talk to my ex again, but after I truly forgave him and moved on, I was able to remember that he wasn't *all* bad. Today we have a cordial, even friendly association. I still remember what he did (LOL), but I also remember what God has done, is doing, and will continue to do for me, and that trumps everything.

B. Young

I've been through some tough times, but my divorce was definitely the most difficult experience thus far. It was, and truthfully sometimes still is, very trying. I struggled with blame, forgiveness, and self-worth. But at some point in the process, that blessed day came when I remembered whose child I am. I spent countless hours alone with my heavenly Father, whose mighty hands held me while I fought to regain my strength, resilience, and personal power. I then prayed more, and with His ever-helping hands, I picked myself up, dusted myself off, and looked ahead toward my peace.

I realized that I hadn't given myself enough grace, but I was able to rely on God's grace while I tried to figure out what was next. As time passed, I found my voice, peace, and purpose again. I learned myself again—what I loved, what I enjoyed—and I dedicated time to those things: exercise, reading, vacationing, and spending quality time with my family and those who uplifted me. I no longer thought of myself as a failure, which I often did. I am growing stronger and more confident in His light every day, and I know that my happily ever after is still attainable. I wake every morning with thanksgiving in my heart, knowing that God knows the desires of my heart and has a plan of prosperity, hope, and abundance for me. "Take delight in the LORD, and he will give you the desires of your heart" (Psalm 37:4).

Women would do well to remember that we deserve to be loved with the same force with which we bless those we love. We need to define, know, and protect our self-worth so that no one has to do so for us. We must hold each other accountable for living the lives that God has predestined for us.

T'Ann S.

I married my high school sweetheart in a Cinderella wedding. Four years later, we had our firstborn son, and then we had our second four years thereafter. My life felt like a fairy tale. We traveled around the world in style, attended Broadway plays and operas, and hobnobbed at political and social galas. I was living my "best life" inside a happy bubble.

Suddenly, the bubble burst. My husband started drinking, gambling, and lying. After nineteen years of marriage, I found myself in the fight of my life! We separated and three years later, our divorce was finalized. Soon thereafter, I was laid off—unemployed with two kids in a very expensive private school, and my ex refused to provide for his children.

I committed my life to doing whatever it took to take care of my two sons. I prayed over them daily, asked the Lord to strengthen me to be the best role model for them, and called on "my village" to help me navigate my new single-parent reality.

Eventually, I accepted a promising position in a neighboring state and got everything cleared to take my boys with me. We were about to start our new chapter when Hurricane Katrina hit our city. We were already all set to move, so we just packed up and headed out a few days early. The aftermath of this hurricane left my hometown devastated. I know that nobody but God protected my boys, my mom, and me from suffering loss and devastation during that natural disaster. He surrounded me with my family and new friendships. He even blessed me with a new relationship.

A year later, I was engaged to a good man who was actively involved in church and was kind and attentive toward me and my boys. One Saturday evening in March 2009, my fiancé was not feeling well for an entire weekend, which was unusual. When I called to check on him Monday morning, he did not answer. I decided to go check on him and found him unconscious. I gave him CPR, but he was nonresponsive. I called 911 and when the EMTs finally arrived, they pronounced him dead. I was devastated!

My prayer life and Bible study kept my mind at peace, but I did struggle. My emotions were raw from the divorce and now mourning the loss of my fiancé, best friend, and partner. I was truly overwhelmed—drowning—and I decided to see a therapist. I learned breathing techniques and how to manage my stress. Yes, it is okay—even good and biblical—for Christians to get counseling. Consider Proverbs: "For lack of guidance a nation falls, but victory is won through many advisers" (11:14). "Where there is strife, there is pride, but wisdom is found in those who take advice" (13:10). "Plans fail for lack of counsel, but with many advisers they succeed" (15:22). "Listen to advice and accept discipline, and at the end you will be counted among the wise" (19:20). See also 1 Peter 5:7; 1 Thessalonians 5:11; and Hebrews 3:13.

A couple years later, I began to date again. At forty-seven, I implemented strategies from counseling, and I was learning to overcome my trust issues and insecurities from past experiences. Thank God! I met and married a wonderful man, and we recently celebrated our nine-year anniversary.

If you're going through a difficult time, practice self-care, pour into yourself, and invest time in you—spiritually, mentally, physically, financially! My words to live by are, love like you've never been hurt; let go and let God!

D. W-White

Hello, Journal! "I's married now" (again)! Last week, I married a kind and loving man whom I love dearly. I'll tell you about him later, but it's just been a while since I've written, and I wanted to share my news. Thank You, God, for blessing me twice with what some women search their whole lives for and often never even find once—the love of a good, godly man . . . and I wasn't even looking! You are so good to me!

This is a journal entry from June 5, 2008. Seven years prior, I lost my first husband to acute myoblastic leukemia. I never would have thought I would be someone's wife again. For many years, I couldn't even imagine being with someone else. But then I not only missed my late husband but also started missing the marital relationship and all that entails. Beyond being sad that our children were missing their father, I started feeling sad that they were lacking a father figure in their lives. I began thinking that I didn't want to grow old without someone by my side.

Nevertheless, my children were my priority, and I was worried about bringing someone into their lives who might not be a good person and who might not stay. So, I began to pray and ask God to send me someone who was spiritually, emotionally, mentally, financially, and physically fit, as I like to say—"Fit to the fifth!" God answered my prayer . . . and two became six. Both my new husband and I received additional gifts when we married each other: he was blessed with an amazing bonus daughter and an awesome bonus son, and I was blessed with two wonderful bonus daughters—all between the ages of ten and sixteen.

Blended families can mesh fantastically and have few hiccups, or blended families can have trouble adjusting to their new family unit. If you choose to enter into a blended family relationship, here are some things to consider:

1. The children did not choose to be in a blended family. They may not want to be in a blended family. Give them time, space, love, and boundaries. Don't be the evil stepmother, nor the pushover parent, nor the distant observer. Offer them the same love, respect, choices, and consequences that you offer your biological children.

2. Prioritize the biblical order of the family. The Bible does not say

   - Let marriage be held in honor among all—unless it's a second marriage.
   - Wives, submit to your own husbands, but not if he's not your first husband.
   - Husbands, love your wives, as Christ loved the church . . . unless she's not your first wife.
   - Children, obey your parents, unless it's a stepparent.
   - Train up a child in the way he should go, unless he's not your biological child.
   - Honor your father and your mother, unless it's a stepfather or a stepmother.
   - What God joined together, let no human being separate, unless it's your second time around.

   It's natural to prioritize your children when you are a single parent. If you've been widowed, you may feel a need to put your children first, thinking, *I'm all they've got*. If you're a divorcee, you may feel the need to put your children first due to feelings of guilt or fear that they'll prefer their other biological parent. Either way, in a blended family, both parents need to agree to prioritize the biblical order of the family, prioritizing one another and the marriage. Together, parents can make sure that each child knows he or she is an important, irreplaceable, valuable, and loved member of the family.

3. Seek Christian marriage and family counseling before and during your marriage! Proverbs includes more than forty passages that encourage believers to seek wise, godly counsel. The New Testament also includes passages that encourage building one another up and holding each other accountable: "But encourage one another daily, as long as it is called Today, so that none of you may be hardened by sin's deceitfulness." See also Galatians 6:1–2; Ephesians 4:25; 1 Thessalonians 5:11; and Hebrews 10:24.

Ultimately, life happens, but God is good in spite of life's difficulties. Whether you're trying to heal from the trauma of a loss or struggling to figure out how best to thrive in your new reality, you can "cast all your anxieties on him because he cares for you" (1 Peter 5:7). Think about it like this: Imagine you're rolling your thirty-pound piece of luggage through the airport, and the wheels fall off. You have to carry that heavy bag to your destination. Then Dwayne "The Rock" Johnson comes by and says, with one eyebrow raised, "Give that to me. I'll carry it." Would you give it to him? Yes! If you're dealing with something heavy and someone who can handle it much better than you offers to take care of it, it would be foolish not to take them up on the offer. God is ready, willing, and more than able to help you handle what is difficult.

Adria E. Luster

Sometimes it's a rough journey when you're navigating through the storm. When I reflect on my life, I now realize that I spent the first half dodging puddles and thunderbolts. Now that I am enjoying the rays of sunshine, I am glad I can look back and help someone else avoid the pits of mud that I trudged through.

I was born to a single mother, who married my stepdad around the time I entered school. While I didn't necessarily feel it within our home, I did notice that others within his family made a difference between me and my younger siblings. I dreamed of one day forming a family that did not include "stepchildren," because I never wanted one of them to feel the pain I experienced. Well, they say if you want to hear God laugh, tell Him your plans.

In my quest to create a loving family, I married my high school sweetheart at the age of nineteen. Looking back, I realize I had boarded a train that was bound to wreck. We had great intentions and truly believed that love would "conquer all," even though neither of us had matured enough to fully understand what "all" included. Additionally, neither of us fully understood our goals and aspirations. We would later find that our differences caused rips that would eventually tear apart the fabric of our marriage.

Having been raised in a Christian household, I had been taught that marriage is a lifelong commitment. Consequently, we struggled to maintain our relationship, but at some point, the wounds of battle became unbearable. I remember crying out to God and asking Him if it was His intention for me to suffer in this miserable union. One of the things God revealed to me was that when He divinely orders a plan for a person's life, it does not result in chaos. When I reflected, I recognized that at many points, He gave me direct signs that our marriage was not part of His plan; I had just chosen to ignore them. I became contrite and began to ask for forgiveness while asking for strength to endure my divorce.

Being merciful, God answered my prayer and miraculously worked on my behalf throughout the almost yearlong ordeal. Looking back, I can truly say it was one of the hardest trials of my life. My favorite passage is Psalm 23, and I would often quote it to myself when I felt like I was about to lose control during my "walks through the valley." In my moments of despair, one thing I managed to focus on was loving and respecting my two young children. I truly believed that they were my blessing from this union, and I hoped they would one day understand that it was better for them to see their parents living joyful and fulfilling lives separately, instead of living together in misery.

While a relationship is not a living being, when it dissolves it can feel like a death and can cause a long grieving process. At the same time, the lessons learned (and there is always a lesson) can result in tremendous spiritual and emotional growth once we learn to accept responsibility for our actions and truly ask God, as well as the other parties involved, for forgiveness. This step is one of the hardest, and for many, this is the barrier to complete healing. Requesting forgiveness requires the trespasser to humble themselves. In every divorce, there are faults on both sides. People might say, "I divorced him because he was unfaithful; I wasn't at fault!" However, this is not true. Even if your only offense was ignoring the signs God showed you, both sides played a role.

After seeking forgiveness, we have to let go. This is another difficult step in the healing process. There's no reason for you to remain in the same room once it's emptied and there is nowhere to rest. It's like a person showing up to work every day and sitting in the parking lot at the job they've been fired from for eight hours and receiving no pay. Sounds silly, right? Put the key in the ignition, turn it, shift the gear to drive, and move on. No, it's not easy, but with God's grace and mercy, you can move. You can be restored.

It wasn't easy after my divorce. As a single mother, I struggled both emotionally and financially. There were times I had only twenty dollars left after paying bills. On certain nights, we had what I nicknamed "Weeknight Brunch," for occasions when we had pancakes for dinner because we'd run out of food. Then there was "Movie Night," when we took turns watching our favorite recorded videos because the cable was cut off. I sometimes felt despondent, but I remained committed to allowing God to guide my steps, even if the road was rocky at times. Now that my children are adults, they often reflect on these hard times as some of the happiest of their lives. I am so thankful.

Eventually, I met a man who also had two children. Collectively, our children were what some refer to as "stairstep," ranging from ages four to seven. He was also divorced. He became a shoulder for me to lean on as I navigated through the process of singleness. While I enjoyed occasional dates with him, our relationship began to grow once we began to spend time together on weekends as a family, and our children bonded so well. I will openly admit that it was not always easy, since he had both an ex-wife and a "baby mama." Children, unwise to the muddiness of broken adult relationships, often talk openly to their parents about new people in their lives. At times, this caused some friction, and interference from our former partners felt so unbearable sometimes that we considered taking a break. Both of us experienced despicable behavior from our former mates—harassing phone calls, threats of violence, verbal tirades, and any other thing seen from a scorned lover in a movie. Nevertheless, we decided to move forward with our relationship, though we were both still hesitant to step into marriage again. We decided to take it slow.

Of course, I don't have to tell you that I felt the fear of marrying for the second time due to the failure of my first marriage. I began to pray and ask God to guide my steps so that I would be moving according to His will. I knew that it was necessary to seek His counsel instead of solely relying on my heart, and I vowed to do so. One of the main qualities that I desired for a future partnership was someone who treated both me and my children with love and respect. In addition, I wanted someone who would support me as I worked toward my life goals and aspirations. In my first marriage, attending college was an issue of contention, since higher education was considered a disruption of my wifely and motherly duties. This negatively impacted my self-esteem because a degree was a personal ambition that I had set for myself. To my surprise, my new partner seemed to be in full support of my goals. In fact, he often bragged to people that while I had a master's, I would one day be going back to school. With his financial and emotional support, I did go on to complete two more degrees, eventually earning a doctorate.

After our relationship became more serious, we began to spend holidays together as a family, and I made it a point to treat all four of the kids equally, whether I was giving out love or punishment. It wasn't always easy, but I always asked myself, "Am I treating them as I would want someone to treat my child?" So, when it came to my partner's children, I never tried to force a relationship with them and allowed them to respond based on their feelings. They began to call me Mom—unprompted (and we weren't even married yet)—and my children felt most comfortable dropping the formality of "Mister" and simply calling my partner by his first name, as they still do today.

When I reflect on this relationship, I realize that I never saw any of the "red flags" as I had before my first marriage. I was also guided to a prayer I had previously written in my journal, where I actually listed the qualities I desired in my future husband. Surprisingly, they were a clear description of my new partner. I took this as indication that God was directing my steps because I was taking the time to reflect and allow Him to guide me. I knew that I loved my partner, and we had decided that our marriage would occur once we both felt the time was right. It wasn't long before that time came, and I still recall the nontraditional manner in which he proposed to me. He had been pondering on the matter for some time and, unbeknownst to me, had asked each of his children how they might feel about it. He told me later that they both said it was fine and laughed when he recalled how his then four-year-old daughter said, "I thought she was already my other mom." In other words, she could apparently feel the genuine love that I had for her even though we weren't legally a family.

After working an underpaid and unrewarding corporate job, I decided to seek employment as an educator with a schedule more closely aligned with my children's. I sent my kids to spend the summer with my mother while I searched for a position. A week before the children were scheduled to return, I was finally hired. When I excitedly told my partner, he told me we would be going to the courthouse the following week and getting married because I would be writing his name on the board for my new students. I looked at him and said, "Are you asking me to marry you?" He responded affirmatively. I then said, "I will if my children say it's okay." He asked me what might happen if they said no, and I let him know that we'd wait until they said yes. It was important for me to show them that I respected them, since this decision would directly impact their lives as well as mine. Of course, when I talked with them, they were ecstatic. My son told me he was glad that he would now have a little sister and a big brother, since "everyone would be married now." I laughed when I realized that as a six-year-old he believed our upcoming marriage would be a commitment that included all of us. He was right.

Looking back, I now see that the children's attitudes created a stronger bond within our marriage. Just as our children assumed, my husband and I weren't just committing to each other; we were all committing to our new family. From day one, neither of us considered ourselves as *stepparents*, and that term was never used within our home. My husband and I had one rule when dealing with our children—maintain a united front. No child would ever feel that he or she could go to "my mom" or "my dad" and pit us against each other. In addition, we never allowed ourselves to be referred to in this way, because everyone was equal, and we were the mom and dad for all four children. Even if we disagreed on how to handle a situation concerning our kids, the children never knew, because we discussed it behind closed doors. A few years later, I realized that God definitely had destined me for this role when his daughter's mother suddenly passed. It was a tough time in her eight-year-old life, but I was there to comfort her and welcome her with open arms. In the past twenty-five years, as our children have grown, we have even been blessed with grandchildren.

If I were to advise someone on how to overcome a painful divorce and learn to love again within a blended family, I would suggest they seek forgiveness, learn from the mistakes of their past, and allow God to direct their future steps. In hindsight, I truly thank God for the storms I endured because they led me to the beautiful rainbow of my loving family.

Miracles and Blessings

Life is unpredictable. But God is unshakable, and His love is unfailing. Death, divorce, single parenting, blended families—the challenges of life may sometimes weigh us down to where we don't "feel" God's love. But the Word tells us that His love endures forever; it is not altered by our circumstances. It's not even diminished during the times we question His presence.

If you see a storm on the horizon, He loves you and will see you through. If you're in the midst of a storm, He loves you and will see you through. If your storm is subsiding and you can almost see a rainbow, He loves you and will see you through. God sent His only Son to die for you, and His Son Jesus, well . . . He can rebuke the winds and the waves (Mark 4:39). So, when those ties that bind get tested, and even if they are torn, just hold on, and you will emerge whole, stronger, transformed.

PART THREE
MANAGING COMPLEX SOCIETAL CHALLENGES

10

Navigating the Digital World

Godly Practices Despite Secular Challenges

QUINITA OGLETREE, GENALYN L. JERKINS

> I have given them your word and the world has hated them, for they are not of the world any more than I am of the world. My prayer is not that you take them out of the world but that you protect them from the evil one. They are not of the world, even as I am not of it. Sanctify them by the truth; your word is truth. As you sent me into the world, I have sent them into the world.
>
> John 17:14–18

When Jesus prayed for the disciples in John 17, He acknowledged that they were not of the world but must live in the world. Similarly, as followers of Christ today, African American women are called to embody their faith and values in all aspects of life, including their presence on social media platforms. As African American women navigate the landscape of social media, they face the challenge of remaining grounded in their identities and values while being exposed to the influences and pressures of the digital world.

However, the biblical passage reminds African American women, and all believers, that they are called to a different standard. They are called to be rooted in their identity in Christ and to let that identity guide their interactions and pursuits on social media. Ultimately, the passage in John 17:14–18 reminds us to approach social media and all aspects of life with a sense of purpose and mission. We can make a meaningful impact by being in the world but not of the world, using our platforms to share our faith, advocate for justice, and contribute to a more positive and uplifting digital world.

By 1990, the World Wide Web had been created, leading to social media's beginning. During this decade, some of us may have even received AOL CDs in the mail and created our first email addresses. We did not know then how quickly technology would become part of our daily lives. In some ways, it has made our lives easier. When we woke up this morning, some of us were awakened by the alarms on our phones. Some of us read our morning devotionals from an app on our phones. Within a couple of hours of waking, many of us have checked the news, emails, and social media accounts from our phones. We now carry almost all of our personal information that drives the management of our lives (schedules, contacts, entertainment, credit cards) on a device that fits in our hands. We are more connected than ever because technology allows us always to be reachable.

In today's rapidly advancing digital age, the powerful influence of technology, particularly social media, permeates every corner of the globe. Social media has emerged as a transformative force able to connect individuals, disseminate information, and shape public opinion. This impact is not limited to a particular region or demographic but extends nationally and worldwide, shaping how we communicate, share ideas, and interact with the world around us.

Artificial Intelligence (AI) can process vast amounts of data, derive patterns, and make decisions, introducing a new dimension to the technological landscape. From personalized content recommendations to automated content moderation, AI algorithms shape the information we consume and our online interactions. However, this integration also raises important questions and concerns regarding data privacy, algorithmic bias, and the ethical implications of AI's decision-making capabilities. As technology and social media continue to evolve and expand, it has become evident that this phenomenon is here to stay, playing a significant role in shaping societies, cultures, and how we perceive and engage with one another. Nevertheless, as with anything created, there are positives and negatives.

Positives of Technology

One of the most significant contributions of technology is enhanced connectivity and communication. With the advent of social media platforms, messaging apps, and video conferencing tools, people from around the world can now connect instantly, fostering relationships and collaborations regardless of geographical barriers. Moreover, the internet has become a vast knowledge repository, providing easy access to information on almost any topic. This accessibility has revolutionized education, enabling individuals to pursue online courses and degrees, breaking down traditional barriers to learning.

Technology has also boosted efficiency and productivity in various industries through automation, cloud computing, and digital tools, streamlining processes and allowing businesses to optimize their operations. It has also been a catalyst for innovation and creativity, unleashing new possibilities and breakthroughs in fields ranging from digital art and entertainment to scientific contexts. In the realm of healthcare, technology has significantly improved medical services, offering advanced medical imaging, telemedicine options, and wearable health devices, empowering individuals to take charge of their well-being.

Additionally, technology has the potential to contribute positively to environmental sustainability, with renewable energy technologies and smart grids aiding in reducing carbon footprints. Social media has allowed marginalized communities, including those populated by African American women, to raise their voices, share their stories, and advocate for social change. Through technology, global collaboration has become more feasible, enabling researchers, organizations, and governments to work together in addressing pressing global challenges, such as climate change and infectious diseases. In summary, technology in the digital age has enriched our experiences, expanded opportunities, and created a more interconnected and dynamic world.

Social Media

We are digitally connected because over 90 percent of the population of the United States uses the internet.[1] Social media has become an integral part of our daily lives because this is how we tend to connect digitally. More than 72 percent of Americans are social media users.[2] In 2023, 54 percent of social media users in the United States were women.[3] More than half the global population of women have at least one social media account. Social media is used positively, including connecting with family and friends, supporting causes, networking for jobs, starting businesses, and learning new hobbies. Christian women also use social media to share the Word of God and evangelize others. We have watched everyday people become social media influencers and go viral.

Positives of Social Media

Social media allows everyone to have a voice or platform. This has been especially helpful to African American women, who are often unseen, unacknowledged, and voiceless. African Americans have used social media to call people to acknowledge police brutality, health disparities, discrimination, and other social justice issues. One way to do this is by creating hashtags or having Twitter conversations. Examples of hashtags include #sayhername, #blackgirljoy, #blacklivesmatter, #supportblackbusiness, and #metoo. This social activism has created spaces for Black voices to be heard and stories told.

The pandemic caused by COVID-19 shut down the whole world because we had to quarantine. People were not able to congregate or socialize in person. Therefore, technology became a way to socialize and use digital technology positively. It allowed families and friends to stay connected through videoconferencing and social media. Digital networks created ways for people to stream movies, or other shows they could watch together, and talk with each other. Apps have allowed us to play games with our social circle and meet new people. Others of us have used videos and apps to learn new hobbies, such as playing the piano, gardening, or crafting.

In the world of social media, we will find someone who thinks as we think. We have watched several African American women simply be themselves, and their audiences found them. They used social media to showcase their humor, fashion, beauty, and lifestyle content. These women did not have to wait for someone to fund them; they just needed their cell phones or microphones or cameras.

The power of having a platform is undeniable, and it is no surprise that funders are eager to jump on board with those who show promise. Several Black women have been blessed to have been discovered by funders who recognized their potential and provided the resources to help them expand their reach. As the Bible states, a gift opens doors (Proverbs 18:16), and these funders were able to use their resources to usher the gifted into the presence of the great.

One such person who benefited from this support started by making vegan meals on video. Her platform grew as she continued to create engaging content, and she eventually gained enough recognition to expand beyond social media. She now has books, a clothing line, a podcast, and even her own television show. Her journey is a testament to the power of persistence and the importance of having people who believe in your vision. Another began with her own Instagram series on social media. Her comedic talent was quickly recognized, and she was hired to write sketches for television. Today she is an award-winning writer, executive producer, cowriter, and star of her own television show. Her story is a reminder that sometimes, all it takes is a small platform and a bit of recognition to launch a successful career. With the right support and resources, you can turn your passion into a career.

The Community: Gena's Story

Staying connected became a lifeline during the pandemic. Perhaps it was the pandemic plus other challenges of routine life for a dear friend and me. Sadly, the pandemic only compounded the lows that life was already dealing each of us. Breakups in significant relationships, new church homes, employment transitions, relocation in living arrangements, and other variables did not "send out a memo" to carefully schedule when they would flow into our lives. Even though we were in a pandemic, life continued to happen. Life issues overlapped and created peak points of stress that further exacerbated depression or discouragement.

The connection was all that we had. My friend and I made conscious decisions to connect. In a world that was very isolated physically, my friend and I created a touchpoint of accountability weekly; every Sunday morning at 7:30 a.m. by phone. We connected for nearly a year, chatting about things we had experienced during the week. These times of regularly speaking sanity into the chaos of one another's lives were held as precious. My friend envisioned connecting with women regularly to uplift one another, and a Bible study was created to focus ourselves on the Word of God. We put out a few fliers, and about thirty women showed up for a virtual gathering. The audience grew and by our fourth virtual meeting, more than two hundred women gathered on Saturday mornings for a couple of hours. Thinking the pandemic would be brief, we ended the study after a few months. However, the pandemic continued.

So, we transitioned from meeting weekly on Saturdays to *Meet Me Mondays*, which became a whole vibe, as women gathered from across the nation. *The Community* (our new name) grew to more than twelve hundred women. Our mantra: *Better together!* Literally, virtual connection has served as a lifeline.

Negatives of Technology

Living in the digital age means we are always available. Often, we are interrupted by notifications. Alternatively, we have emails throughout the day. When we socialize with family or friends, we often see people engaged with their phones instead of with the people who are present with them. Lockboxes and apps have been created to stop people from accessing their phones or certain apps on their phones because they realize their phones are impacting their lifestyles and productivity. Some phones have a do-not-disturb feature, or they allow us to create settings to filter out calls, messages, and notifications. We must not allow technology to take over our daily lives. It is easy to want to multitask and play games or check our social media accounts while talking with our family and friends or watching television. However, multitasking means we are not giving anyone or anything our full attention.

Another negative is harassment that occurs in digital spaces: cyberbullying. Cyberbullying is increasingly common among teenagers, especially older teenage girls.[4] Almost half of US teenagers (46 percent) have been bullied or harassed online.[5] Cyberbullying includes offensive name calling, spreading false rumors, receiving or being the subject of explicit images, physical threats, and being followed constantly (asked where you are, what you are doing, or who you are with by someone other than a parent).[6] The effects of cyberbullying include anger, isolation, depression, illness, and humiliation.[7] The US government created a website to prevent cyberbullying because of its impact on people. However, federal laws do not prohibit cyberbullying,[8] though all states have anti-bullying legislation.[9]

Sextortion is a form of blackmail where nude or sexual images or videos are shared unless you do what is demanded of you. Data from Homeland Security reports that they received over three thousand sextortion tips.[10] Teenage boys and girls are targets and are usually being "catfished" by adult predators. Catfishing is when someone pretends to be another person online, often masking their true identity by using another person's pictures. In this case, adults are pretending to be teenagers to get teenagers to share compromising pictures of themselves. They then use these pictures to blackmail the teenagers into doing whatever they request, including more pictures of the teens. Several teenagers have taken their lives because of sextortion.[11]

While the power and expansion of technology, including social media and AI, have brought numerous benefits, it is essential to acknowledge and address the negative aspects that accompany these advancements. Technology has also significantly impacted lifestyle and productivity. Constant connectivity and distractions posed by smartphones and social media platforms can lead to addictive behaviors, decreased focus, and diminished productivity in both personal and professional settings. And the rise of cyberbullying and sextortion has become a concerning consequence. The anonymity and broad reach of the internet provide a breeding ground for online harassment, intimidation, and the exploitation of individuals, particularly among vulnerable populations, such as children and teenagers. These negative implications highlight the need for responsible technology use, robust digital literacy, and effective measures to address and mitigate harmful consequences.

Relationships

Social media makes it easy to find someone who will affirm or validate you. It is felt to be okay to be yourself and informal in this space because you have access to subgroups that you might not have access to physically. However, there is a dark side to social media. It can be used to divide people rather than connect them. Knowledge about algorithms is one precaution against the dark side of social media. Algorithms calculate what digital content you view, what you want to follow, and connect you with content that reinforces what you already believe. For example, if a person has extreme views, they are more likely to see extreme events. One way to prevent this is to follow various pages that provide different perspectives.

Loneliness

The US Surgeon General published a report about how loneliness affects Americans mentally and physically.[12] While technology connects us and our friends and followers can number in the thousands, we need more *depth* and quality in these relationships. Regardless of our followers, retweets, and likes, we should not equate clicks to the meaningful, quality, genuine relationships each of us need.

Do we realize that social isolation impacts mortality?[13] Why is isolation occurring in a world more connected than ever? Why are some people lonelier than ever? We need people who know us beyond our social media or digital footprint. Our social media pages have been "curated"—that is, they connect and engage us with content based on algorithms social media companies employ. This content is interest based and not relationship based.

Managing Your Tech Time

Almost everyone underestimates the time they spend playing games or on social media. You can check this on your own device to see where you stand. Often, when people are on social media, they keep scrolling, and then an hour or two has passed.

Taking a break from technology and social media is essential for several reasons. First, it allows us to recharge and prioritize our mental and emotional well-being by reducing constant stimulation and information overload. Second, it encourages real-world interactions and fosters deeper connections with loved ones, providing an opportunity to be fully present and engaged in offline experiences. Last, it promotes self-reflection and introspection, enabling us to gain clarity, find balance, and rediscover personal interests and hobbies that our digital lives may have overshadowed.

There are several ways to manage your relationship with social media and technology. One way is to set time limits for phone or app usage. Another way is to go on a social media fast to take a break. You can also remove apps from your phone.

Comparison and Competition

Women may slip down the dangerous slope of comparison by having the ability to see other women's daily lives, locally and internationally. Social media often presents a perfect version of people's lives, curating the experiences of someone's life in a way that often highlights their achievements, appearances, and experiences. Social media provides people's highlight reels, and we only see the best of their worlds before comparing that to the highs and lows of our lives. Our lives may appear to be lacking. According to social media, everyone is on vacation, having five-star meals, and living with perfect families and children. This can lead to constantly comparing and focusing on what our lives are lacking when compared to the lives we see on social media. FOMO (fear of missing out) can occur because of this.

One study examined the predictive relationship of social media on body esteem in women, especially adolescents. As a result of frequent social media use, adolescents are continually exposed to appearance-related media content. According to the study, this likely reinforces a thin ideal and fosters appearance-based comparison.[14] With little external validation, adolescents may begin to have negative self-images. This is because social media has shown them unrealistic standards of beauty (body type, hair texture, and complexion).

We could ask whether social media is doing as intended: connecting us with people we already know. But it often comes across as media telling us about people we do not know. Therefore, we are taking on unneeded and unwanted information. Do we really need to know what is on our FYPs (For You Pages), reels, or stories?

I think we need to recognize the impact technology and social media can have on our well-being and sense of self. The constant connectivity and pressure to conform to societal norms and standards can leave us feeling adrift and disconnected from our true priorities and spirituality; it can make us feel lost. Moreover, the distractions of the digital world can overshadow the importance of self-care and maintaining a healthy balance between our online and offline lives.

However, getting lost can also offer a glimmer of hope. Getting lost is a part of our journey, suggesting an opportunity for growth and self-discovery, even in the challenges of technology and social media. When we are open, we can explore and learn from our experiences, finding our way back to our values, purposes, and sense of self.

I think it's important to approach technology and social media with mindfulness and discernment. Be aware that these platforms can lead you astray and recognize that getting lost can be a part of the journey toward finding your way back to a more meaningful and purposeful online and offline existence.

What Does the Bible Say about the Digital Age?

Today's technology was unavailable during biblical times, but the Bible has a relevant word for the digital world. Proverbs is the book of wisdom, and it provides us with some guidelines and suggestions for our digital footprints.

Know and Understand

> The beginning of wisdom is this: Get wisdom. Though it cost all you have, get understanding. (Proverbs 4:7)

Foundationally, you need to understand digital technology before using it. What is the purpose of this social media or this app? Why are you on it? With whom will you be connecting? Does it help support the calling God has for your life? When it comes to technology and social media, it is crucial to apply this wisdom. It is essential to seek understanding and discernment in your digital life, using technology as a tool for growth and learning rather than being consumed by its distractions. By approaching technology and social media with a mindset of wisdom and insight, you can navigate these platforms with intention, ensuring they enhance your life rather than hinder your overall well-being and relationships.

Guard Your Temple

> Above all else, guard your heart, for everything you do flows from it. (Proverbs 4:23)

You must remember that everything digital can be accessed without access to you. There is a saying, "Garbage in, garbage out." So, what are you allowing in from the digital world? If you would not let it access you physically, why do you let it access you digitally? Regarding technology and social media, this verse is a reminder to be mindful of these platforms' impact on your heart and mind. It encourages you to protect your emotional well-being by being intentional about the content you consume, the interactions in which you engage, and the time you spend online. By prioritizing your mental and emotional health, you can cultivate a healthier relationship with technology and social media, ensuring that your actions and attitudes reflect wisdom and positivity.

Seek to Serve, Not to Be Famous

> Better to be a nobody and yet have a servant than pretend to be somebody and have no food. (Proverbs 12:9)

Often people are trying to be influencers and get funding for their posts in the digital world. This verse reminds us of the importance of maintaining a balanced perspective in using technology and social media. It cautions against the pursuit of virtual status and popularity at the expense of our true needs and priorities. It encourages us to focus on the essentials of life and avoid becoming overly consumed with portraying a certain image or seeking validation through online platforms. We must be mindful of our purpose in creating content, always questioning whether we are creating it for the likes and the followers, because content creators want to be viewed as important or famous.

Think before You Post

> Fools show their annoyance at once, but the prudent overlook an insult. (Proverbs 12:16)

> Whoever is patient has great understanding, but one who is quick-tempered displays folly. (Proverbs 14:29)

> A hot-tempered person stirs up conflict, but the one who is patient calms a quarrel. (Proverbs 15:18)

> Like one who grabs a stray dog by the ears is someone who rushes into a quarrel not their own. (Proverbs 26:17)

Remember, whatever you write can always be found once you write or post it. You should not always respond with the first thought in your mind. Process your thoughts first. Develop a habit of having someone review your writing before posting. Just because you wrote it one way does not mean it will be perceived in that way.

In the digital realm, where emotions can run high and conflicts can escalate quickly, it is crucial to approach online engagements with prudence, patience, and a focus on peaceful resolutions. The verses in Proverbs caution against impulsive reactions, hot-tempered responses, and unnecessary involvement in quarrels not our own. They urge us to be mindful of our words, to exercise self-control, and to seek understanding and reconciliation rather than fueling online disputes. By applying the teachings of these proverbs, we can contribute to a more harmonious and uplifting online environment, where conflicts are resolved with wisdom, kindness, and the pursuit of peace.

Watch What You Post and How You Respond

> Evildoers are trapped by their sinful talk, and so the innocent escape trouble.
>   From the fruit of their lips people are filled with good things, and the work of their hands brings them reward. . . .
>   The words of the reckless pierce like swords, but the tongue of the wise brings healing. (Proverbs 12:13–14, 18)

What are you saying in the digital world? Is it edifying or perhaps sinful? Is it full of good things, or is it reckless? Does it hurt or heal? These verses are a reminder to speak truthfully and wisely online, as deceitful or careless words can lead to negative consequences. These verses also emphasize the importance of seeking knowledge and understanding before forming judgments or sharing opinions in the digital realm. Moreover, they highlight the value of listening attentively to different perspectives, promoting thoughtful discussions, and responding with kindness and grace in one's interactions on social media platforms.

Final Thoughts

In today's rapidly advancing technological era, the power and influence of technology, particularly social media, have become a worldwide phenomenon. We must be aware of our digital footprint and our children's. Children, as digital natives, are particularly susceptible to the influences and challenges of technology and social media. It is crucial to provide them with guidance and support as they navigate the digital landscape. Just as African American women face pressures and potential harm, children are vulnerable to the negative effects of comparison, cyberbullying, and exposure to inappropriate content. It is important as parents and caregivers to instill in children a strong foundation of values and ethics, teaching them to use technology responsibly and to be aware of the potential risks. Open and honest communication, setting boundaries, and monitoring their online activities are essential for their well-being and digital literacy. By equipping children with the tools to navigate the digital world safely—and by promoting their critical thinking skills—we can empower them to make positive choices and create a healthier online environment for themselves and others.

Social media platforms offer unparalleled connectivity, information sharing, and the potential for positive impact. However, with this power comes a need for responsible use and awareness of the negative aspects. Comparison, competition, and the perpetuation of unrealistic standards can impact the self-esteem of African American women. Additionally, issues like cyberbullying and sextortion pose severe threats to our well-being and that of our family members. It is crucial to approach technology and social media with wisdom, seeking understanding and discernment, guarding our hearts, and prioritizing our mental and emotional well-being. Taking breaks from technology can help us recharge, foster real-world connections, and rediscover personal interests. As we navigate the digital landscape, it is vital to cultivate patience, promote peace, and avoid unnecessary conflicts. By applying timeless wisdom from Proverbs and the whole of Scripture, we can navigate the complexities of technology and social media, contributing to a more positive and uplifting online environment.

Home and Career

A Balancing Act

VICKI HARRIS

> She watches over the affairs of her household. . . .
> Her children arise and call her blessed.
> Proverbs 31:27–28

In this era of fast-paced living, demanding positions, and social unrest, how do we navigate home and career? For mothers and caregivers, marrieds or singles, life is a balancing act that requires the power of prayer, a Christian lifestyle, and dedication to juggle multiple roles to have a successful home and career.

We as African American women have had a role in the workplace of this country from the beginning. It is common knowledge that the horrific ravages of slavery and Jim Crow laws took their toll on our population. For far too long, we were relegated to hard labor, low-ranking jobs, and poverty because of racism, classism, sexism, poor educational opportunities, segregation, and other societal ills. After centuries of oppression, civil rights laws and resistance movements began to pay off, and we started to see changes in our social status regarding access to education, freedom of movement, and opportunities for jobs. The social ills are still present, but by the grace of God, we can remember the dedicated, consistent work ethic of our foremothers and fathers. It is heartening, and not unusual now, to see communities of home-owning African Americans who have college-educated children and abundance that goes beyond their material needs. Do racism, oppression, an abundance of poverty, and social ills remain? The answer is an overwhelming yes, but we can still point to some of the blessings our ancestors yearned to see.

African Americans have achieved at every level of society, and can even boast of a Black president and first lady, in the persons of Barack and Michelle Obama. But changes over the decades have shown that we are in a world that has shifted African American women to the boardroom, the cockpit, the pulpit, university, health clubs, and billionaire clubs. We are in "primetime," meaning we are totally immersed as anchors in our homes and simultaneously engaged in dynamic professional careers. We have energetic hourly workers, sometimes managing two jobs or more, and women who are entrepreneurs, on Wall Street, and in politics, medicine, law, education, the military, fashion design, sports, entertainment—the list continues. God moved current generations from pioneers and trailblazers to primetime decision-makers, entrepreneurs, and movers and shakers. There are lots of demands, but thankfully, there are resources on how Christian African American women can navigate the fast-paced life of home and career.

Demands, Demands, and More Demands

Here are a few scenarios.

> I am a wife and mother of two children. I own a successful hair salon and have six employees. I work long hours and have a real challenge spending time with my husband, children, friends, and often feel too tired to go to church. It seems like my business is dominating my life, but I am determined to make a home that is pleasing to God and to honor *Him* in my business.

> I am a single mother of four children. I work two hourly jobs to make ends meet and pay a large portion of my earnings for childcare. My goal is to be successful enough to earn a promotion with more money so I can quit one job and have more time

with my family. I am proud of my children, their success in school, and their involvement in our church. However, I must admit, most of the time I am exhausted.

I am a wife, mother of three children, and leader in the church. I teach a full course load at the university, write blogs, regular print, and online columns for publications. I also give forty to fifty speeches a year, appear regularly on TV and radio, and have a new academic book that will be published soon. My lifestyle can be summarized as busy, busy, busy.

These scenarios are about Christian African American women who are representative of the new era of lifestyles. This new generation of hardworking moms and career women in the prime of their hectic lives, regardless of financial status, is active and industrious. I am a member of this primetime, working women's group: married, a mother of three children, a Christian, and a chief officer of a large publishing house in the United States with dozens of offices worldwide. I love my husband, my children, and my coveted position in this global organization. I am considered successful, but not unusual. For centuries, African American women have been uniquely central to the economic well-being of their families and a foundational cornerstone in the workplace of our nation.

At work, a continuous stream of deadlines, memos, reports, evaluations, events, conference calls, meetings, and other responsibilities all translate to long hours and late days. Everything is hurried, fast-paced, and rushed. At home, everything is done after hours or on weekends, which means shopping, hair or doctor's appointments, dry cleaning handling, music lessons, and children's school events, among other things. All must be carefully scheduled. Work that needs to be completed at home gets crammed between after-school activities and helping kids with homework assignments. Family meals are once a week, maybe, while social and church events are completed with exhaustion. At least two days of each yearly vacation are spent sleeping, after lots of forced fun. Everything, including vacations, must be completed on a scheduled timeline. The hustle, bustle, and high demands of good living bring into question the true quality of life. It is easy to fall prey to the abundance of demands, the dreaded weapon of exhaustion. How do you avoid the overwhelming busyness of home and career and strike a balance that enriches, rather than depletes, the soul?

Can You Do It All?

In my own reflections and in conversations with other professional women, I ponder the question, *Can we really do it all?* Can we lead or colead a healthy home life while competing with men and women who are not parents and seem to have lifestyles of greater freedom and fewer responsibilities? Increasing numbers of women are choosing careers over marriage and are postponing motherhood, or are not becoming mothers at all, to compete and climb the career ladder. But what if we want healthy, delightful homes and dynamic careers as Christian mothers who want to please God? Can we have it all?

As a matter of fact, this question is not new for the African American woman because we have always done it all. The difference now, when contrasted with the past, is that we have women who are in positions of greater authority, of decision-making, and of power. The real difference between those who are thriving and those who simply appear to be thriving is the former will often have a relationship with our Lord and Savior, Jesus Christ. Women who put God first in every aspect of their lives will make good decisions and thrive with contentment and a quality lifestyle.

The Art of Compromise: Better Known as "Making a Way"

In this world of gifted, talented African American women, you may sometimes wonder, *Is there anything some women cannot do?* I have a colleague who is a professor but knows how to design and sew clothes, cook like a chef, sing, design media platforms, and she leads a Bible study. I asked why she became a professor, and she said it was about the lifestyle. She could teach at night and be at home during the day with her small children. She indicated that her true desire was to become a chef, but she has decided to defer that dream until her children are grown and living independently. She is making a way to achieve her dream.

As an adult, I chose to attend college and maintain a demanding job while being involved in ministry at the same time. I found a way to do it all. I have a friend who works from home because she also serves as a caregiver for her mom and needs to be present in her home daily. Making a way means finding resources through others, including online and through inquiry, about all available resources.

My Story: Building Character and Sticking to Your Mission

In my history, there were not many successful people in our community. In fact, there was only one African American church and school. Thankfully, at these two places, we were able to learn insights on how to remain focused on our own identities and how to develop strong character to sustain us in our purposes. The focus on character was one of the main areas that encouraged me. When I struggled with friends, school, and societal issues, it was my grandmother who gave me the greatest wisdom of all and helped instill character in me. She instructed me not to worry about peer pressure and what others thought, but to simply make sure I treated others well because it mattered to God and to her. She encouraged me to remain true to my character and to try my very best to treat people well. She instilled confidence in me and pride in being an African American woman.

I'm thankful for a praying grandmother! She was the *rock* and matriarch of our family. She was a great example of balance and a role model for me, her children, and many other African American women. For several years, she worked full-time as a maid to the wealthy in our community. I watched her daily routine: getting up very early to pray and read her devotions. Like the Proverbs 31 woman, she always started her meals for the family in the morning, and by the time evening came, it was done. We had church services every single day and all day on Sundays. She was always very prepared. It was my grandmother, this missionary to the poor, who served her community all while working every day.

My mom was a social worker, foster care parent, and adoption advocate for most of my young childhood. As a family, we learned early that our neighborhood needed help from others. It did not matter if help came from the church family, a pastor, or other community leader, ours was a community that reached out to help one another, if possible.

My mom was a promoter of character as well and said I should always be honest with myself. She helped me demonstrate character in my moments of decision-making about schedules, life, and purpose. She would always ask us to be good citizens, and she taught her family to focus on building character rather than one's outward appearance or personality. Mom would state that it was your character that would give you the strength to say *no* to things that were being asked of you, things that were not part of your overall mission in life.

I learned to stick to my mission in life. My mother said we should not take on everyone else's mission but pursue our own. For years, I would try to please people, doing everything they asked of me instead of focusing on what was honestly important to me. These actions would leave me feeling void of strength and unfulfilled because all these things were not part of my purpose. I love to serve, and still do, in ministry but I have determined *when* to say yes. Because of this, I always try to bring the best that I have to my home, my career, and my calling in the ministry.

Making a Way for Childcare

In the good old days, the ones who cared for our kids were their grandmothers, aunts, cousins, or other relatives and friends who shared our values and loved our children. These were people who also worked at an economical or almost barter rate. Today African American women are able to have more quality time with their children because their economic means allows them to have excellent help with childcare and housekeepers to clean their homes, wash clothes, and perform routine chores. I have a colleague who hired an au pair (nanny) to care for her children so she could travel with her husband more often. Women are finding creative ways to make excellent daycare happen. However, if a responsible family member is available to help, by all means, take advantage of their help. Extended families are part of the African American tradition and are a strength for helping to sustain, love, and support the family. Overall, the goal is to find a way that works and is pleasing to God.

Home and Work Balance: Self Matters

Books and the internet are full of ideas and suggestions for balancing home and career. These ideas change over time, but some of them are basic:

1. Ensure that you have babysitters, au pairs, or caregivers who warrant your confidence so you can focus when you need to be at work or absent from home.
2. Set boundaries between work and home. Even if you work from home, keep work and home separated so you can be productive but also enjoy time at home. Know your limits and do not allow yourself to get overwhelmed. This includes setting time for enjoyment and regular vacations or staycations.
3. Ensure that you can be reached by your family's caregivers or children if an emergency arises. This way, you can feel confident that "no news is good news" and that all is going well. But, if needed, you will be immediately contacted so you can make arrangements or handle a situation yourself, if necessary.
4. Make time for yourself each day. When life gets stressful, I find that I need to pull away and get refreshed from the fast-paced activities and day-to-day demands. I make time for healthy meals and physical fitness time at home or work. Take breaks, even if it is just fifteen minutes twice a day. Block out time for yourself in your planner, just as you would a meeting. Read Scripture, call a friend, or simply close your eyes and meditate on the goodness of the Lord.
5. Become a part of a caring church community, whether it is online or in person. Go through life with friends or a prayer partner so you will feel connected and can be uplifted by others.

6. Ask for help when needed. Whether at home or at work, call on someone to help you to avoid being overwhelmed by circumstances. Ask the Lord for discernment on who to ask.
7. Prioritize your own well-being and give yourself grace. Everyone makes mistakes, misjudgments, and errors. God gives grace daily; accept it and move on to the next thing.[1]

Boss, Wife, Mother, Caregiver: Loved Ones Matter

Your husband, children, or any person you are caring for matters to you. They are God's gifts to you and your assignment for the season God chooses in your life. Take care of yourself—mentally, physically, and emotionally. The reason you want to be healthy and care for yourself is to contribute to the lives of your loved ones.

1. Be present in the moment. Focus and give time and attention to your loved one(s) on a regular basis. The reason the Proverbs 31 woman was called *blessed* is not because she was an entrepreneur, but she had time to be a positive presence in her home.
2. Plan for time with loved ones so it is consistent; for example, an afternoon together every weekend.
3. Share responsibilities within the home with your spouse or older children.
4. Be intentional in creating balance by making wise choices.
5. Ensure that you and your family get enough sleep and rest; it is good for you physically, and it replenishes the soul.

Of course, there can be challenges, but strong family relationships are the key. According to one parenting website, for some women, a heavy workload, travel, or shift work can mean getting home after their families are in bed or leaving before they wake up or needing to sleep while everyone else is awake. "You might not be able to control the hours you work or how busy your work is. But you can build strong family relationships by making time for each other when you can, appreciating each other and communicating about how things are going."[2]

In our family, we held regular family meetings together even when our children were young. This was an opportunity to discuss what was happening in each of our lives. We worked on all our schedules to ensure everyone in the family felt their activities were important.

I want to emphasize family vacations. We take family vacations annually, not because we have a lot of money—we don't by the world's standards. However, because we have a plan for saving money, we ensure that when the time comes for a family outing or vacation, we can take it. Yes, times can get hard, but we always make time for family and fun. We are grateful to the Lord that He helps us to sustain this.

You, too, can pray about your job and career. Ask the Lord to give you guidance and direction as you make decisions about how to make a quality lifestyle for the seasons of your family members' lives.

Work- and Career-Related Activities

I'm a believer in developing a time-management plan that will help prioritize personal and professional goals. I worked on processing what is truly important in my life, prioritizing those main things (God, family, career/calling). I also focused on developing a system and vision for the future while building the right relationships in order to become a strong, balanced professional.

In this life, there are going to be highs and lows, but if you have a healthy amount of balance, it will sustain you through life's challenges. I also want to encourage women to seek out older women as mentors or coaches, those whom you feel are demonstrating a healthy balance. They won't be perfect, of course, but they'll be seasoned, competent, mature, and caring.

In fact, family-friendly work arrangements can also help you improve your home life and give your career a boost. There are several basic principles you can consider in your position at work to ease on-the-job stress:

1. Say no to things that are not priorities.
2. Engage in whatever counts as meaningful and productive.
3. Delegate as much as possible. You cannot do everything. Allow others to help you carry the load.
4. Consider working from home, or pursuing flexible hours or even part-time work, if necessary and possible.
5. Use technology to its fullest to make work, meetings, and other tasks easier.
6. Ask the Lord for a good mentor(s) who can help you navigate your career and give you insights about decisions that need to be made. Mentors can help you avoid costly mistakes.

Remember, you have choices; use your options to reduce stress, and use alternatives if needed and available. Remain flexible and allow yourself to stay open to redirecting or changing routines whenever necessary.

Family Mission Statement, Goals, and Personal Evaluation

Family Vision

Every family should have a mission or vision statement that guides their life. Our Harris Family Mission Statement is as follows: "To be a family that strengthens, encourages, motivates, and supports each other's gifts and talents to be all that we can be for the glory of God." We've always kept this mounted on a wall in our family room for all to see, and at one point, it was at the front door. As guests would enter, it became a great talking point. We did this by making sure everyone in our family strived to know their God-given gifts, talents, and purposes in life.

Personal Mission

I encourage others to have an individual mission statement as well as that family mission statement. My personal statement is "To live a life of noble character, honoring God while developing those around me to become the person God created them to be."

Try to find resources that will help you establish your personal mission statement. Some time ago, I was given a book by one of my pastors. It took me a few months to take time to read it, but . . . wow! When I did, it was exactly the right time in my life to do so. This book changed my life and helped me to structure my life for a greater purpose.

I was working a great job and married with two kids, but I was struggling with my identity—not as a wife or mother but with knowing my own purpose in life. I knew that what I was doing was good: I was working part-time as an office manager and recruiter and I loved it. But I knew that God had more for me. I could feel the Lord beginning to structure my life in a way that would add more capacity.

I accepted a full-time human resources role in one of the largest Bible publishing houses in the United States. After being there for a few months, I was asked to start a training and development program to enhance the culture of the organization. Much to my surprise, my experience was in alignment with the book I had just completed reading. I urge you to find Christian resources that will contribute fundamental principles and strategies to your life and help you balance all that God has given you to accomplish.

Goals

Our family has a regular, systematic approach to goals we set annually and review regularly to ensure we are accomplishing work-and-life balance. The internet has volumes of "goal setting plans for families," but here are some basic steps:

1. Encourage everyone in the family to contribute when setting goals. This way, when there is a positive outcome, every member will feel successful.
2. Create goals that are specific, attainable, important, and have a timeline. But be flexible; changes may be needed.
3. Write down your goals in creative ways. Have everyone involved with designing a goal board. Display it to keep each member motivated and accountable.

4. Uplift and cheer on other family members throughout each activity.
5. Congratulate each other on your accomplishments. When you reach a goal you've all made, plan a celebration—a little one or a big one.

Examples of family goals are

- Eating meals together regularly
- Learning Bible verses
- Planning new experiences
- Being physically active together or one-on-one
- Watching movies or playing games
- Expressing gratitude verbally or in writing
- Cooking nutritious meals together

And the list goes on. Some benefits of setting family goals are improving family bonds, better communication, and a sense of shared purpose among family members. See if you can develop your own lists of benefits within your family unit.[3]

Evaluation

I take time away to conduct an annual evaluation of every area of my life to ensure I am healthy. Therefore, I would recommend you do a checkup—emotionally, spiritually, and physically—and assess where you are in your life.

You may start by asking yourself these questions:

- Do I have a healthy balance?
- Am I taking time for just me?
- Am I heading in the direction I want to go?
- Am I facing barriers in my life? What is hindering me?
- Who is missing in my life?
- To what do I need to say no?
- What do I need to start, stop, or continue?

After completing your evaluation, share the results with someone else. A reevaluation of your life will allow you to reap the benefits of a healthy, well-balanced life.

Final Thoughts

My husband and I are hardworking parents with a strong work ethic, strong values, and Christian morals. Together we learned how to balance home, family, careers, and being called to ministry. We structured our home foundation on orderly routines, time management, and communication so that every area is being cared for and nurtured. This practice ensures long-term success.

I accepted the fact that by the grace of God, I can balance it all and still be emotionally healthy and have peace. Remember, when your family members have needs and demands, you can make a way to meet those needs because you can do all things through Christ who strengthens you (Philippians 4:13). When the job places pressure on you to be "on," sharp, and present, you can do it. If God gives you peace and you feel like you have enough time for "all the things" in your life, you probably have a good home-work balance.

My prayer for us as African American women is that we begin to take time to rest from striving and heal from all that we face daily. I pray that we take lessons learned and insights given to live a better-balanced, healthy life. May we spend time in meditation with God first and then begin to reach out and help others through the difficulties we all face. My prayer is that we will help and support each other's destinies.

12

Generational Wealth

Pursuing Wisdom and Prosperity

JOYCE M. DINKINS

> Keep this Book of the Law always on your lips;
> meditate on it day and night, so that you may
> be careful to do everything written in it. Then
> you will be prosperous and successful.
>
> Joshua 1:8

As we consider wisdom and prosperity, let's explore generational wealth from a biblical perspective. Let's reflect on Scripture as well as Black history and consider personal stories that relate to and illustrate financial literacy and generational wealth. We'll examine how managing money helps us to care for ourselves, our families, and our communities. We'll prioritize God's wisdom about seeking wealth and giving to those who are in need. As we seek God first, we live our best lives, leave our richest legacy, and maintain our peace (Matthew 6:33–34).

While we focus on principles of godly money management and success, we'll note the racial wealth gaps that exist without poring over negative statistics because that ignores the root of these disparities between Black people's and others' wealth. Black people, including Black women, have been and are pivotal models of wise, biblical principles—curating our coins, cash, credit, and selves as we also care for others. Our godliness and stewardship—against all odds and naysayers—will continue working to enrich us and our future generations.

Exemplary Women

Let's remember a few exemplary women to whom God gave a measure of wisdom, money, influence, and power. These are individuals from the biblical record, a Black icon, and a young woman I know personally. They model how God redeems and inspires us to pursue our best lives, benefit our families, and bless others. They have made a positive impact on the world, nurturing families, encouraging communities to thrive, and helping individuals achieve dreams.

First, these biblical women prioritized God as they managed their assets. The referenced verses provide fuller illustrations, revealing more of their stories:

- The daughters of Zelophehad negotiated land ownership to benefit future generations of their father's tribe. They were of the clans of the descendants of Joseph (Numbers 36:1–10).
- Africa's Queen of Sheba sought Solomon for godly wisdom. God used her as a key financial backer *for* the king, the wealthiest person ever (1 Kings 10:1–13).
- Women were among the disciples who served Jesus: at His birth (Luke 2:1–19), for His ministry (Luke 8:1–4), and at His death and resurrection (Matthew 28:1; Luke 24:1–10).
- Jesus taught the truth about His kingdom by citing this poor widow's gift in worship (Mark 12:43).
- Women were leaders and investors in the early church (Acts 2:1–4, 42–47).
- Through business relationships, women have served communities as they spread the gospel (John 11:17–40; Acts 16:1–16).

In our modern history, women are on the record as industrious, worshipers, and people who prioritize evangelism. Take for example Mary Ellen Pleasant. As an abolitionist, Pleasant funded the African Methodist Episcopal Zion Church, served the Underground Railroad, supported Black journalism, and fought for justice on behalf of herself and her community through the courts and in her business dealings. In the 1890 census, Pleasant was listed as a "capitalist," who lived and worked in San Francisco. She had relocated from Virginia in a wise, timely move.

Working humbly in other people's houses, she invested in mining and real estate. She managed an inheritance left by her first husband. Pleasant was a powerful businesswoman during San Francisco's Gold Rush era. She's featured on California's "National Historic Trail" and is publicized in author Lerone Bennett Jr.'s "The Mystery of Mary Ellen Pleasant" (*Ebony* magazine, September 1993).[1] Other records report her real estate portfolio included land in Canada, though she died insolvent, in part due to racism.

A personal example is my daughter, who is also a great-granddaughter of formerly enslaved ancestors. Loren has served and helped to lead the company founded by her father (my former husband). She is a key leader in that company, recently bought by venture capitalists. She has served clients internationally, invested in others through church affiliations, and supported her community alongside other successful Black women in an international Black women's nonprofit. According to Loren, her work "contributes to reducing mental health stigmas in the African American community, provides wellness presentations delivered to African American faith-based community sites, and highlights the accomplishments of youth through programming."

These women are representative of Black women pursuing wisdom, managing wealth, and inspiring others to have a positive impact in African American communities.

We Are Wealth Managers

> Honor the LORD with your wealth, with the first-fruits of all your crops; then your barns will be filled to overflowing, and your vats will brim over with new wine. (Proverbs 3:9–10)

I was about three, the youngest in our family, growing up in a poorer neighborhood of a wealthy village near Chicago. In so many ways, I was far from my grandparents' lives enmeshed in chattel slavery and sharecropping. Though they lacked formal education—they did their best to learn through churches they established—they were determined to ensure that their children were very well-educated. Forsaking the denials and drudgery of the South, my parents relocated to gain opportunities that would enrich their next generation. My childhood home developed from their dreams for a better life.

Their first savvy step moved our family into a few dilapidated rooms inside a boarding house. The village didn't fully enforce covenants against the dwelling. (Covenants were racist practices restricting Black ownership of [a deed to] real estate in better neighborhoods, even after the Fair Housing Act of 1968.)[2] We walked to schools that served primarily White children and the wealthy. We gained the best instructors and facilities, and there were opportunities in the wealthy areas of this community for Dad's painting work to keep us fed and sheltered.

We slept on a dining room floor beneath a table until our parents could clear out vermin and roaches. Dad refurbished sagging ceilings, repaired holes in the walls, and eventually bought out the remaining tenants and property owner. That was my first childhood lesson in real estate investing, especially in fixer-uppers. It was part of a popular wealth-building strategy that became the focus of one of my jobs later in life.

Why me? I'm not a professional financial, or wealth, adviser.

Given my upbringing alone, I wondered why the editors invited me to write this. Even as I questioned my capability, God prompted me to reflect and write about what I have learned and experienced.

My family is blessed to live on almost forty acres, gifted to my husband and me, passed down through three generations by his enterprising grandfather, Sam Taylor. Granddad's beginnings were in poverty: shoveling coal in Alabama for a few dollars a day until he migrated. He somehow bought this land and established a small family business that became a nationally recognized electric company, now more than one hundred years old.

My own grandparents, impoverished Georgia sharecroppers and ex-slaves, had little opportunity to dream, though I have received plenty from their strivings, as well as from my parents'.

I have, however, decades of my own experiences with gains and losses, as married, then divorced, then a single provider for my child, and then a remarried Christian. My husband and I have raised a blended family. We also have been servant leaders helping to plant churches in several states, and we have engaged in international mission work throughout our almost forty years of marriage.

God has shown me that this chapter dovetails with my family financial planning: matching donations of time, talent, and treasure to trustworthy nonprofits; emergency saving; forecasting annual income taxes against retirement distributions; founding a limited liability corporation (LLC); renewing insurances; preplanning and prepaying for our final rites; updating our wills; contracting editorial work; and pursuing personal writing. My most important activity is investing in prayer for my family and extended family each day.

While building *generational wealth* is important, that wealth can be fleeting. More than monetary gains for ourselves and future generations, *gaining wisdom in using our wealth* is crucial. As the Queen of Sheba realized, wisdom has the greatest worth: "From all nations people came to listen to Solomon's wisdom, sent by all the kings of the world, who had heard of his wisdom" (1 Kings 4:34). We can gain and retain through God-given wisdom. Without that, is our other wealth ever sufficient and lasting?

Some Steps for Gaining Financial Wisdom

Solomon attested: "For lack of guidance a nation falls, but victory is won through many advisers" (Proverbs 11:14). Granddad Taylor told his family, "Do not let a poor man tell you anything about how to manage money." I don't sense that his words were meant to mock; he was pointing to the role of wisdom from experience and offering his advice as a means to succeed in building one's finances. Advisers—tax preparers, lawyers, estate planners, investment realtors, bankers—are experienced in helping people manage their finances. However, it is important to remember that all true wisdom comes from God.

Begin with Wisdom

When the Queen of Sheba consulted Solomon, she already owned plenty; what she sought was the wisdom God had given him. Again, God used her as a key financial backer for *him*: "And she gave the king 120 talents of gold, large quantities of spices, and precious stones. Never again were so many spices brought in as those the queen of Sheba gave to King Solomon" (1 Kings 10:10).

Wise Women Give as They Grow

Millions of our role models from previous generations have furthered their training and education in order to capitalize on their skills and gifts. This helped some of them immensely. They gave, shared, and sacrificed to help their own and others' families, neighborhoods and churches, communities, and institutions. Black women continue today to contribute and serve mightily; it's part of our legacy.

Wise women know God as the source for giving and the call for them to give. There is not enough room to enumerate all that God gives. Here are a few references:

- "For God so loved the world that he gave his one and only Son, that whoever believes in him shall not perish but have eternal life" (John 3:16).
- God gives His Spirit to all who trust in Him for salvation (Acts 2:38–30).
- God calls us to give to the needy, which reflects our love for Him and our neighbor (Matthew 6:1–2).
- God teaches us that giving is an act of worship that models our lives after His (Mark 12:43).
- God has called His people to practice giving and sharing since the beginning of Christianity (Acts 2:42–45).

Wisdom and Giving Begin at Home

My brother-in-law, a credentialed financial adviser with decades of life and business experience, and a trustworthy Christian minister, reemphasized that the great percentage of good (or bad) financial habits begin at home. Then the more technical financial understanding comes from consulting with other experts.

At home, our family can teach us to value work, save, build credit-worthiness by paying our bills before they are due, and pursue a wise lifestyle overall. At home, we can learn to budget. We can also learn the value of gaining appreciating assets (such as a house) rather than collecting too many assets that depreciate (cars, clothes, shoes, makeup). Once we have a good foundation and we are ready to obtain an appreciating asset, we can call on family and the brokers, bankers, and other advisers for that detailed guidance.

When I was a child, my mother's teaching ignited our joy in giving. She prayed with her family daily, giving God thanks. When we ate, she simply asked us not to take the last piece from any serving plate; rather, we were to leave food for someone who hadn't yet eaten. Although we were poor in comparison to most families in our village, my mother would give me a dime tied inside a handkerchief to place in the church offering on Sundays. It was as though she had entrusted me with gold to give away. Giving brought joy.

Healthy Habits Are Wealthy Habits

Our immediate families and extended families pass on health-giving attitudes that can save and preserve our lives and the next generations'. Many advise that good healthcare is a *primary* asset to teach our family. Habits of healthy eating prepare us to function well, enjoy life, and be mind-and-body competitive. We should consider a diet full of vegetables and fruits; vigorous exercise; a balanced regimen of mental and physical work; avoidance of alcohol, smoking, and illicit drugs; and managing stress. Seeing our bodies as gifts from God, we can train our children to have healthy lifestyles that can preserve them and offer a witness to others.

Growing up, our family routinely gleaned melons, peaches, and zucchini squash from neighbors' gardens, not to mention raw honey from a beekeeper. We ran and climbed and feasted in the neighbor Rainier cherry trees. Hours of yard work and housework gave us a work ethic and appreciation for responsibility and our belongings.

When my dad gave up smoking cigarettes, that provided an indelible health lesson. I was thirteen. Though I bowed to peer pressure in college, recalling his action helped me give up cigarettes and alcohol in my twenties. I was also seeking to protect my body as I sought to become pregnant with my first child.

Good Habits Transfer

We can "catch" good practices from family; they "rub off" on us. Family influences our integrity, perseverance, respect for others, frugality, and more. These traits are as valuable to our lives as receiving material wealth.

My parents raised us with second- and third-hand everything—not as a thrifty trend but as a lifestyle. They reminded us to control our expenditures: "Turn off the lights when you leave a room" and "Live within your means." As we observed their good habits, including thriftiness, we also saw how enterprising they were and that we could be too.

Bank, Earn, Save, Grow, and Slow Spending

A number of resources say that Black Americans have been underbanked, often using check-cashing services and payday lending services that cost more than banks would charge. Part of the reason for this is a dearth of banks in some communities.[3] Those lending "services" don't provide basic financial tools like compound-interest savings accounts, mortgages, and equity loans. As we as Black people work and earn income, we must find reliable banks, including those that are accessible online, if not in our neighborhoods or nearby. We can always save something with a budget rather than spend impulsively.

As a quad of elementary-aged children, my siblings and I made and sold potholders. As teens, we did babysitting and yard-care work. We pooled our earnings and each took an allowance of a dollar a week, saving the remainder for needs. We had individual savings accounts and were taught also to contribute to purchases, including the car we bought together and shared for ten years. We each helped pay for our college tuition; otherwise, we would have been unable to attend. We learned care with our choices, practiced paying in cash, kept zero debt, and shunned borrowing. By purchasing all of our clothes from where we worked, we gained deep discounts as we carefully built credit and were able to dress well.

It's wise to minimize pride (the pride of trying to "keep up with the Joneses"). We knew that spending to acquire depreciating assets would disrupt our finances.

During junior high school, high school, college, and graduate school, my siblings and I were employed outside our home. We chose in-state and community colleges, and that lowered tuition and transportation costs. We applied for scholarships and found or purchased used books. Though we would have loved to attend a historically Black college or a prominent private university, that was not in our budget. If we had had enough money, we might have made our savings work for us through certificates of deposit (CDs). That would have allowed us to gain greater interest on our money in order to help keep pace with rising costs of living. Stock market investments were out of our reach and understanding at the time. We simply did not have that wealth to invest, and we did our best with what we had.

Everyday People Counsel and Encourage

We can examine the news from financial gurus and counsel with many experts. But I've found timely help through my family, church, and others. Those in my family, or those recommended by family, can give some of the best financial advice, as they share expertise from their networks. I also cater to local businesses where the customer service is consistent and where I have a relationship with the vendor or service provider. This also supports my own community's well-being and tends to promote good customer service.

I remember the day my local bank manager concluded that I needed to boost my income in order to qualify for a refinance mortgage on the condominium I owned. My father had referred me to this bank manager, so since he knew my family, he didn't simply say no to a lower interest rate with cash out of the equity. A new job offer to work in Christian publishing meant adjustments in my income. I knew the job was my opportunity to serve Christ but needed to hold on to our home, an anchor for me and my daughter.

A close friend phoned at a decisive moment. I shared my dilemma and we prayed. He offered, "You could follow your calling; you just need a second job." With that wise encouragement, I immediately asked for a yearlong freelance contract—in order to become an editor at a new job. The former employer agreed to give me the contract, the bank approved my refinance, and my career in Christian publishing began. I learned a powerful lesson of the value of a second stream of income. You can learn from others' expertise and through experiences with successes as well as losses.

Growing Our Financial Literacy: Definitions, Terms, and Examples

"Like apples of gold in settings of silver is a ruling rightly given" (Proverbs 25:11). Whatever monetary wealth we have, we can grow in our understanding of how to steward it. We just need the right information and counsel. I gathered these basic explanations of terms from personal insights, experiences, and the Consumer Finance Bureau.

- Becoming *literate* means to have the wisdom and skills to make correct financial decisions, know how to create and maintain resources, and know how we might pass on some resources to the next generation. This is a process that can begin immediately.
- Practically speaking, *generational* wealth is what one owns—free of debt—that can be passed on to others. It is "wealth that is transferred from parents or relatives to children or

other members of their family . . . that may take the form of cash, property, or anything else that has financial value, as well as investments in children's education, like paying for college or vocational training. This is also referred to as intergenerational wealth."[4] Estate planners are helpful in identifying assets that can transfer at one's death.

- *Financial well-being* is "the ability to meet all financial needs, today and over time; feel secure in the financial future; absorb a financial shock; and have the financial freedom to make choices to enjoy life."[5] Using an income and disbursements ledger can help your family keep a balanced budget, including tithing, savings, and having more appreciating than depreciating assets.
- Paying little or no interest on debt is a wise move; however, if a payment is late, the lower rate is lost, and the interest on the debt balance may increase dramatically. In addition, other fees may hit your account. Carefully read the fine print on all credit offers to see rates and late payment penalties.
- *Annual percentage rate* (APR) is "the cost of borrowing money on a yearly basis, expressed as a percentage rate"[6] of interest the borrower will pay monthly over the life of a loan. If, for example, you've protected your credit rating by establishing an income, gaining credit, and paying off debt balances with excellence, you can even gain a zero percent interest rate on some purchases in certain markets. That's a smart way to pay for an asset (like a new mattress) that is going to depreciate in value. Maintaining very good to excellent credit affords opportunities to pay less interest as long as your monthly payments continue on or before due dates.

  You can see a credit report by contacting a credit bureau and should check your score annually for free. You can then follow a process to remove negative information, such as a bankruptcy or debts falsely attributed to you.
- *Capital gains and losses* are what you incur when cashing out tax-deferred long-term investments, such as mutual funds in a retirement account. There can be tax consequences depending

on your other taxable income, so it's best to check with a tax professional.
- *Elder financial exploitation* is the "illegal or improper use of an older adult's funds, property, or assets by family members, caregivers, friends, or strangers who gain their trust."[7] People can do the unspeakable to the elderly when prompted by greed. Contact a counselor or an elder-law expert if you suspect abuse of any sort.

Some financial experts advise that financial literacy should become regular study in kindergarten through high school.[8] Though definitions help, wealth-building strategies and tactics require having not only the money to manage but some experience in doing so. Many of us as African Americans have experienced *not* having the money needed to help our families overcome setbacks and grow income that could also boost the next generation with a running start. Progress has occurred. Our ancestors have worked hard and provided invaluable life lessons for us as we move ahead.

We as Black women remain influential, and God has positioned us to be a blessing to our future generations. As we make monetary and other gains, we want to employ and increase our financial literacy and continue to grow in godly wisdom.

Wealth-Building Strategies

Hear a health reminder: The woman said, "He would give all the wealth he had to simply enjoy good health." All the money in the world can help but cannot buy health for you or your children. Medical care costs are excessive. Diseases, pandemics, and more challenges have affected Black and Brown communities disproportionately—and have also affected their credit standings due to medical debt. The best solution is boosting self-care for one's families; drinking water, eating well, and exercising are doable. But planning ahead helps too.

Experts urge everyone over the age of eighteen to have a health plan that includes a *durable power of attorney* (someone appointed to handle your medical decisions if you can't make them). A *living will* or *advanced directive* states your wishes for whether you would like to be kept alive in the event that doctors have been unable to resuscitate you. A *last will and testament* spells out the distribution of your assets to family and friends after you die. It will also name a guardian for minor children or other dependents.

Handle Credit and Debt

According to a recent study by the Urban Institute, young adults in Black communities had significantly lower credit scores (including due to medical debt).[9] Of course this also would be the case given historical wealth gaps that began with slavery and continued through discrimination against Black people. Studies have looked at the median credit scores of young adults in primarily Black communities and found their median credit scores were lower.[10]

Credit is important for renting, buying a car, accessing lower interest rates, and homeownership. Proposed solutions include creating a federally backed credit bureau. According to the policy proposal, a federal credit reporting agency could reduce racial disparities in credit reporting. Some action has been taken to remove medical debts from credit reports—a type of debt that disproportionately affects Black and Hispanic communities. Imagine how managing one's health could yield good results financially.[11]

Real Estate Investing Begins at Home

My parents used equity from their first home, the rooming house, to purchase and refurbish another sort of "investment property." Instead of living off-campus, my brother and I resided there at a huge savings. Our parents eventually sold the home and invested in their retirement home and five-acre farm. When Dad became seriously ill, he sold the farm he had improved and bought a fourth property in a high-tax suburb. My sister and her husband became joint tenants, an arrangement providing security and care for my parents but also excellent schools for the grandchildren.

Acquiring, improving, and selling real estate became a model for me. I learned to invest strategically, buying well-located property that might not meet all of my wants.

Manage Insurance as a Wealth Builder

High-value life insurance can pay funeral costs and leave wealth for family. There are no federal taxes owed on life insurance gains. Other types of insurance will protect your assets, cover accidents, provide income during illness, pay off mortgages, and more.

My dad's life insurance policy did not cover all of his funeral costs. Financial literacy wasn't the problem; some insurance companies practiced charging Blacks more for products and offering small face-amount burial insurance that provided little value.[12]

My elderly mom received an insurance payment following a car accident. She added to money received for releasing her joint-tenant rights in her home. The total amount threatened continuation of her Social Security income. We prayerfully and promptly sought advice to clarify the expenditures that could be made for Mom's needs. She repaired her car, purchased burial insurance, preplanned her funeral, and paid for the creation of her will. She hired an estate lawyer to help establish an irrevocable trust to protect her money for her long-term care.

Mom was healthy. She prayed, attended church, and loved on her family. She never smoked or drank liquor. She rode a bicycle into her eighties and traveled independently by car and airplane.

She moved across the country to live with my family (and her youngest grandchild) when she was diagnosed with Alzheimer's disease. The monies in her trust provided for her long-term care in an assisted living residence and finally in a twenty-four-hour secure care facility near me. The night she passed away in my arms, she was at peace. And she owed no one. She left no debt. The money in her trust bequeathed gifts to her grandchildren and to the charities she supported.

My mother taught us to pray, use wisdom, save, give, and she showed us what courage looks like in life as well as in death. I think financial literacy and growing generational wealth requires all of that. As Black women, we certainly can pass courage to our future generations, an invaluable asset.

Invent Your Business

Sadly, Dad had that lousy insurance. But he figured out, without much formal education, how to create a wealth reserve for my mother, and he counted on her children to help her. He owned the rights to another small business he started after handing down his painting business to the youngest of his four sons. (My brother continued to build that business as his own.)

A plaque on my office wall boasts the painting sundries Dad invented, patented in his eighties. He pooled the gifts and energies of his offspring to build a new business that passed to Mom at his death. When the business sold to fund the irrevocable trust, the money provided enough to care for her insurance and some medical expenses.

Owning and passing down a successful business provides career advantages, income and tax advantages, independence, employment security, and may allow you to pass on other advantages. "While more than half of entrepreneurs rely on personal savings or income to fund their startups, there generally will come a time when outside financing is required, and securing that financing can be tougher for women . . . only 1.9 percent of venture capital (VC) funding goes to women-founded startups. But other funding options do exist, including loans and grants earmarked for women-owned businesses. . . . And some venture capital firms specialize in funding women entrepreneurs."[13]

Discuss with your financial adviser before you launch your new business. As entrepreneurs, Black women are usually one-person businesses.[14] But one person can be successful through inventiveness, collaboration, and by seeking God's wisdom.

Final Thoughts: Our First Asset

While barriers to financial well-being and wealth building exist, God's wisdom is golden, free, and profitable for all generations. Wisdom in our minds and hearts remains our best asset. As King

Solomon advised from his renowned experiences of success and failure, "Above all else, guard your heart, for everything you do flows from it" (Proverbs 4:23). As we pursue success, let's practice godly wisdom, knowing as Christ followers that "life does not consist in an abundance of possessions" (Luke 12:15).

13

The Church

Breaking the Unholy Triad of Sexism, Classism, and Racism

KELLIE CARTER JACKSON

> Love your neighbor as yourself.
> Mark 12:31

Sin is sin and yet I cannot help but think of all the harm and violence caused by sexism, classism, and racism in particular. The change we want to see in the world begins with the church, not a building or facility, but the body of Christ: we Christians. Let's first turn the mirror on ourselves. We expect the world to be cruel and unfair. We expect the world to push power and accumulation. Satan's primary goal is to steal, kill, and destroy (John 10:10). But Christians are called to a different standard. Our work is to help heal and repair a fallen, secular world. In other words, the church should be the place where equity, love, and care for others is modeled for the world. We are living in a time period when people are turning away from the church. Bad faith actors, scandals, celebrities, nationalism, and White supremacy provoke some to walk away from the church. But I believe the solutions to our biggest "isms" can only be found and healed by Christ alone. The work starts with us. We are salt and light (Matthew 5:13–16).

Defining the "Isms"

So much of my identity has been shaped by the fact that I am a Black person, a woman, and born without wealth. I think of the countless ways people are marginalized, disadvantaged, and destroyed because of human-instituted power dynamics. The Bible is clear about how we ought to treat one another: "Love your neighbor as yourself" (Mark 12:31). The Bible is also clear that unity is God's desire for us, and division is a weapon of the enemy (John 17:21). We are all God's children and are, thereby, all neighbors. Therefore, it is vital to discuss how sexism, classism, and racism conflict with our lives. While it is impossible to cover all of the grievances and history in this article, I will do my part to share three stories, personal and anecdotal, to reveal truth from the Word of God. Together we can work to dismantle the barriers that keep us from loving our neighbors.

First, defining each "ism" matters.

Sexism is discrimination and prejudice based on gender, and is primarily against women. Sexism is more than offensive language and jokes; it can cause harm, including violence and death. When we examine sexism against women, we are essentially grappling with *patriarchy*. Patriarchy is a system of power that benefits men while simultaneously subordinating women. While men are the beneficiaries, women can support patriarchy and do its bidding. Sadly, too often the primary enforcers of patriarchy have been women. So much sexism has been ingrained into our culture as a "way of doing things" that we forget to ask questions. Women and men can push back against patriarchy because the systems of power that promote the subjugation of women and the disproportional promotion of men affect everyone.

Classism is a system that promotes the wealthy and disdains the poor. Classism requires poverty and a permanent underclass. Classism and capitalism work together to foster wealth and material accumulation by some, resulting in hoarding. Of all the themes in the Bible, money and possessions are the second most-referenced topic. Scholars estimate that money is discussed more than eight hundred times. The Word repeatedly warns about the pitfalls of the love of money and the ways God wants us to treat the poor and powerless.

Racism is about prejudice and power. In the United States alone, structural racism and anti-Blackness are deadly. The public has often seen what happens when unarmed Black people are stopped by the police. Racism impacts public health, education, access to housing, justice and incarceration, and economic security. Racism affects how we internalize ideals of beauty and how that influences art and culture. Racism fosters hyper-surveillance of Black people while simultaneously denying protection. The oppression of Black people through slavery, segregation, and structural racism is historic, consequential, and pervasive.

Common in all three of these "isms" is falsehood. These are lies that breed belief in the inherent superiority of those in power and the inferiority of the powerless.

Sexism

When my husband and I moved to Boston, we joined a church we loved. We were excited because it helped us feel like we belonged. It was one of the oldest churches in New England and was full of rich history and warmth. The ongoing joke in New England is that it is cold . . . and the weather is too. For many of its residents, it can be hard to connect with people in a transitional town. People come to Boston for school, professional programs, or fellowships that last anywhere from a year to several years. But in my experience, it was hard to meet people who were there to stay. However, when we joined our new church, we became close friends with people who had lived in Boston their entire lives, and they welcomed us into their community.

My husband and I grew up serving in the church from youth choir, in the college ministry, in the nursery, and during Vacation Bible School. We strove to always invest in the community to which we belonged. I will never forget the day we were asked to serve as deacons of the church. We were honored. We felt seen and valued. Yet my question was about gender: "So, you want me to be a deacon *or a deaconess?*" I asked because the deaconesses were typically the wives of deacons. They wore white on the first Sundays of the month and fancy hats in a traditional Black Baptist style. They often sat behind the deacons in the church.

"No," the head deacon responded, "we want you to be a deacon. We want you to have a leadership role in the church, serve communion, visit the sick and shut-in, and offer your input. We want to see more women in this role." I was shocked but honored. I loved serving. I loved attending the meetings and helping shape the church community. I remember the first time after church when we gathered in groups of two or three to visit the local nursing homes where our elderly members were residents. We would serve them communion, pray with them, and spend time connecting. The people we visited longed for our fellowship and care. I never felt like I was doing the Lord's work more than when I was in the home of someone who was "sick or shut in." Being able to lay hands on and pray for fellow believers, see them, hug them, and serve them blessed me tremendously.

One cold, wintry Sunday morning, I was preparing to attend church. It was the first Sunday of the month, so I knew we would be serving communion. I dressed in my traditional all-black attire and wore a red pashmina scarf, knowing that the men would be wearing red ties. It was particularly cold that Sunday, so I wore black slacks instead of a dress. I headed off to church, thinking only of what I needed to accomplish that day.

When we reached the point of the service for communion, I was handed one of the golden plates with the elements that symbolize Christ's body and blood. Each deacon stood next to the rows of churchgoers and passed the communion plates across the aisle. When I got to about the third row, a man sitting at the end of the row looked me up and down. I smiled and passed him the communion plate. He gave me a smug look of disdain and refused to take communion from me. *I was confused.* I looked around and checked myself to see if I was missing something. He shook his head and waved me away.

My face suddenly flushed with heat. I thought, *Did this man just refuse to take communion from me?* Instantly, I knew it was because I am a woman, and even worse, I was wearing pants. Part of me wanted to shrug off his disdain. Communion was a sacred act between him and God. I was merely a vessel. *Leave me out of this*, I thought. But I was angry. This elderly man had taken something so sacred and intimate and muddied it with sexism.

While it would be easy for me to talk about sexism in the classroom, workplace, social spaces, or legislation, this interaction stood out to me. I believe many of the Black women reading this book will find that some of our churches have struggled to reckon with gender. Many men in leadership have been unwilling to relinquish their hold on power and problematic ideas regarding women.

For example, in 1963, during the March on Washington, which featured Dr. Martin Luther King Jr.'s famous "I Have a Dream" speech, not a single woman was invited to make one of the major speeches or be part of the delegation of leaders who went to the White House. Rosa Parks and Jo Ann Robinson, leaders of the famous Montgomery bus boycott, were not allowed to speak. Mamie Till, who had lost her fourteen-year-old son Emmett to horrific violence, and who had campaigned for justice for her son, was not asked to speak. Freedom riders and Student Nonviolent Coordinating Committee (SNCC) leaders, such as Diane Nash, Fannie Lou Hamer, and Ella Baker were never given the mic.

Dorothy Height, who was President of the National Council of Negro Women, wrote, "Nothing that women said or did broke the impasse blocking their participation. I've never seen a more unmovable force."[1] The omission of women was intentional. Among the leadership of the Southern Christian Leadership Conference (SCLC), women were only meant to be silent helpers. Anna Arnold Hedgeman was the only woman invited to be on the march's administrative committee, and she vehemently opposed going forward with a program with no women speakers. In the end, Daisy Bates, who had guided and advised the Little Rock Nine, was the only woman on the official program to speak before the crowd. Her speech, entitled, "Tribute to Negro Women Fighting for Freedom," was only 142 words.[2] Her brevity was intentional too. In her 1977 memoir, Hedgeman recalled listening to all of

The Church

the speeches made by men. She was incredulous. With all the talk of justice and equality, Hedgeman wrote, "Wryly, it occurred to me that women, too, were not yet adequately included in man's journey toward humanity."[3]

On many occasions, I am confronted with the absurdity and violence of marginalization and erasure against women. When it comes to civil rights, equality, justice, and most certainly the Lord's communion table, we are all one. In some ways, my experience with a man's denial of Christ's sacred ritual was not only trivial but sad. We have to remind each other that as the Christian church, we are to be set apart from the world and held to a higher standard of love and care. This means that when our brothers and sisters engage in this divisive and abhorrent behavior, they are, in fact, acting like the world. They are acting like unbelievers and in lockstep with countries such as Iran, Afghanistan, India, and even America as a nation when it regulates women to subjugation. Patriarchy is a result of sin. As biblical voices inquired, "Do we not all have one Father? Did not one God create us? Why do we profane the covenant of our ancestors by being unfaithful to one another?" (Malachi 2:10).

Throughout the Bible, women led. Esther was the Queen of her people. Deborah was a judge and prophet. Rahab was courageous in negotiating the protection of the Hebrew spies. God used Mary to be the mother of His own Son, Jesus. Women ministered alongside Jesus and His disciples (Luke 8:1–4). Priscilla and her husband Aquila helped to establish the early Christian church (Romans 16:3). These are a few examples of how God empowered women and used them to model leadership and His love. Subjugating and subordinating women has never been part of the plan God created for people. Both men and women are made in and from His image.[4]

When it comes to leadership within the church, the Bible and scholarship are full of examples of women leading, preaching, and serving congregations. I can recall one of my male pastors discussing a conversation with his girlfriend, who later became his wife. He said flippantly, "I don't believe women should be pastors; there is no place for them in the pulpit." Rather than rebuking her boyfriend, she said, "Oh, really? Let me ask you a question: If a woman preaches the gospel from a pulpit, is she sinning? Is she, by preaching Christ, somehow in opposition to Him?" He paused. He did not have an answer, but at that moment, he knew anything he came up with would be wrong. The church is in a special place to model for the world what leadership looks like when women are empowered.

In the New Testament, spiritual leader Priscilla instructed others (Acts 18:26), and Paul referred to her as a coworker in the ministry of Christ (Romans 16:3). She preached, taught, and served communion, likely to men—while wearing what we might consider a dress by today's standards. At best, sexism is laughable because it is utterly absurd, trivial, and self-loathing. Christ came through a woman! At worst, sexism is violent, destructive, and reflects the values of a society that is far from God's purpose for His people. When the man at my church refused to take communion from me, he did more than insult my attire or gender; he refused Christ's ultimate sacrifice. I was not angry, but sad. He was robbing himself. His refusal was not the end of my story. I shared with the leadership team, mostly comprised of men, what had happened. They were offended. One deacon said to me, directly, "That was wrong." The men continued to work with me to shift the culture of the church from one that reflected the sexism of the world to one that reflected Christ. The work was not mine to do alone. Godly men took the lead on promoting equality. I felt seen, heard, and valued. The good works of the church can be light to the world.

Classism

When I was in graduate school in New York City, I lived in university housing, in a small apartment on the first floor with very little natural light. It almost felt like a basement. Because of its proximity to the main lobby, I often heard or saw lots of people as they left for work, went for a run, or returned from classes. One person I saw almost daily was my building super, Richard. If you needed anything, he was your guy; he managed all of the maintenance for the building, which was no small job. He took care of folks moving in or moving out and all the dirty jobs in between: dealing with rodents and bed bugs, removing trash—you name it. Richard was a chatty person. He always stopped tenants to see how their day was going or to tell a joke. He was jovial. I was also one of the few Black people who lived in the building, so it was nice to be able to talk to another Black person. I learned that we had a strong work ethic in common.

One day, Richard stopped me in the hallway as I was about to enter my apartment. He knew I was training to be a historian. "You know there's a movie about my family," he said. My interest was instantly peaked. "Really," I said. "What is it about?" He told me he was one of ten children. His family lived in Harlem, and one day in the 1960s, a photographer asked to take pictures of his large family, which was later made into a documentary about it. He gave me a copy of the DVD and told me to watch it. He wanted to know what I thought. I took the DVD and went into my apartment. I wanted to decompress from a long day of classes, so I propped open my laptop, popped in the DVD, and started watching.

Within three minutes, I was blown away. The photographer who asked to take pictures of his large family was Gordon Parks, one of the most famous photographers of the twentieth century. He got his start as the first Black photographer to work for *Life* magazine. The year was 1968, and America was on fire. *Life* wanted to understand why Black people across the country were rioting and angry. Parks proclaimed he could live with any Black family for a week and tell that story. One day, while walking through Harlem, he met Richard's mom, Bessie, and her ten children outside of a grocery store. Parks asked her if a story could be done on her family. With Bessie's permission, he spent one week visiting them without his camera. It was then that he became "Uncle Gordon." The following week, Parks brought his camera and took some of the most striking and haunting images of the Fontenelle family to discuss the story of poverty in America.

Norman Sr. and Bessie lived in a tiny apartment with their ten children. Money was always scarce and so was food. Times were especially tough because winter was approaching. Both parents were unsure about how they were going to feed their children and keep the family warm. Chronic unemployment compelled Norman Jr. to drink, and in his drunken rage, he would beat on Bessie and the children. Bessie's youngest child, three-year-old Richard (and later my super), would get sick from eating plaster that fell from the dirt-covered walls of their apartment. On Thanksgiving, Parks photographed the family all huddled around an empty oven to keep warm; it was their only source of heat in the apartment. On March 8, 1968, *Life* magazine made Parks's story the cover. The image selected for the cover is one of Parks's "most arresting: a wailing five-year-old Ellen Fontenelle, with a tear fully formed at the bottom of one eye, just before it descends her cheek."[5]

The story was so gripping that letters came in from all over the country from people wanting to support the Fontenelle family. Enough money was raised to purchase the family a home in the suburbs of Long Island. For a short time, life was good. The children had food and good schools to attend. They were growing a garden in their backyard. But within three months, the house burned down. Richard's brothers Norman Jr. and Kenneth were killed in the fire. Once the house was destroyed, life plummeted for the remaining family members, who all moved back to Harlem. One by one, siblings lost their lives to the streets, drugs, violence, AIDS, incarceration, and mental illness.

When I finished watching the documentary, I understood that the only two living members of the Fontenelle family were Richard and his sister Diane.[6] I sat in my apartment thinking about all of the hardships that poverty imposes on its victims. There have been times when I had money and times when I had none. There are times when I was a nobody and times when I had some recognition. In the African American community, the instability of class and wealth are well known. Capitalism will not get them free; only Christ can do that. Fame and celebrity will not save them either; only Christ can do this.

We are most like Christ when we meet the needs of the vulnerable. I thanked Richard for sharing the film with me. I wanted to draw attention to the powerful themes in the film. I told him I was going to use this film in my classes. Parks used his article to expose and educate on the violence of poverty. I wanted to follow suit. He began his article on the Fontenelles by writing,

> For I am you, staring back from a mirror of poverty and despair, of revolt and freedom. Look at me and know that to destroy me is to destroy yourself. You are weary of long hot summers, I am tired of long hungered winters. . . . My children's needs are the same as your children's. I too am America. . . . Look at me. Listen to me. Try to understand my struggle against your racism. There is yet a chance for us to live in peace beneath these restless skies.[7]

In the film, Diane recounted the unimaginable losses of her family. Tearfully, she lamented the death of one of her brothers: "He just wanted love. We all wanted love."[8] Diane admitted that due to poverty, she turned to drugs as well—but she also turned to Christ. Her life was changed when she found Jesus. She found love and a home and a church that embraced her. She even found employment in a job that did not require her to be on her feet all day, which was a specific prayer request. In 2013, forty-five years after the *Life* magazine article debuted, the Studio Museum in Harlem revisited the Fontenelle's story with an exhibition that featured Gordon Parks's photographs. Three days after the show opened, Richard died from a heart attack.[9]

We are all navigating an unjust world. Classism is a weapon. It weakens and sometimes eradicates a person's potential to improve themselves and their circumstances. It is not a sin to be poor, but poverty and oppression are a result of a broken, sinful world.

Racism

Few things have impacted Black life more than the lie of White supremacy. Throughout history, White supremacists have weaponized *whiteness* and perverted Christianity and the Bible to subordinate and exploit Black lives and labor. It can be argued that slavery and even segregation gained acceptability only through the approval of White churches. There are articles that cite priests sanctioning the whipping of an enslaved person.[10] In the twentieth century, there are photographs taken inside a White church where dozens of members of the Ku Klux Klan are dressed in full regalia and standing in the pulpit. The minister is shaking hands with Klan leadership, all under a banner that reads, "Jesus Saves." The image was taken in the 1920s during the height of lynching in America. We know that this is not the Jesus we serve or the Jesus who saves. Racism, in order to be rendered effective, has to create and maintain rationale regarding supposed Black inferiority and White superiority.

Outside of the KKK, there are also less-recognizable forms of structural racism that permeate Black life, such as the racial-wealth gap. I have never seen this gap amplified more clearly than in church building funds. Black churches often struggle to renovate or build new facilities because generational wealth is virtually nonexistent in Black churches. Inheritances are few and small. Accordingly, every effort to maintain basic facilities can be a struggle, and building campaigns can go on for years, even decades. Structural racism has stunted the growth of Black communities.[11]

During a capital campaign for a Black church, two members of the church came before the congregation. They wanted to announce the amount of a large sum of money they prepared to donate. The gift was a sacrifice, a step out of faith. They donated $20,000 to the church building fund. I was impressed. It is hard for many Black people to save $2,000, much less give $20,000 away. The congregation erupted in cheers and applause! People shouted, "Praise, Him! Look at God!" But $20,000 was still quite far away from their goal of $800,000. Even when Black Americans earn significant money, it pales in comparison to White Americans' incomes.

For example, I can recall a friend telling me about a White church that needed a new building for its growing population. The pastor did not want to have a prolonged capital campaign to raise funds for a new facility. So, instead, he said to his congregation that they were going to take just one special offering, and if they received the money they needed in that onetime offering, they would build a new church. They needed $13 million dollars. They got it. Six people each gave one million dollars. This story has always stunned me. It is incredible what generational wealth can do. Moreover, many larger White congregations not only hoard resources but segregate their lives from interacting in meaningful ways with the fullness of Christ's body.

The effects of racism and anti-Blackness in the church are global. South African Archbishop Desmond Tutu once popularized a joke about colonization by saying, "When the missionaries came to Africa, they had the Bible, and we had the land. They said, 'Let us pray.' We closed our eyes. When we opened them, we had the Bible and they had the land."[12] The joke is somewhat of a truth. Europeans' missionary work often served to implement colonization and gain control of Black land and resources.[13] Understanding and appreciating Black culture was a farce. Missionary work was paternalistic in nature. Many White spiritual leaders used and weaponized their power, perpetuated atrocities, and claimed that they knew what was best for Black people.

Silence and Complicity

Silence and complicity have been the status quo for White churches that refuse to acknowledge their long history of racism and exclusion in their practices. In and outside America, scholars, activists, and Christians have worked to call out White supremacy and the incalculable violence it causes to people.[14] The Scriptures tell us repeatedly that God cares deeply about the vulnerable, the poor, the exploited, and the despised. In the Scriptures, I have found nothing more scathing and clear than the message in the book of James regarding how capitalism and racism are rejected.

> Now listen, you rich people, weep and wail because of the misery that is coming on you. Your wealth has rotted, and moths have eaten your clothes. Your gold and silver are corroded. Their corrosion will testify against you and eat your flesh like fire. You have hoarded wealth in the last days. Look! The wages you failed to pay the workers who mowed your fields

are crying out against you. The cries of the harvesters have reached the ears of the Lord Almighty. You have lived on earth in luxury and self-indulgence. You have fattened yourselves in the day of slaughter. You have condemned and murdered the innocent one, who was not opposing you. (James 5:1–6)

Capitalism and White supremacy ideology in America go hand in hand. Money fortifies the power of the ideology of whiteness.

I study the American abolitionist movement. One of the key differences between Black and White abolitionists were the goals of the respective organizations. Many White abolitionists wanted to abolish slavery, and that was about it. But Black abolitionists understood that abolition was only the beginning; it was the first step toward justice and liberation. Black abolitionist Joshua Easton, for example, saw the fight for freedom as political and spiritual. In 1837, he prophetically claimed,

> Abolitionists may attack slaveholding, but there is a danger still that the spirit of slavery will survive, in the form of prejudice, after the system is overturned. Our warfare ought not to be against slavery alone, but against the spirit which makes color a mark of degradation.[15]

The spirit of slavery is alive and well and seen in nearly every aspect of our lives. Simply put, division is the root of the problem. Racism is a sin. At the core of sin is separation and division from God and one another.

Silence and inaction are also sins. We Christians have a responsibility to speak up and speak out against the things that divide us. It means we all, including White Americans and others, will need to learn history and its impact today and, equally important, unlearn how White supremacy has fostered White people's perspective, power, and position. We all have a duty to live out these principles of love and unity. The fight against racism is a daily battle that cannot be combated with hashtags, slogans, or "thoughts and prayers."

The Church

The Message Bible eloquently sums up what remains our daily duties as Christians.

> So here's what I want you to do, God helping you: Take your everyday, ordinary life—your sleeping, eating, going-to-work, and walking-around life—and place it before God as an offering. Embracing what God does for you is the best thing you can do for him. Don't become so well-adjusted to your culture that you fit into it without even thinking. Instead, fix your attention on God. You'll be changed from the inside out. Readily recognize what he wants from you, and quickly respond to it. Unlike the culture around you, always dragging you down to its level of immaturity, God brings the best out of you, develops well-formed maturity in you. (Romans 12:1–2)

The Message version is clear. Every day, we have work to do.

Final Thoughts

Nothing is more toxic than when we moralize wrongdoing—when we adopt a culture of degradation among the least of these. Rarely does society fear the repressions of harming unpowerful people. God commissioned the church to be a defender of the weak and a safe space for the marginalized. I have long felt that the chief barrier in the Black church is capitalism, and in the White church, it's racism. Both struggle with sexism and hoarding. At the heart of the problem is a desire to be all powerful and, thus, be like God. But this is a fallacy and idolatry. God has all power, but He is love (1 John 4:8). Power is what He has; love is who He is. Striving to be like God must be a journey toward love and its transformative power. Cultural shifts are uncomfortable and hard, but possible and positive.

The church is a place of transformation, a place of healing, reconciliation, and restoration. Anybody can call out the ugliness, or even ignore it. Vision is needed. What does the church look like when it values women, the poor, and people of color? Let women, the poor, and people of color tell leadership what they want and need. More importantly, let women, the poor, and people of color lead (Acts 2:17–18). You are called to love God with your whole being and to love your neighbor. You must not forget, as Christ said, "A new command I give you: Love one another. As I have loved you, so you must love one another" (John 13:34). I believe this love can best be displayed by putting the interests of others ahead of your own (Philippians 2:3–4) and by working to dismantle the systems and ideas that fortify violence, harm, or harmful neglect of the poor and people of color.

The unholy triad that we all live with can at times feel insurmountable, but nothing is impossible with God. Together we can and will experience the promises of God here on earth, and certainly in eternity. I aim to encourage all my sisters and brothers of the faith, "Let us not grow weary while doing good, for in due season we shall reap if we do not lose heart" (Galatians 6:9 NKJV). Christ cares about women. God can and will use us.

PART FOUR

GOING THE EXTRA MILE FOR SELF AND OTHERS

14

Discipling through Love and Relationship

ANGELA ABNEY

> Do nothing out of selfish ambition or vain conceit. Rather, in humility value others above yourselves, not looking to your own interests but each of you to the interests of the others.
> Philippians 2:3–4

Women today are seeking the wisdom needed to be successful in their families, relationships, and careers. I learned early in life that discipleship and service develop wisdom and a path for success in life. As a young child, I watched my Christian mother as she worked as a nurse, midwife, and social connector for her family, friends, and patients. She always looked out for the interests of others before considering her own needs. As I became an adult and grew in maturity, I found myself following in her footsteps as a caregiver to family, friends, and those in need. I could not help but draw parallels between what I saw my mother do so often and how deeply love is intertwined in life's tapestry. I began to see love as the sustaining factor in discipling and service. For me, it was simply doing what came naturally, but my reflections reveal how my desire to engage in discipling and service became a reality through love and relationships.

Divine Impartation through Discipleship

Discipleship is one of the greatest legacies of Christ (2 Timothy 2:1–2). Christ's relationship with His followers evidences this method of leadership. He discipled all who were willing to follow Him, such as the men who dropped their jobs as fishermen. Jesus challenged them to drop their nets and follow Him, and He would make them fishers of men (Matthew 4:19). This same principle can be applied to the role of women in ministry because they have devoted themselves to outreach and service in the church and community. The discipleship of women is both an outreach and the keenest act of spiritual development shared by seasoned women with a heart and depth of lived experiences. These women impart to other women who need spiritual guidance and counsel. This is known as *divine impartation*: the passing of wisdom for spiritual growth. By imparting and modeling wisdom, older women, or more experienced women, ensure the sustainability of their role in society.

Discipleship Is a Shared Experience

I remember engaging in discipleship that resulted in being a shared experience. In that moment, I knew whatever I encountered would be life defining. Somehow, I just knew this would become a trial of my faith. There I was, waiting. The wait time felt different. In this situation, I felt pregnant with anxiety, yet equally peaceful. The dichotomous inner conflict became silenced when a sweet young girl greeted us at her door.

"Hello, my name is Angela Abney," I said. "Your mom works with my daughter. Do you remember her?" My daughter stepped forward to embrace the girl, who led us to the living room. I asked her to check with her mom to see if I could visit with her for a short while. She came back and said I could go to her mom's bedroom. I took a deep breath and began to walk toward her bedroom. While walking, I whispered a prayer for wisdom and guidance.

I was not a stranger to entering situations that required me to offer a simple prayer for a person who is facing a medical challenge. Oddly enough, today felt different. The atmosphere in the home felt sad and empty. You see, the mom (I'll call her Arial) was one of my daughter's supervisors. Her house was beautiful. Judging from the family photos, they were a lovely family.

There I was, on the threshold of her bedroom. As she lay in her bed, her voice was like a whisper. I walked to her bedside. As I gazed at her, I felt my maternal instinct kick in. She reminded me of my children. I shared that I was there to pray for her. She reached for my hand, and in that moment, I knew I would be offering more than a simple prayer. She needed me. She needed care. Her home needed love and life breathed into it. I am sure you have also probably searched to find your true purpose in life. I get it; I have worked in ministry for years. I know what to do when it comes to service and leadership. I have never felt I was the kind of person who had a special talent or gift. Inside, I felt just ordinary for most of my life. The day I met Arial, I felt like I was walking in my God-given purpose. Beyond all that I know and have attained, I feel that discipling women is my greatest purpose. Caring for Arial and her family became all-encompassing for me.

Like a soldier, I felt like I was prepared. God showed faith in me by trusting me with this precious family (John 13:34–35). This experience allowed me the opportunity to disciple the women around me, who learned how to see a need and how to get involved to make a difference. The women emulated what they saw and applied what they learned to their lives. Further, other members of Arial's family were influenced to grow in service to others based on what they learned through our discipleship experience. The most desired takeaway from my time with Arial was to show those I discipled how to effectively serve as servant leaders and engage in community outreach.

Servant Leadership and Caring

I grew up as an only child, and as such, I was known to have singular vision when it came to sharing. As I grew into adulthood, I found myself dedicated to servant leadership. My vantage point became the ability to see needs and solutions. I looked around Arial's home, and I saw needs all around. There was a need for personal care for Arial and care needed for her children (ages twelve, seven, and three). There was also a need for housekeeping and food. Her husband (I'll refer to him as Chris), who worked long hours and worried about his wife and children, also needed care.

I hosted a meeting with my ministry team, women who previously worked several ministry assignments with me. This time was just as compelling. The women rallied around me as I shared my vision of care for Arial's family. It was my mission to have caregivers in the home, as long as needed, who would clean and organize it. I spent long hours caring for Arial. Most days, I stayed until Chris returned home from work. Cooked meals were always ready for him. Their daughters would stay with my family on weekends. My ministry team watched as I coordinated the work of getting this home back in order.

Gradually, I worked to train specific women to assist in caring for Arial. As weeks and months progressed, I attended doctor's appointments with her. I drove her to chemo treatments and infusions. I became her next of kin, and her doctors and nurses all recognized me. Arial and I enjoyed deep soul-searching conversations. She trusted me and I felt honored to love her through her darkest moments. (See Philippians 1:7–11.)

I did not know how long the assignment would last. I remained open to the prospect of it ending when the time was right. I felt it was important to demonstrate how to go the distance, regardless of how long one must serve. When you are in service to humanity, it requires you to remain engaged if you are needed.

Selfless Discipleship

There is an aspect to discipleship that requires a selfless mentality. Jesus taught this ideology as a principle to exemplify. He instructs us to love our neighbors as ourselves and thereby counter the perspective of receiving credit for another's success. The real motivating factor for the discipler is to fervently want for others what you would want for yourself. The act of pouring into another is the essence of discipleship. The pouring is the impartation of skills, life lessons, and vision. The discipler shares wisdom and expertise, to pass on knowledge through tutelage. The well-known adage "Give the man a fish, he will eat for a day. Teach a man to fish, he will eat for a lifetime" is applicable when sharing through impartation.

We are called to live our Christian way of life by following the example of Jesus Christ, more specifically through epitomizing the example set by Jesus through discipleship.[1] As Jesus led His disciples, He carefully taught them by precept and example. They watched as He showed them to love without condition when He ate with publicans and sinners. Further, Jesus did not seek to position Himself above those He discipled. Rather, He sought to show them His humanity through humility by washing their feet (John 13:3–12).

Relevance of Mentorship

There can be a thousand detours in life, but only one God-given path to purpose and wholeness. As women, we are required to multitask through life without a simplified plan of execution. Our heavenly Father knew we would need a plan of guidance as we journeyed through life. His plan included an instruction manual, which is His Word. The Holy Spirit was dispatched to be the guiding force to godly living.

African American women have been the backbone of the Black community for centuries. Black women in the church are known for their steadfast devotion, devout living, and spiritual insight. Traditionally, Christian African American women connect their children to home and church. This practice is a central influence for impartation of the wisdom from generations of old to the generations to come. Lessons learned and taught are the crux of the truest nature of divine impartation and the epitome of adults teaching their young how to be adults, professionals, leaders, and, yes, wives and mothers.

There were great examples of heroic women in biblical times. Queen Esther showed her courageous strength as she stood to save her people (Esther 4:16). Likewise, Naomi demonstrated the positive influence of discipleship by guiding Ruth on how to win the love of Boaz (Ruth 3:11). This kind of heroism is exemplified by women today who are following their examples as they are discipled and gain shared life experience.

Evolving through Lineage

Examination of my own lineage and the lineage of women I mentored has shed light on why African American women benefit from spiritual discipleship. Reaching back to analyze their mothers helps these daughters to better understand the power of unspoken love and formidable strength that they express and experience. I share because it has been the catalyst to unearthing my own voice. I find great satisfaction in expressing God's love and demonstrating how to pass discipleship and service from one generation to another.

This consciousness of love acts as the driver to incentivize your servitude. I have had deep reflection about my journey after my time with Arial. I cannot credit one experience as the impetus to my discovering the totality of the call on my life or as an expression of my humanity. As a woman, I sat with my thoughts in hopes of emerging with a clear understanding of what causes me to love the way I love, which has led me to a life of service.

Purpose of Love in Discipleship

I began with the story of Arial because it is important for you to understand how I mother as I mentor. Learning to connect the dots between who you are presently and how you got here is essential to understanding yourself and why you think the way you think. Though my time with Arial was special, I realize I have had several experiences that required me to engage fully in a person's life or career. It has caused women I have discipled to reflect and understand their capacity to share love. There is a natural assumption that all women have experienced love from their mothers, but the truth is, we have all experienced it in different ways.

Understanding this concept helps the discipleship process work well, when you share authentically and in a way that people need. For example, I once had a teacher who had difficulty acclimating to working on a team. I modeled how to engage with colleagues during meetings by preparing her with questions before the meeting.

As a ministry leader, I demonstrated how to minister in a confined setting. I would take women into retirement communities to teach them how to do outreach ministry. That environment was a great place to better understand how to operate in service through love. Some of the ministry disciples referenced lessons learned as acts of unconditional love. The correlation between what they heard and what they felt carried the same weight in their hearts. It was surmised that love is shown in different ways. This realization can be transferred by adopting the mindset to love people who need to be loved, thereby proving love to be an action word. The Holy Spirit helps one to understand how mercy and grace are the foundation for love. Since love is actionable and no one can do it on their own, it takes the power of God to transform hearts and minds.

I have found that people really care about how you make them feel. I discovered this to be true from a young woman I discipled over twenty years ago. She recently found me on social media and wanted to share her love and admiration for me. She was happy to share, "You probably don't know just how much you impacted my life. I cannot tell you what you said to me back then, but I do remember how you made me feel." It is in instances like this that you can see the long-term impact of your efforts to be an effective discipler.

Discipling Daughters through Mothering and Trust Building

The experiences I share with my three biological daughters are ongoing and our relationships continue to grow over time. Mothering is a powerful connector for offspring, through the power of impartation and respect.

For me, it was all about making a lasting connection with my daughters. It is a virtual passing of the torch into womanhood and Christendom. I remember looking at my first daughter on the day she was born and feeling an overwhelming desire to continue a lasting connection that began in the womb, much like the connection I felt with my mother. Imagine feeling like the earth was shaking, but no trembles were evident. It was more of a spiritual exchange of revelation and love. The feeling continued to grow as I gave birth to two more daughters. Gender has significance regarding my desire for them to really know and understand my humanity and passion for service and, likewise, the budding stages of their own womanhood.

As an African American woman finding her voice, I spent time in deep reflective research about how I became the woman I am and why I perpetuate love the way I do. It was an effort to carefully prescribe the lineage of love passed from generations of mothering in my family, church, and community.

By exploring how mothering lent itself to me as a person and how it shaped my attributes as a caregiver, a clear picture became evident of my internal makeup as a woman and as a believer. I found that much of who I am and the way I show love are connected to a rich history of loving mothers in my life, both living and deceased, who were disciplers. This legacy is ingrained in me from the core of my spiritual beliefs.

The greatest accolade I have received came from watching the efforts of my daughters to disciple other young women through service and time. Whether it is mentoring in the community or visiting and caring for others in the nursing home, they seek opportunities to share the kind of love they have witnessed and felt from their mother.

Women, both those who have been mothered and those who have not, play a critical role as spiritual leaders. Mothers have always spoken into my life. There is a humility that comes from desiring and adhering to the voice of mothers, both naturally and spiritually. In essence, I could not impart myself to other daughters and women if my own biological mother and my spiritual mother had not taken time to speak to and nurture me as a woman. The responsibility of enrichment can be seen and felt as women reach out to connect to a source.

The cycle of impartation begins with building trusting relationships. Trust is one of the biggest hurdles women must overcome in order to glean the wisdom needed from spiritual mothers.

Think of how Naomi imparted into Ruth: Following the death of Naomi's sons and husband, she encouraged her sons' wives to return to their families. However, Ruth pledged her devotion to Naomi and refused to leave her. Ruth trusted Naomi and allowed her wisdom to guide her in obtaining favor with Boaz.

The Next Generation

Honestly, the consideration of the other woman must be your mission. It must be about us because you are me and I am you. We are charged with being servant leaders. As I reflect on the influence of discipleship, I hope to answer the following questions:

Why is discipleship important? It is important to continue to share the love of Christ through love and leadership.

How can the attributes of discipleship translate in the corporate setting? The attributes can be adapted in any environment where leadership skills are needed to build human capital through modeling and advice.

Is discipleship relevant in the twenty-first century? Discipleship is needed in current times. In fact, this is a great model for relationship building and servant leadership.

How do I know if I am ready to be a discipler? You will know that you are ready when you see the need. This need can be a novice coworker, a friend, or even a community member. If you can help through wisdom, knowledge, or expertise, you are prepared to disciple.

How can I let love guide me as a discipler? Love will guide you as you engage with authenticity and share with integrity of character and sincerity of heart.

The strongest indicator that one has found a path to discipleship is they strive to emulate Christ through their actions. There are takeaways from the discipleship experience:

- Hear and respond. Your response is obedience to the call.
- Conduct a needs assessment. Survey the environment.

- Connect with the person in love.
- Relationship building is critical.
- Commit to the cause or need. Be prepared to render aid.
- Ask for assistance if needed. Delegate to include others in the work.

The View of a Disciple

>Enter and exit, there you go.
>I am here for you whether the winds do blow.
>For you and for me, there we shall meet.
>Each day is a new start.
>We begin at the same part, in an ongoing saga, which has not stopped.
>Each day feels the same while nothing seems to change.
>When will life return to normal? we ask.
>Normal is no more, as it is heretofore, both a relative and muted point.
>For in these uncertain times, there is a truth that remains.
>Commitment to resilience
>With inspired fortitude and belief
>For them and for me.
>
>Abney, 2023

There are many lessons I have learned in life. As a mother, I have worked to impart the need for serving; I call it living by example. My daughters have had front-row seats to observe genuine servanthood. This was evidenced when one of my daughters said, "I have learned so much from you about forgiveness and serving." She went on to explain that she had watched how I cared for my father. She believes my love, forgiveness, and care for him extended his life. I feel completely humbled by her words. Sometimes one does not see the light others see in and through them.

> You are the light of the world. A town built on a hill cannot be hidden. Neither do people light a lamp and put it under a bowl. Instead they put it on its stand, and it gives light to everyone in the house. In the same way, let your light shine before others, that they may see your good deeds and glorify your Father in heaven. (Matthew 5:14–16)

I have asked myself many times, "Where do we go from here? Who are we to disciple, and how will we know?" Without a definitive answer to the questions posed, I must move forward ready to inspire and encourage new disciples. My contribution to society will keep the work ever present. There is no need to look afar, as paths cross and divine encounters happen each day. The soberness of mind, singleness of heart, and desire to make a difference is all you will need.

The next generation needs wisdom and life experience. From a social context, where everyone wants their voices heard, it is more ardent for godly women to rise and lead with God's love and wisdom. In the final analysis, this is the required mindset to truly make a difference in the lives of women.

15

My Journey Caring for Parents with Alzheimer's

A Story of Unconditional Love

KAMALA V. WILLIAMS

> Honor your father and your mother, so that you may live long in the land the Lord your God is giving you.
> Exodus 20:12

In this space, I share my journey and lessons learned as a caregiver for my beloved parents who both lived with Alzheimer's disease. My sharing is not only about caregiving and the accompanying responsibilities; it is about so much more. I share my story because I wish I had had better insight from someone experiencing a caregiver's role. Caregiving can be a rewarding experience; however, with it come overwhelming responsibilities, unexpected sacrifices, and often self-denial. Hopefully you will gain from my experiences. I invite you to come with me as I share some of what I have learned and experienced on this journey while walking in step with God, learning a deeper level of dependence, and growing in faith.

Ultimate Example

A caregiver is someone who provides direct care for children, elderly people, or the chronically ill. Caregiving includes providing for the needs of any who cannot provide sufficient care for themselves. The concept and practice of caring for children, widows, the sick, and the disabled are exemplified throughout the Bible. Perhaps the most compelling and amazing example of care is the act of love shown toward us by our heavenly Father. "For God so loved the world that he gave his one and only Son, that whoever believes in him shall not perish but have eternal life" (John 3:16). When we look to the Word, there are numerous examples of how God sympathizes with those who require caregiving, such as widows, the elderly, children, and those who are differently abled.

> But if a widow has children or grandchildren, these should learn first of all to put their religion into practice by caring for their own family and so repaying their parents and grandparents, for this is pleasing to God. (1 Timothy 5:4)

The Bible also includes many examples of Jesus's profound demonstrations of healing, forgiveness, and love for those with disabilities. Finally, of all the commandments, the first to include a promise involves how we treat our parents: "Honor your father and your mother, so that you may live long in the land the LORD your God is giving you" (Exodus 20:12). Caring for our parents is covered in this verse. *Caregiving* may not have been the term used in biblical days, but Scripture gives us models of caregiving we can apply in our lives today.

Our modern lifestyles can make caregiving challenging. Being informed and prepared for the role of caregiving has become increasingly important because of our often hectic and much-too-busy lifestyles. Advanced medical practices, longevity, and the increase in the diagnosis of dementia-related diseases are all reasons not just to be educated and prepared for the possibility of the need to assume a caregiver role but, in a broader sense, to be aware and supportive of those in caregiving roles. It might be surprising that according to one website, there are some fifty-three million Americans providing unpaid care to an adult with health or functional needs.[1] With these alarming numbers, it is imperative that we educate, arm, and prepare ourselves.

As the caregiver for my parents, my first order of business was to do everything I could to uphold their dignity and advocate for them. *Advocating* meant I needed to serve them in ways that were (in my estimation) in their best interests. That required me to develop a deep understanding of the various stages of their disease and to be constantly and consistently in tune with where they each were in their individual journeys through their illness. I needed to speak for them during medical appointments and during countless hospital emergency room visits. I had to educate myself and represent them in every way.

It meant asking store and restaurant managers for family restrooms and making them aware that these bathrooms are necessary, not just for small children but also for families like mine. I had to speak up when my father was exhibiting unusual behavior and people stared, and I became keenly sensitive and aware of others who were caring for a child or an adult with special needs. As with any advocacy role, it is frustrating and exhausting.

Not everyone I encountered, even in the medical profession, has been sensitive to the special needs of my parents or the burden that I carry. Remembering, recording, and reflecting on their personal lives has helped me through the process as the custodian of my parents' dignity. Jesus has displayed the ultimate example of love. I am always reminded that just as Christ has shown His love to all, He commands people to love each other (John 15:12).

A Glimpse into Who They Are

I share the story of my parents to give you a glimpse into the lives they led before Alzheimer's disease and the need for a caregiver. This reflection helps me advocate for them, to insist that they be treated with respect, which is sometimes a challenge in a fast-paced and insensitive world.

My dad was the sixth of seven children. He was raised in a

small college town in central Texas and was quite the student. His 1950 high school yearbook has him listed as "most likely to succeed, most versatile, most studious, a member of the student council, choral club, president of the athletic club, and member of the male quartet, football, basketball," and what was known as the "Hi-Y teams." He attended college, earned his bachelor's and master's degrees, and dutifully served in the United States Army. But not just any mate would do for marriage; the woman who caught his eye was my mom. My dad worked for the Postal Service for more than thirty-three years and retired from there. He would no doubt, by any of his three daughters' or five grandchildren's accounts, overwhelmingly earn the "Best Dad" and "Grandfather of the Year" awards every year!

My mother was a country girl raised in rural east Texas. This community of close relatives was tucked away in a peaceful countryside environment surrounded by tall pines and farmland with livestock. Her mother passed away when Mom was very young, and her extended family was instrumental in her upbringing. They wanted her to continue her education, so they moved her to the city to finish high school. She attended college and earned both her bachelor's and master's degrees. She caught my dad's eye, they married, and raised their three daughters. Mom taught public school for more than thirty years, retired, and would no doubt, by any of her sons-in-law's or grandchildren's accounts, be the best mother-in-law and grandmother ever created!

Both my parents led engaging lives. They were involved parents when we were growing up. They served in church, spent time doing things that mattered to them personally, and were very involved grandparents. Those realities made it difficult to acknowledge and accept that they were no longer capable of living alone and taking care of themselves without assistance.

A few instances made it clear to me that my role as daughter was about to change as well. During this period, I found solace in Galatians 6:7–9 and was reminded that I will reap what I sow and that I should not get tired of doing what is right because a harvest is waiting. My parents sowed good seeds throughout their lives, and I believe I have sown good seeds through my act of caregiving. Although I do not recall the term *caregiving* being used by my relatives or my mother, I had seen the act of caregiving long before I became a caregiver myself.

Moving beyond Denial

My parents raised my sisters and me to value and show appreciation for family. Caring for the family was modeled. Over the years, I saw my great-aunt take care of her siblings, my aunt care for my grandmother, and my mom care for my great-aunt. These caregivers undoubtedly influenced my decision to embark on the journey of providing in-home care for my parents when that became needed. Somewhere deep inside me, I knew I would be the caregiver of my parents. I said it often to myself, to them, and ultimately to my then-husband.

When my husband and I purchased our second home, one criterion was to have a space to accommodate my parents. The idea was, when my parents needed care, I would be the provider. This was thoroughly understood by my family. It would be only a few short years of living in the home before we moved them in with us. Making the decision was not difficult for me; however, it was not what they ever planned or intended. The approaching struggle included moving beyond denial.

I suppose denial is some kind of universal language that we all speak and understand. Our fluency and proficiency with this language convinces us that if we believe hard enough, then that which we are seeing is not really what we are seeing, or even that what it is we are seeing will go away. We all want to see the people we love in the most positive light, and we especially want to avoid seeing the ones we love slip away in front of our very own eyes. Denial for me was a place of safety. Avoiding what I knew would be a very uncomfortable situation for as long as I could was coming from a place of self-preservation. My parents had been such a strong support system in my life and in the life of my family, so remaining in a state of denial rather than acknowledging where they were heading would not have been good for me or for them.

Recognizing the signs that something was different about my dad was a process. There were early signs, like my mom writing everything on a calendar so my dad could have a reference and reminder of activities, and changes in hygiene habits. This progressed to seclusion and isolation from settings that made him uncomfortable, like church. He, like many Alzheimer's patients, experienced *sundowning*.

Sundowning describes being in a state of confusion that starts in the late afternoon and can last into the night. Someone may experience confusion, anxiety, aggression, ignoring direction, pacing, and wandering.[2] My mom's solution was to go to bed earlier. That did not prove to help, because while she may have gone to sleep, he roamed the house, getting into all sorts of trouble.

My dad had the advantage of being protected by my mom, who ran interference while doing her very best not to let the secret out that something was changing with him, that something was wrong and he needed help. His early diagnosis and treatment helped in the long run.

My mother, on the other hand, was a different story. My sisters and I had not noticed any signs of dementia or changes; we had been so focused on my dad that the changes she was experiencing had gone mostly undetected. She was the one holding things together, or so we thought. We were at the bowling alley celebrating her eightieth birthday when a lady from her league (she was an avid bowler) pulled me aside to let us know that we needed to keep an eye on her so she would not be taken advantage of or get hurt. I wasn't exactly sure what the lady meant, but I knew I felt like I had been punched in the gut. To this day, I remember that sinking feeling. I drove my mom and her neighbor home that night in silence. I got Mom safely in her house and started my forty-five minute journey home.

I remember that was a long ride with thoughts of what I would, could, or should do with this information, and how soon. Even though I was prepared to help care for my parents, I wasn't actually prepared for the news when it came. My husband and I had only recently accepted, and were even still struggling with, the fact that my dad was incapable of being alone for any extended period of time. We were managing that, or better yet, my mom was managing that, and now I was hit with "you need to keep a closer watch on your mother."

What would all of this mean? That conversation threw me for a loop and sent me spiraling down what I came to know was a period of depression and great mourning. I had to face the reality that I was losing Mom as I knew her, and this was especially painful as she was always my "go-to girl." I leaned hard into Scripture that would encourage me, as well as Bible stories of faith and determination. God reminded me repeatedly that I needed to be strong and courageous and that He would not leave me (Joshua 1:9). The changes, the decisions, and the transitions initially sent me into a tailspin, but the experience has brought me to where I am now, sharing my journey as a caregiver.

Some Decisions Don't Come Easy

There are times when decisions can be deliberated over for long periods of time, and there are times when decisions need to be made quickly. When it comes to the safety and care of a loved one, decisions should be made with the thought and consideration of all involved and, most importantly, in the best interests of the people most vulnerable. In my case, after much prayer and a review of my options, the decision was made to bring my parents to our home. I felt the Lord leading me in this decision. He had prepared me for "such a time as this" (Esther 4:14). I knew, whatever was ahead of my parents and me on this journey, God would give us what we needed, and He would be there for us.

This decision was fully supported by my husband and my adult children. Although it was an easier decision for me, this did not come easy for my parents. For *years*, my parents asked me to take them home. I sometimes tried to convince them they were at home, but some of their long-term memory remained intact. My parents would call out their home address to let me know exactly what they meant by *home*. It was not until they embarked on the final stages of Alzheimer's that the constant requests to go home subsided.

During the first eight years of their care, I became astute at distracting them and diverting their attention to other things. This was not always easy; it was often frustrating and very tiring. To manage the stress of it all, I had to implement strategies to calm both them and me. These were strategies I learned while attending caregiver conferences, support groups, personal counseling, and through other resources. For my parents, I played music, and we went on walks to the neighborhood pond. I sat at the kitchen table for countless hours and did activities with my parents. I read with them and to them, and we recalled stories from their past. I was creative in identifying things they enjoyed and that kept their attention. I discovered that Mom's need to feel useful had not waned because her memory was failing.

They also attended a monthly group with others who required caregivers, sponsored by a Christian organization. Mom had been a teacher and always loved children. I found a television station with kids dancing and singing that would hold her attention for hours sometimes. I found an exercise station that made her feel like the instructors were talking directly to her and that she was the only person who mattered. My dad would not follow the exercise routine, but he would count along with the coaches as Mom exercised.

A great deal of effort was placed on my parents' engagement. I found God to be faithful! As I spent time in His Word, I was always directed to the right people and places. I learned how to follow Him closely and my faith grew. I found so much joy in them being with me and in having the honor to care for them.

Making the decision to move my parents in and provide care for them at home was only the first step in a series of life-altering steps for my parents, my family, and me. For my personal well-being and my family's well-being, I sought a professional counselor's help. My counselor helped me learn to cope with my own feelings of anxiety, resentment, loss, and grief, which is surprising because my parents were still with me. I learned breathing techniques and meditation practices and other activities that helped me to stay calm. My own immediate family was giving up a lot of personal time with me. I was not always able to focus on their specific needs as much as I would have been able, had I not taken on the caregiving responsibilities.

For those reasons, my family and I decided that we needed time away alone together, to stay connected to one another. We took several mini-vacations a year and some lengthy ones as well. It really didn't matter where we went, how far it was away from home, or how luxurious the accommodations were; we just knew it was important to have time together, just the four of us. Making this commitment to one another and planning for these family getaways was one of the best things we could have done for ourselves!

Planning, Planning, and More Planning

A friend recently reminded me that everything that has a beginning has an ending. It seems so simple; however, planning for the end of life is something most of us don't want to think about. I also remember a sign that said, "Failing to plan is planning to fail." I will always remember that sign and its broad implications. I did not think of my parents as planners before taking on my caregiver role, but they lived frugally, spent conservatively, and invested sufficiently. I am blessed that my parents were planners, and I am grateful that the Lord's plans prevail.

As my role as a caregiver expanded and their needs became greater, there were sufficient resources for their care, thankfully. There is no way to know what challenges we might face in the future or what condition we may find ourselves in if we are blessed to grow old, but planning for that possibility may be the best thing we can do for our families. Mom never wanted to talk about death; her only comment was that she and the Lord planned for her to live a long time. What Mom did was share the details of her personal affairs.

Mom always showed me where her important documents were, and she wanted me to understand her business affairs. Both of my parents' personal documents were orderly and easy to follow. Because of this, taking over the custody of their affairs as their caregiver was rather smooth, albeit overwhelming. Having adequate legal documents was important both for my parents and for me to take on the role of caregiver. It is a lesson of planning I learned from and appreciate dearly. I am now very open with my children about my business affairs, and I make sure they know where important documents are kept. I have obtained legal counsel to ensure that my children have the same ease if the need arises and am unable to care for myself.

I am naturally inquisitive. Long before I can remember family medical history being a thing, I always asked my parents a lot of questions. I wanted to know my family's medical background. Some of the responses to questions included, "They died of old age." Not sure whether that meant they were senile; I knew that meant forgetting. I was not sure if that had been a disease or how it was medically characterized. After seeing my paternal grandmother suffer from Alzheimer's and my maternal great-aunt suffer from the same disease, I became interested in my mother's health. I asked about her medications and her doctor's visits. I even went to the doctor with her for a few visits long before she was diagnosed with Alzheimer's so that I could have a clear understanding of her health and medical treatments. This made for ease in the continuity of her care. My father did not have any major medical challenges and was not under the ongoing care of a doctor. There were some minor things my sister managed, but his ongoing care came after his Alzheimer's disease was identified.

Conversations about end-of-life plans are never easy but necessary. I have learned from my parents the value of sharing information and keeping documents orderly. I have also found it less threatening and uncomfortable when discussions about my business affairs, medical conditions, and end-of-life wishes were eased into everyday conversations. I am also glad I can have these conversations and make decisions with my children now, when I am fully conscious and cognizant and when I am not threatened with feelings of them taking over my life.

Adjust, Readjust, and Adjust Again

The decision to provide in-home care came with challenges that were not initially considered. Similar to what would be done to "child protect" a home, we had to modify our home for the safety and care of two adults with Alzheimer's disease. We learned as we progressed through the journey. Safety was always the priority, which meant some inconveniences for us. In addition to safety, our lifestyles changed drastically!

At the front of every plan was the consideration of my parents. *Is this something they can attend or be involved in?* Would this be a safe space for them? There was the expectation that these adjustments would continue throughout my caregiver journey. Just as in life, nothing stays the same. I was more prepared than I knew. However, the challenges were great. Sometimes even strangers would remind me that God would not put more on me than I could bear (1 Corinthians 10:13). As I bore witness to the difficulties and challenges of caregiving for parents with Alzheimer's, I came to fully understand and appreciate the essence of 2 Corinthians 12:9:

> But he said to me, "My grace is sufficient for you, for my power is made perfect in weakness." Therefore I will boast all the more gladly about my weaknesses, so that Christ's power may rest on me."

Along with relying wholeheartedly on the Lord for strength, our family also learned how to not take things so seriously and to laugh in lieu of crying. And, boy, did my parents give us reasons to cry and laugh. My dad was the amusing one. He kept us on our toes. As he experienced sundowning, he was a wanderer and a runner. That meant at every chance he could get, he was going to break camp! Not funny at the time, but there were several times he escaped what must have felt like captivity to him to roam the free world. God's hand of protection was on him and with him because he was never far away and was never injured. On the other hand, I am sure some years were taken from my heart's capacity to perform its duties due to stress. There was much to laugh about as well, like the time I woke up in the middle of the night to find my dad standing over me in my bedroom saying one of his favorite sayings, "Boo." We learned to lock our bedroom door at night.

Oh, and this is one for the ages: One morning, I could not find my dad's dentures. I searched the house and the trash can, thinking maybe he threw them away. After losing all hope of ever finding them, I took him to the dentist to be fitted for another pair (which, of course, was not a onetime visit process). Somewhere during the final stages of him getting his new dentures, I was putting something away in the China cabinet. I put my hand in a teacup and felt something strange. I jerked my hand back and looked inside the cup. You already know . . . there were the dentures. If you had no idea, before there were nice little covered containers for dentures, they were often placed in a coffee cup. Silly me for not checking the cups when I was looking for the dentures.

Something my husband and I never envisioned when we decided to keep my parents at home was the intrusiveness that went along with being a caregiver. As my parents' medical needs increased, more care provider services were added. Home visits became routine. We shared our home and space with countless people from different agencies that changed frequently. Our space was no longer "our" space; it became the space of everyone involved in caring for my parents. Our privacy was limited greatly. And over time, I learned to pick my battles and not be annoyed when things were not done in my kitchen the way I would do them. The greater purpose: for my parents to have the care they needed, whether my dishes were stacked in the dishwasher the way I would stack them or the clothes sorted the way I would sort them. These adjustments were constant and ongoing.

Balancing It All and Self-Care

There have been very high highs and very low lows on this journey as a caregiver for my parents. I have made continuous changes. Initially, I worked from home, but then I went back to work outside my home full-time. That required me to hire outside caregivers to come into my home to care for my parents. Early on, I was blessed to have found caregivers who were more like family than outside help. My husband was retired, so he was home some of the time and was there with my parents when I was late getting home or if I needed to work late. My children were also a great help with caregiving. Before leaving for college, my son was my mom's transportation from the bowling alley on Monday nights. When my daughter returned from college, she was a fill-in caregiver on weekends and other days that I did not have a caregiver.

We were a team. We encircled one another, and we encircled my parents with love and care.

As a family, we found balance in knowing when we needed additional help. We learned that we could not possibly do it all. Having caregivers come through the evening, and eventually on Saturdays, gave us some time to live life as we should. I have to admit, things were not always balanced, and it cost me my physical health. I neglected my own annual health exam and found myself having a colectomy. Something that could have been prevented had I not missed my colonoscopy. I was not prioritizing or managing time for myself. I learned the hard way how important it is to seek help, take time out to reset, and build a network of support.

It was easy as a caregiver to put the needs of my parents in front of my own needs. Caregivers often experience caregiver burnout.[3] I was blessed to have a husband who supported me and encouraged me to take care of myself. We found things that worked specifically for us. We were committed to our date nights and our family vacations. Self-care was critical in order to provide the best care for our loved ones.

Unconditional Love

My parents supported me my entire life. Every whim I had, they entertained, and every reasonable and unreasonable request was granted. I cannot remember my parents ever really telling me no in response to anything I wanted or needed. One of my dear friends reminded me that even standing at the door of my wedding, as we looked at the chapel filled with guests, my dad demonstrated his unconditional love for me. It did not matter that there were photographers, videographers, musicians, and a soloist all on hand for a grand wedding. Out of love for me, my dad asked if I was sure I wanted to do this. When I replied yes, he reminded me with conviction that I did not have to go through with it if I didn't want to. I knew how deeply my dad loved me and would do anything for me. It did not matter to him the money that had been spent—he would not have been embarrassed had I said, "No, this is a mistake." Knowing what I know about my dad, he would have politely walked to the front of the chapel and said, "Wedding off."

This memory also reminds me of God's awesome plan for the perfect mate if you ask, listen, and obey because not all husbands would have endured this caregiving journey. The love my parents showed me was extended to my husband and my children. My mom loved my husband as if he were her own son. That made it even more painful for him when she progressed in her disease and became aggressive toward him. Even through some of the ugliness he had to endure, he never asked me to move my parents or suggested that we could no longer care for them. For his exemplary long-suffering, I am eternally grateful. My parents supported my children at nearly every event in which they participated. They traveled across town to see them in their various activities. They cheered them on and encouraged them just by being there. They gave them everything they asked for and so much more. Seeing my children experience their grandparents as their support and then witnessing my children return tender, loving-kindness toward them has been one of my life's treasures.

Lessons Learned and Final Thoughts

Being a caregiver is a lifestyle adjustment. The adjustments to your living space are minor compared to the adjustments to your life and your family. As a caregiver of parents with Alzheimer's disease, the journey had been tough. There were twists, turns, bumps, bridges to cross, and even forks in the road. The journey is a great responsibility and should be taken with caution. My family and I have been blessed to care for my parents in our home. Our love for one another has deepened, our faith has grown, and our trust in the Lord has been strengthened. I offer these suggestions to anyone contemplating in-home caregiving or a caregiving role, and to those who may support a caregiver:

- Know, record, and share family history.
- Pay attention to the signs of any disease.
- Early diagnosis and treatment matters.
- Create space for family dialogue and decision-making.

- Plan financially for your own extended life and end-of-life requests.
- Prepare all legal documents for your senior years (make decisions early).
- Educate yourself about your loved ones' disease and available resources.
- Support and self-care are critical.
- If you are not the primary caregiver, relieve the primary as often as possible. Offer to do other tasks, and be empathetic to the role and responsibilities they have incurred as the primary caregiver.
- Trust in the Lord!

As I continue to make what I consider to be the best decisions for my parents, I will plan for the next steps. And I will adjust what needs to be adjusted in order to stay in balance for myself and for my family. I know that given the choice, I would do it all over again! Thankfully, I have learned to trust in the Lord with all my heart, leaning not on my own understanding but in all my ways to acknowledge Him, and He has directed my path (see Proverbs 3:5–6).

16

Overcoming Grief

Sistas Sharing Journeys, Lessons, and Insights

NORVELLA P. CARTER

> Where, O death, is your victory?
> Where, O death, is your sting?
> 1 Corinthians 15:55

One can grieve in many ways and for various reasons. I remember grieving over the loss of a job, a failed relationship, the death of a dream, and the loss of the family pet. Pain, suffering, and grief come from a multitude of circumstances that cause heartbreak. However, I do not think many people would argue that the greatest of all heartbreaks is the physical death of someone you love. If you love someone and death strikes, you will grieve. It does not matter whether you are a devoted Christian or a nonbeliever; you will grieve.

Who wants to read a chapter about death and grief? I never did, until it hit home in a big way. Then I had many questions, such as, "Why is grief so powerful and all-consuming? How do I overcome the pain and suffering that come with the death of a loved one?" I remember writing in my journal:

> One reason grief is so powerful: death is inevitable. If you outlive someone you love, grief is going to happen and cannot be avoided. Death and grieving are not respecters of persons. Every human being is impacted. . . . If you are old enough to understand or have the capacity to mentally comprehend loss, you feel it. Death is permanent, cannot be reversed and is one of the most powerful facts of life for everyone. The death of my loved ones brought shock, pain, suffering and devastation.

I wrote this passage after my husband and I experienced the death of two children within thirteen days of each other. I had heard about people who had multiple deaths in their families, but I did not imagine it would ever happen to me.

My Personal Story

My husband and I grew impatient one Sunday morning while listening to a visiting pastor preach at our son's morning church service. We were visitors ourselves and felt a little disappointed that we chose a Sunday when the official pastor was not present. The sermon that morning was based on Romans 8:28: "And we know that in all things God works for the good of those who love him, who have been called according to his purpose." He repeated the phrase "all things" multiple times and gave examples of circumstances that "all things" encompassed, including some we thought were gruesome. His goal was to emphasize that any circumstance we would face as Christians would be transformed into something good and that we needed to trust God to do so.

Within months of that sermon, our daughter Tracie, who was successfully battling breast cancer, suddenly passed away. Our son, William, who was a captain in the Army and studying to be a chaplain, spoke a powerful and uplifting message at her funeral service. A few days later, while preparing to return to Iraq for a second tour of military duty, William succumbed to an unexpected virus and passed away. In less than two weeks, my husband and I suffered the loss of two children.

Both Tracie and William loved the Lord and had ministries that impacted their families and multiple communities. So, my husband and I knew then, and we know now, they are with the Lord. Still, we suffered intense pain and sorrow. In the midst of our grief, we remembered the words of the visiting pastor: "All things work together for good . . . all things . . . all things . . ." We were faced with the challenge of sincerely believing the Word of God, trusting it to be true, and applying it to our personal lives. It was a real struggle for us. We understood Lamentations 3:22–23: "Because of the LORD's great love we are not consumed, for his compassions never fail. They are new every morning; great is your faithfulness."

My husband and I had to trust the Lord daily for His mercy to get through the gripping days and tearful nights. We had to trust the Lord's sovereignty and decisions about life and death. Regardless of our feelings, we had to trust that everything, even the deaths of loved ones, would be transformed into something good.

Years have passed since the deaths of Tracie and William, but our Lord has been faithful, and tremendous good has engulfed our family. My husband and I have eighteen grandchildren, among them are our grandsons Trace and William, namesakes of their aunt and uncle. Little by little, the Lord turned our sorrow into joy, letting others know that we do not grieve "as others who have no hope" (1 Thessalonians 4:13 NKJV). Now we remember the visiting pastor fondly and believe he was ministering directly into our souls for the days that would come.

All things . . . all things . . . *really*? Do you believe it . . . *really*?[1]

Personal Narratives: Struggles and Triumphs

As you read the narratives, ask yourself, "What is my real struggle?" Everyone grieves differently and must deal with their own issues of loss. Often, there are multiple struggles, but each has a "lesson-learning" journey. The learning is often an example of God using your journey to transform your thinking and belief system so you can grow and develop in a way that pleases Him. He renews your mind so you can release faulty thinking (if that is an issue) and embrace the will of God (Romans 12:2). As you read, ask God to help you identify your struggle(s) and pray for guidance. Look with expectation for direction, relief, and a special kind of peace only He can give.

Dee

Grieving Mama and Daddy: When God Appears Silent

Some of the most difficult seasons of my life occurred when it felt like God was silent. This seemed especially hard when I was already going through major and challenging situations. I experienced grief during the years of my mother's illness as she battled liver cancer. Several years later, I went through it again as my daddy battled failed kidneys and endured dialysis that sapped so much of his life's strength. Losing both parents within what seemed like a few years was devastating. These were emotionally dark days for me.

When it seemed like everything was going wrong and my help seemed to be nowhere in sight, in each of these instances, it left me feeling forgotten, in despair, and simply rejected. My major frustrations in these seasons came from simply thinking that God's silence meant His absence. But I was wrong!

The author of Psalm 88 had not only been through similar types of heartbreaking situations, but he also wrote about them. He expressed his feelings of being overwhelmed, cut off, forgotten, grieved, rejected, terrified, and in despair. Worst of all, he was crying out to God, wondering where He was in all his personal suffering. The psalm ends, "Darkness is my closest friend" (Psalm 88:18). However, the hope this psalm offers is not in its ending but in its beginning: "LORD, you are the God who saves me; day and night I cry out to you" (Psalm 88:1).

The psalmist who wrote this Scripture so openly acknowledges that there is hope for salvation in the Lord—even when God appears silent. This Scripture assures me that just because God is silent does not mean He is absent, and it certainly does not mean He is not working behind the scenes on my behalf.

This psalm is a great reminder that darkness in my life is never greater than where my help comes from. God is my help in times of trouble. He can heal me in grief and any other type of situation. God is the source of my hope, and I can always depend on

His never-ending faithfulness. God can handle my despair. That means He can handle yours too!

Michelle

My Husband, the Love of My Life: A Tearing Apart of Oneness

In my marriage, I saw the most beautiful, exciting, God-created institution on planet earth. Life has problems, but I had a lifelong friend, lover, and partner with whom to navigate each and every struggle. I had joy. Our plans, dreams, and life itself merged and we understood oneness.

Unexpectedly, my husband passed away of a heart attack. It seemed as though life stopped. I thought, *How can I continue without my husband?* I could not function coherently and was in a state of shock. I was numb. I immediately began to realize the incredible support a spouse gives in a marriage.

My husband had been there every day, listened to all I had to say, and inquired about my day. We were together constantly and slept together each night.

The void was overwhelming, and I felt like I was dangling in the air. After more than four decades of marriage, my emotions were too painful to comprehend and I felt a deep, low-grade undercurrent of sorrow that was continuous.

I led (and continue to lead) a large, national women's ministry, but now I had to lead my own household alone, without my daily supporter. I had major adjustments and could only take one day at a time. Holidays became anticlimactic and I did not look forward to celebrating, especially during Thanksgiving and Christmas.

I had to turn to the Word of God and His sustaining power. One of my favorite attributes of God is His sovereignty, meaning He is in control of all things, including me. He knew the exact time I would be born and when I will make my transition (Psalm 90). I had to trust that He would take care of me, and He does. Immediately when Lloyd transitioned, what got me through every moment that day and the days to come was that the truth of God is sovereign and He alone determines the outcome of all things. I repeated this daily. I had to make major adjustments living without my husband, but after about two years, I began to really enjoy and appreciate the memories I have of him. I began to thank the Lord for my time together with him. Soon I was planning my life without my husband, knowing that God would give me comfort and direction. I started seminary to earn a degree, I continued serving in my church, and I led my national organization. God was handling my sorrow. He will handle yours as well!

Phyllis

My Son, My Son, My Only Son, How Could This Happen to Me?

My son passed away from a chronic illness. For me, it took about two years in Christian grief counseling to determine that my most upsetting grievance was that I did not believe certain things should happen to me. I felt privileged and protected because I am a Christian. I am a deaconess in the church, I pray for people, I teach Sunday school, I love church—I love Jesus. But my belief system was faulty.

When my son transitioned to be with the Lord, I was mad and offended at God. I had to confess and admit it because the Lord knows my heart and knows it was true. My deep-rooted belief was never spoken verbally, yet it was present in my heart. When I was convicted of my mindset, I repented and asked God to forgive me for my faulty thinking and belief that "works" could exempt me from problems. I humbled myself before the Lord and repented for doubting that He knows best in every situation, including the transition of my son to be with Him. I asked the Lord to help me and to relieve my grief.

These Scriptures in the books of Matthew and John were helpful to me:

> He causes his sun to rise on the evil and the good,
> and sends rain on the righteous and the unrighteous.
> (Matthew 5:45)

The same grief that happens to an unbeliever can happen to me. The difference is how the Lord helps me through the pain and suffering: to grow as a Christian.

> I have told you these things, so that in me you may have peace. In this world you will have trouble. But take heart! I have overcome the world. (John 16:33)

I had to study and internalize the fact that all people have trouble and suffer from a range of problems. My benefit is that I can give my grief to the Lord and trust Him to deliver me as I go through life's pain, problems, and trouble. I began to look at problems with a different mindset and focused on the deliverance God would bring. This change brought healing from grief and relief to my soul. God can handle my devastation and questions, and He can handle yours too!

Loretta

We Were on Vacation When the Accident Happened

It was summer and time for our vacation. Excitement filled the air as we packed for our annual family reunion and Fourth of July celebration in California. My husband, my only daughter, and I flew from Texas to join the family event. We always enjoyed the picnics, swimming, seeing family, going to tourist attractions, and simply having fun and relaxing. A group of us were at an amusement park when my sister received a family member's call that solemnly and firmly asked us to return to the family home. In my heart, I knew something tragic was about to change my life forever.

We arrived at the homestead. Cars were everywhere and young people were in the street and yard of the family home, crying. A policeman took us aside privately and shared the devastating news. My daughter, niece, and two young men, while on their way to breakfast, were killed in a car accident earlier that morning. My daughter, the youngest, was nineteen and the other three victims were in their early twenties. My life began to spiral into an unknown zone of grief that was incomprehensible. In the months that followed, the pain, tears, sorrow, and depth of grief paralyzed me, and I could not leave my house for weeks.

The most difficult part of my grief was the loss of my plans and dreams for my young daughter. I had to hold on to the belief that my baby girl, my niece, and the two young men were with the Lord in heaven. I had to release my plan and accept God's plan for me and all who lost their lives. I had to meditate and focus on God's Word. I held on to this Scripture:

> Very truly I tell you, you will weep and mourn while the world rejoices. You will grieve, but your grief will turn to joy. A woman giving birth to a child has pain because her time has come; but when her baby is born she forgets the anguish because of her joy that a child is born into the world. So with you: Now is your time of grief, but I will see you again and you will rejoice, and no one will take away your joy. (John 16:20–22)

My experience of grief has a time limit, and I will see my daughter and loved ones again. I will rejoice and have joy. I am so grateful to Jesus for His salvation and hope for the future. There are no real goodbyes; in God's eternity, we will be together again. And sure as God can handle my anger and brokenness, He can handle yours.

Jolee

Grief? No Time for It! I Want Justice!

My son was killed by policemen. They said it was a mistake, but I never believed them, and "mistake" does not bring my son back to me. I could not begin to think about grief until I saw justice for what happened to him. But years passed and there was no justice. I couldn't sleep, I was a "zombie" at work, and most people seemed to forget about what happened. I was being eaten away by anger, fits of rage, and overall instability.

I began to realize that I could not handle my emotional state, and I had to depend on Jesus to help me. I quit my job, went to another state, and started going to church. My church members prayed for me, I began to pray for myself, and I began to study my Bible. I also joined a national prayer group of mothers whose sons were killed by the police. I am still on my journey, but my pain has been lifted and I can sleep.

I know that Jesus is the Great Justifier, and I depend on Him, not people or the justice system. This Scripture helped me cope: "Do not take revenge, my dear friends, but leave room for God's wrath, for it is written: 'It is mine to avenge; I will repay,' says the Lord" (Romans 12:19).

I still do not know all of the circumstances surrounding my son's death, but I have to depend on the Lord to bring justice. God knows how to make things right. I had to seek the Lord and ask for a release of my rage and anger, which were tied to my inability to forgive. I memorized this Scripture and it helped me: "Get rid of all bitterness, rage and anger, brawling and slander, along with every form of malice. Be kind and compassionate to one another, forgiving each other, just as in Christ God forgave you" (Ephesians 4:31–32).

It is interesting to me that anger and deep-rooted sins emerge when you are grief-stricken. By studying the Word in my church and working with the mothers in the national prayer group, I learned that forgiveness is really for *me* and *my* well-being, as well as the persons I had a grievance against. When the Holy Spirit enabled me to forgive, it did not mean condoning the policemen's behavior; it meant I gave their justice, punishment, and fate to God. Forgiveness took away the rage that is self-destructive and it freed me. I thank God for enabling me to move through the depths of my grief and to become a functioning, helpful person again. God was able to handle my rage and inability to forgive, so I know He can handle yours.

Carlotta

Why Didn't I See the Signs: Suicide or Self-Inflicted Accident?

My son moved from another city and was living with me while he searched for a new job. I was happy to have his company. We talked each morning before I left for work, and he was excited to share information about some of his interviews for a new position. One morning, he did not come into the kitchen as usual for a chat. I went into his room and there he was, lifeless, still in the bed. Frantically, I called an ambulance, and they gave me instructions on how to try to revive him until help arrived. I traveled with him in the ambulance while they worked on saving his life. I waited in a room at the hospital and called family and friends, who immediately came to be with me at the hospital. A doctor came out and said they did all they could to save his life but that he had passed away.

My son was young—only twenty-seven—healthy, and did not have a history of a disease. How could this happen? Weeks later, a report from his autopsy revealed he died from the use of the illegal drug fentanyl. I was asked about his mental health and whether he was depressed. I was sick with grief, but more than grief, I felt horrible about not recognizing the signs of my son's drug use. I was also embarrassed to tell anyone how he died. I felt both guilt and shame. I told people he died of a heart attack, but close family knew the truth. I believed my family members were privately talking about me behind my back, and I withdrew from all family activities. I preferred not to have been born than to have this happen to my son and me. Job cursed the day of his birth, and I did the same (Job 3:1–4). I went about my daily routine and did my job at work, but I was rotting away on the inside.

Finally, I sought help from my church leaders and professional Christian counseling. A Scripture I love and believe that helped me is John 17:15: "My prayer is not that you take them out of the world but that you protect them from the evil one." Jesus prayed that I would not be taken out of the world of trouble but that I would be delivered from the evil one. I was destined to overcome this tragedy only through Christ. The Lord delivered me from being destroyed by this experience.

I began to understand that God is the creator and giver of life, and only He can decide when it ends. In Christ, if it is time to live, nothing and nobody can take you out of this life. In Christ, if it is time to die, nothing can keep you here. Doctors, accidents, and even your own choices do not begin or end life on earth. God is the ruler of everybody and everything. He can handle my pain and crushed soul. He can handle yours too.

Know Your Story

Every person has their own journey through grief, and it cannot be rushed, postponed, or avoided. Your pain in the loss of a child through miscarriage, abortion, stillborn death, newborn death, or whatever the circumstances is yours to suffer. Your pain in the loss of a brother, sister, family member, or friend is yours to experience. Whoever and whatever the loss, ask God to reveal the true source of your pain. Ask Him for the strength to go through the suffering and for relief as you endure. Therein lies your story, and it is yours as a testimony as you move forward in your life.

Lessons Learned

Know the Savior

One of the key Bible verses I learned as a child is John 3:16: "For God so loved the world that he gave his one and only Son, that whoever believes in him shall not perish but have eternal life." I love this verse because it serves as a framework for my belief system about God and my future.

God does not change and He loves us, regardless of our ignorance, unbelief, temper tantrums, and rebellion. Jesus Christ came to earth as a human being, substituted Himself to pay for the forgiveness of our sins, and died to save us from destruction, even though we did not know Him (Romans 5:8). The good news is that God, in His power, resurrected Himself from the dead. He demonstrated resurrection to show us that we, too, will be resurrected after death to be with Him in heaven—when we believe and accept Jesus Christ as the Lord of our lives.

This belief and knowledge make the death of a loved one bearable, and it is good news. We share this good news with others so we can all know the truth about life and death. We share the good news as we yearn to see our loved ones again—recognizing that we will all be changed and transformed in heaven—and enjoy our lives in eternity with God (1 Corinthians 15:49, 53).

Go to God in Prayer

Tell God how you feel in your prayers. He already knows your thoughts and will give you the expressions you need to share with Him and gain relief.

> I sought the LORD, and he answered me; he delivered me from all my fears. (Psalm 34:4)

> In my desperation I prayed, and the LORD listened; he saved me from all my troubles. (Psalm 34:6 NLT)

Tell a few trusted Christian friends how you feel, and ask them to pray with and for you. Bear each other's burdens (Galatians 6:2).

Study the Word of God

Study your Bible to learn how to live your life fully. Hosea 4:6 says, "My people are destroyed from lack of knowledge." Daily Bible study is life changing and will show you purpose for living and how to navigate your individual struggles.

Seek to understand suffering as one powerful way to grow.

The death of a loved one brings grief, but it also brings an opportunity to deepen our relationship with God. God sustains us and gives us peace that is beyond all comprehension. Paul wrote to us in the Scriptures about suffering:

> We also glory in our sufferings, because we know that suffering produces perseverance; perseverance, character; and character, hope. And hope does not put us to shame, because God's love has been poured out into our hearts through the Holy Spirit, who has been given to us. (Romans 5:3–5)

He is the God of all comfort (2 Corinthians 1:3), and suffering will compel us to draw nearer and closer to Him. The study of "suffering" is a powerful way to grow in our faith and can bless us during our grief and beyond.

Personal Insights

Celebrate Life (See Psalm 98:4)

Funerals and memorial services are called a "celebration of life," and rightfully so. We should celebrate while people are living but also celebrate their lives once they have transitioned, hopefully to be with the Lord. We should applaud the singing, celebrations, and uplifting "homegoing" services of Christian believers that churches facilitate for grieving families.

Elevate Your Praise and Worship (See Jeremiah 20:13)

Regardless of your struggles, find ways and times and places to worship God. Go to your church and engage in corporate worship with other Christians. The church service, prayer times, singing, and sermons will uplift your spirit.

It is a joy to worship during church services, weddings, and special events, but it is life changing to bow before our Holy God and worship during the time of our greatest need. God promises to comfort us and stabilize our minds during times of great grief and stress. We should take time to increase and elevate our praise and worship.

Embrace Your Pain (See Romans 5:3–5)

Strangely enough, it is important to embrace your pain in order to emerge from the depth of your grief. To *embrace* it means to acknowledge, receive, and experience your deepest level of pain and suffering. Therefore, it is important to take private time with the Lord to cry, mourn, and let your emotions pour forth. If the pain for your loved ones goes on for too lengthy a time period, seek professional help from a Christian counselor or physician who can advise on the grieving process.

Seek Balance in Routine and Relationships (See Ecclesiastes 3:1)

If your normal routine is overwhelming, take time off and give yourself a chance to grieve and rest. Engage in your routine, little by little, as you are able. Do not expect life to be the same, but function as much as you can. Do not spend too much time alone in deep grief or you may get overwhelmed. At the same time, do not become inundated with too many people.

Seek balance and plan for interactions and events. For example, if you are in deep grief and want to attend church, ask friends to be with you in church and protect you from crowds and interactions that may overwhelm you. Plan for an early exit, and depart quietly and discreetly if you know that talking to people is premature. You may need more private time with limited interactions.

Seek Christian Counseling (See Proverbs 19:20)

If you experience the death of a loved one and cannot seem to get through it, seek a professional Christian counselor who will help you in prayer and the study of Scriptures that are needed for healing your heart. It is not wrong to retain the services of a qualified Christian counselor. Grief is confounding and perplexing. The deepest part of your grief may not be readily apparent.

A grief counselor can help sort through your emotions and identify the root of your pain, as you navigate a path out of depression and despair. God has prepared professionals to help. I spent two years in counseling after the deaths of my children, and I am grateful for their service. Along with seeking counselors who are Christian, do not hesitate to change if you have a need or service that is not being met. Pray and ask the Lord to guide you to the professional most appropriate for your needs.

Seek Out Successful Overcomers (See Revelation 12:11)

In my personal story, I shared about my two children passing away. As I reflect, I recall experiences that really helped me during my time of grief. For example, when my friend learned about the loss of my children, she introduced me to two of her friends, a husband and wife, who shared their story and encouraged me. The husband said he was driving at night when he fell asleep at the wheel of the car. The car carrying his entire family went over a cliff, and all were injured, but their two children were killed. I was grieved by their story, but I wondered how they could talk so calmly about their experience without tears—and with words of encouragement for me.

This godly couple said the pain I was feeling would be relieved by God because I am a believer and that I had to trust Him to heal me as He had healed them. I needed to see real people who understood my feelings and deep-rooted grief. I needed to see their success after such tragedy. A snapshot of their lives encouraged my faith and helped me to heal.

Such was the case for Loretta and Michelle as well. They found support from a national group. Your testimony could be the answer to someone's prayer. "They triumphed . . . by the blood of the Lamb and by the word of their testimony" (Revelation 12:11).

Final Thoughts

Are you reeling or shaken by the unexpected loss of a loved one or facing the long-awaited, inevitable transition of a person you love? Has your world been "turned upside down" by grief, and your sense of stability and normalcy seems to be slipping? Do you have riveting questions that are unanswered? Pray to God and depend on His sovereignty, believing He is in control of all things. His Word says that in Christ, "all things hold together" (Colossians 1:17). Trust in God during your pain, and believe your unseen victory over your grief is a future certainty.

Once the intensity of the pain subsides, you will be able to see the joy of having a God-given relationship with your loved one. The joy of knowing them, spending time together, and having a connection of love is pure joy. In the midst of missing them, you will be able to see the precious memories that are yours to cherish. You will be able to experience joy in the midst of pain and suffering, and you will be able to declare, "Where, O death, is your victory? Where, O death, is your sting?" (1 Corinthians 15:55).

17

Leaving a Legacy

The Lives of Our Foremothers, African American Grandmothers, and Mothers

PATRICIA J. LARKE, ALTRICIA LARKE,
MYRA HANEY-SINGLETON

> One generation commends your works to
> another, they tell of your mighty acts.
> Psalm 145:4

Our grandmothers and mothers taught us the value of leaving a legacy for African American families. This was the way that our African American grandmothers and mothers lived their lives. They embodied attributes, teaching guiding principles to influence future generations. How they carried themselves—the implicit and explicit messages in the way they talked, walked, and interacted with family members and their community—made a difference in the lives of our African American families and others in the community. Historical evidence indicates that our African American foremothers shared rituals and participated in ceremonies that have been passed on from one generation to another. Our grandmothers and mothers carry the DNA of our African foremothers' rituals and ceremonies, as well as the vestiges of the bondage of four hundred years of slavery in the United States. They are the godly, Christian women who emulated values and executed behaviors that are consistent with leaving a lasting legacy.

Solidifying the Links to Our Foremothers: Heritage, Identity, and Legacy

The heritage of any ethnic group is the full range of inherited traditions and culture. Heritage serves as the basis for identity, social organization, productivity, planning, and responsibilities. The identity of the African American family embodies the characteristics by which the family is definitively recognizable or known. This identity separates it from other groups and is highlighted by the accomplishments of its people, past and present.

Our identities as African Americans are tied to our African foremothers as a people, but we are such a mixture of people; it is our culture that makes us a very diverse group. When the identity and culture of a people are lost, the people as a group cease to exist. Without a transfer of knowledge of one's heritage, it only takes a few generations for a people to forget the struggles and accomplishments that were achieved to get them to the present day.

Distinctions

As African women (and people), we are linked to our foremothers in distinctive ways that helped us survive the American experience. First, we are linked by the primacy given to blood relatives. In Africa and in America, traditionally, Black people were protected and sometimes supported by family members. More than by just Dad and Mom, support has come from brothers and sisters.

A second distinction is the primacy given to *extended* families versus *nuclear* families. Appreciation and close communication are usually maintained with extended family such as grandmothers, grandfathers, aunts, uncles, nieces, nephews, cousins, and relatives who are considered "kinfolks." From African times through slavery in America and until today, close contact with the extended family is a major characteristic of an African American woman's life.

Finally, in a world where she is known for beauty, brilliance, and flamboyance, strength and spirituality are two of the strongest characteristics of the African American woman's legacy passed through the generations. Women as daughters, professionals, workers, wives, mothers, and grandmothers have been and continue to be responsible for the many tasks related to the success of the family. African American women have a history of spirituality and comprise the majority of members in Black churches nationwide.[1]

Cultural Aspects That Reflect Africanism

Some African American women exhibit cultural aspects in their lifestyles that are similar to those of their African foremothers,[2] even today (of course, these examples do not represent all African Americans, because as a population we are very diverse).

Personal Habits

- We tend to dress in original ways (unique clothing and attire, style with flair).
- We wear our hair in a variety of ways (wrapping, braiding, straightening, cornrowing, and tattoos, in a variety of textures and styles). This also includes headdresses (hats, scarves, headbands, and wraps).
- We love to have verve (motor habits) in our actions through demonstrative gestures, postures, expressions, and anger. This includes movements in walking, dance, and singing.

Family Practices

- We love family gatherings like family reunions, family meals, and Sunday dinners. At these gatherings, we love to cook together (no recipes). This allows for bonding and passing on how to do things from the older generation to the younger.
- We have multigenerational families where members live with each other.

Leaving a Legacy

Spiritual Practices

- We tend to be churchgoers, especially older generations.
- Black women are often known to be prayer warriors.
- Black funerals are a spiritual and cultural experience.

Social Practices

- Some observers say we appear to all talk at the same time.
- We are expressing affirmations of one another.
- We value and show respect to our elders (though this may be seen less in certain circumstances, and vary in succeeding generations).
- We treat close friends like family.

Some traditions and practices may need to be extinguished.

- Black women being a "burden bearer" and not getting professional help.
- As family members, we should not keep family secrets from other members. Often, we are not sharing information that will help future generations understand themselves.
- We should not be keeping up with the Joneses (overextending ourselves to look good and have what others have).

Preserving wonderful aspects of our African American heritage means people worldwide can learn more about us because we played a crucial role in the making of our nation. As African American women, preserving our heritage means our legacy will continue through the generations to follow. We can continue to tell our story.

Three Legacy Cornerstones: Spiritual, Educational, and Social-Action Foundations

While we as African American women have demonstrated many influential values and behaviors for leaving a legacy, we focused on three legacy cornerstones: spiritual, educational, and social-action foundations. These were shared with us by our grandmothers and mothers. We believe these areas are critical to positively impacting generations of African American women. Whereas the lives of each of our grandmothers and mothers give us stories about some aspects of the three cornerstones, we selected specific stories to represent how they helped us develop our spiritual, educational, and social-action foundations.

Patricia

Spiritual Foundation Legacy

The majority of African Americans were introduced to the Bible during slavery, through plantation gatherings and early churches that were conducted in the bush "harbors." These were in small, framed buildings or on their shanty porches. Such early experiences were pivotal to the development of African American spiritual foundations. Praying, memorizing Scriptures, singing songs, and sharing in baptismal experiences are engagements that were passed down through the generations. It is these early spiritual practices that were passed on to my two grandmothers, who were among the first generation of "free people."

Annie McClain James

My first remembrance of my paternal grandmother, Annie McClain James ("Grandma" to her grandchildren), comes from when I was three or four. Grandma was born August 30, 1891, and she passed away at the age of 101, January 4, 1993. Grandma was the mother of ten children. She was witty and always used phrases that conveyed deeper meanings, such as "The bottom rail will come to the top rail." This means that people may say you are on the bottom today, but one day, you will be on the top because the Lord will provide what you need to get to the top. Perhaps this was her interpretation of Matthew 20:16, which states, "So the last will be first, and the first will be last." Grandma James's life taught me lessons that are cornerstones to building a spiritual legacy: teach by example, love people, and spend time with God.

Teach by Example. Grandma *lived out* the Bible. She embodied the fruit of the Spirit of love, joy, peace, patience, kindness, generosity, faithfulness, gentleness, and self-control (Galatians 5:22–23). Yes, self-control. Until my grandma passed at the age of 101, I had never seen her angry or heard her curse or say harsh words to or about anyone. She had such self-discipline because of the Spirit. On one occasion, my grandfather said some "choice words" about his disapproval of my grandmother's three-month trip to visit two of her daughters in Philadelphia and another in the Bronx. Instead of responding with "choice words," my grandmother smiled, said a prayer, and continued to pack her clothes. She ignored my grandfather, who continued to voice his disapproval while using "choice words." Grandma taught me the value of "no response is a response." Her response to my granddaddy reinforced the biblical principle "Blessed are the peacemakers, for they will be called children of God" (Matthew 5:9). When there were conflicts with my granddaddy or my aunts or uncles, Grandma always demonstrated calm temperance.

Love People. Grandma always smiled and she never met a stranger. She always infused love in her words and deeds. Grandma loved to sit on her front porch and speak to everyone who walked by or wave at others who would drive by. If she did not know their names, Grandma would ask, and the next time she saw them, she would call them by name. Grandma taught me to love people, as she would always have guests at her house. She had the gift of making individual people feel that they were the most important in the world.

Cooking and baking, bringing food to the sick, and giving to the poor and needy demonstrated that she cared for people. She would bake a pie just because someone wanted one. I remember her baking me five sweet potatoe pies when I had given her only one pound of sweet potatoes. Over the years, I thought about that. She *loved* me. I felt her love all of my life. She encouraged those who were down and brought joy to those who had lost loved ones. Grandma always told me to be kind to people. She said, "The Lord loves everyone, and you should love others, for God is love."

Spend Time with God. Since about the age of eight, I would visit or see my grandma at least once a week. I spent countless hours in her home. She lived three blocks from me, walking distance from my immediate family. I would visit her house and sit on her front porch or in the dining room, kitchen, or living room. There I would see her reading her Bible. The black book was worn and tattered from reading. She would also read it every night. She always said, "You have to know the Lord and spend time with Him."

Grandma taught me the importance of going to church to learn about the Lord. She loved going to church and was given the title "Mother of the Church." The members affectionately called her "Mother James." While I did not attend Grandma's church, I attended Cumberland United Methodist Church, most of the time alone or with my two sisters. Like Grandma, I loved going to church . . . because she did. From the age of eight to the age of eighteen, I walked to church each Sunday, always passing by Grandma's house, knowing that she was at church, and I was also on my way to or from church. I could feel that connection.

Emily "Mood" Scott Gordan

My grandmother Emily Scott Gordan, whom the family called "Mood," was my mother's mother. Why we called her Mood, I do not know. Grandma Mood was born December 3, 1903, and passed away at the age of ninety-eight. She lived in South Carolina and was a widow and the mother of four girls. She had raised her daughters as a single mother after the death of my grandfather, Theodore Gordan, a World War I veteran. My mother was the third girl. I lived about thirty miles from Mood and did not get to see her as often as I saw Grandma James. We did not have a car, so Mood would get someone to drive her to our house on weekends, or my father would get one of his friends to drive us to Hartsville to visit her, usually on Sundays.

During several summers, family members would spend a few nights with Mood in Hartsville. Every Christmas I can remember, Mood would always spend time with us in Florence. After I got married at the age of eighteen and moved away from home, my Grandma Mood became a pivotal person in the continuation of my spiritual development. She would visit my husband and me often, staying for a week or two, at least six or seven times a year. She visited every place we moved, including South Carolina, Missouri, and Texas. Mood taught me the importance of prayer, faith, studying God's Word, and finding joy in serving the Lord.

Prayer, Faith, and Studying God's Word. Some of my earlier memories of Mood were of her reading the Bible and the prayers written in her faith-based magazine. Everyone knew not to disturb Mood when she was reading her Bible and the prayers from her magazine. Her steadfast commitment to God and her faith established a memorable example to many. All who met her knew that the Lord was first in her life and that spending time with the Lord is important. People would ask whether she was reading her Bible and, if so, would wait until she finished to visit with her. To her, spending time with the Lord was a significant component of building a spiritual foundation and legacy. She said to us family members, "You have to spend time with the Lord and have others respect your devotional times." She was letting us know that praying, studying God's Word, and faith provide the blueprint for dealing with life and its tribulations. The Bible gives readers answers to life's dilemmas. My grandmother's devotion to spending time with the Lord aligns with Psalm 119: "Your word is a lamp for my feet, a light on my path" (v. 105).

Joy in Serving the Lord. Mood showed our family how to love the Lord and how to have fun by embracing the simple joy of living. She loved people and found pleasure in creating humorous moments. When she came to visit us, the community would come to hear her stories and her infectious laugh. Those stories remind me of her joy in serving the Lord.

One particular story of Mood's is how the Lord answers your prayers. She would tell the story about how she fell in the hedges one spring day. She had been spying on Mrs. Minnie to see what she was doing in her yard. They were in competition to have the yard with the prettiest flowers in the neighborhood. Mood was so busy looking at Mrs. Minnie that she fell in the hedges that separated her house from Mrs. Minnie's house.

When asked what she did after falling into the hedges, Mood said, "I started praying and asking the Lord to help me get up, but also to not let Mrs. Minnie know that I fell." She went on to say, "I stayed there for a few minutes, looked up at the sky. I did not want to get up right away, because I did not want her to see me. I started praying, *'Lord, help me to get up, and please, Lord, don't let Mrs. Minnie know I fell in the hedges, trying to see what she was doing in her yard, and Lord, forgive me for trying to be nosey.'* I got up, brushed my clothes off, looked around, and quickly ran back into the house. And, you know, the Lord heard me, and to this day, Mrs. Minnie doesn't know that I was spying on her. See, if you pray, the Lord will answer."

While Grandma James and Mood stories embody a spiritual foundation legacy, our second grandmothers' stories focus on an educational foundation legacy. The stories of "education is our family business" capture how grandmothers imparted the value of education to the next generation.

Attricia

Educational Foundation Legacy: Education Is Our Family Business

I am a third-generation educator. My maternal grandmother, Williard Rainey Billups James, was an elementary school paraprofessional and teacher's aide for more than thirty years. My mother was a teacher and college professor for more than forty years, and one of my daughters is currently a second-year elementary school music teacher. You can say that education is our family business.

Although my paternal grandmother, Staretha Aaron Larke, did not finish her formal education, she instilled in my father the love of education. He was a former agriculture teacher and then a college professor for more than thirty years. His siblings (my uncle and my aunt) followed in his footsteps, starting as classroom teachers before becoming administrators and finally superintendents of school districts.

This business was started by both my grandmothers and their resiliency. Although neither of them gained the degrees and advanced degrees their children attained, these grandmothers instilled in their children the work ethic that allowed them to pursue a career in education and rise to the top of their respective careers. This legacy of education not only has inspired me but has been a ripple effect through all the students, administrators, and teachers my family has collectively served.

Williard Rainey Billups James

My maternal grandmother, Williard Rainey Billups James, was born February 26, 1925, and passed away at the age of eighty-five, on August 3, 2010. My grandmother was the mother of six children—four girls and two boys—and my mother was the fourth child. For more than thirty years, Grandmother was a public school paraprofessional as a teacher's aide. At the age of fifty, she wanted to pursue her dream of going to college and went for three years before having to stop because of challenges with her sight.

She instilled in her six children the importance of education. My aunt became a career educator with more than thirty years of classroom experience. My mother became a math teacher and, after completing her doctorate in education, became a college professor. She was the first African American female to move from the lowest rank of lecturer to full professor at her university. My grandmother's insistence on education has been carried on to every student that my aunt and my mother have reached. My cousin also works in higher education, in student administration.

Staretha Aaron Larke

My paternal grandmother, Staretha Aaron Larke, was born September 9, 1923, and passed away at the age of seventy-seven, on October 7, 2000. As did my cousins, I called her "Grandma." She had eight children: three girls and five boys. While Grandma did not finish her formal education, she made sure that all of her children completed high school, and at least six attended college.

As the oldest male, my father went to college and became a high school agriculture teacher. He later completed his master's degree in special education and his doctorate in Agronomy.

Both of my grandmothers encouraged me to pursue my education.

As a college student, I had an unplanned pregnancy, and it was my paternal grandmother who told me, "Do not give up, do not be ashamed," and to complete my education. She told me, as we were standing in her kitchen, "Tricia, don't let anyone talk you down. You are not the first person this has happened to, and you won't be the last. Have your baby and finish your degree." Her words meant the world to me. I was worried about bringing shame to my family, but her assurance encouraged me to keep my head up and to keep going, despite my plans not going as expected. The biggest lesson I learned that night in her kitchen is that things happen in life, but what you do afterward is what counts. I completed my undergraduate degree and, subsequently, my master's and doctorate as well, just like my parents had. I came to understand the Scripture that says, "I can do all this through him who gives me strength" (Philippians 4:13).

Myra
Social-Action Foundation Legacy

Themes of moral courage and resilience are lessons often shared through the stories of African American women. Their lives provide remarkable examples for others to follow. Their words often infuse inspiration in those who listen. The stories of my grandmother and mother present perspectives of how two women used their voices to create a social-action foundation on which many could stand. While their experiences mingle with joy and pain, their fortitude resulted in lessons that will last. My grandmother and mother were "before their time"; they understood the importance of "Black Lives Matter" and the social activism that is necessary to make the difference in the lives of Black children. These women participated in that activism in rural South Carolina.

Lucille Davis McQueen

The legacy of my maternal grandmother, Lucille Davis McQueen, is marked by resilience, strength, and determination. Born in 1908, in a rural area known as Jedburg in Berkeley County, South Carolina, she was the matriarch of a family with seven sons and three daughters. She passed away at the age of eighty-four. During her life, she experienced overt oppression, yet she embodied a unique style and grace that shone. Complaining was not in her vocabulary. Her strength and resolve inspired many who knew her. My grandmother lived through the Great Depression, Jim Crow, the strict rules of segregation, and the civil rights movement while shouldering care for her husband. He had suffered a stroke at the age of thirty-three. My grandmother never appeared bitter about her position in life.

In the mid-1960s, given changing laws, Grandmother was excited that desegregation was coming to the Berkeley County school system. Acknowledging the school system's unrelenting resistance to social change, she often shared a story demonstrating her moral courage during a difficult time in her life. Information about desegregation was disseminated widely. Her teenage sons were expected to ride the school bus with other children in the community, both Blacks and Whites. After years of oppression, she was excitedly preparing for a major change many of her forebears had prayed to see.

Protest. My grandmother worked in the home of a prominent White family, where she would cook, clean, and care for their children and family. She arose early in the mornings to arrive by foot at their home to prepare breakfast, tend to their children, clean their house, wash their laundry, and prepare their meals. For more than twenty years, Grandmother left her own family to care for that family and attend to their daily needs.

One day, the father of the home shared his strong resentment against desegregation. He felt emboldened to share with my grandmother that *his* sons would not ride the same bus as *her* sons. Grandmother arose to her feet, her fury set ablaze, and asked a clarifying question: "So, are my sons not good enough to ride the same bus as your sons?" Sensing her anger and discontentment, he would not answer. His silence spoke volumes.

In protest, my grandmother took off her apron, laid it on the kitchen counter, and shared that before she would wash another dish, cook another meal, or clean another floor, she would go hungry! While he tried to reason with her as she was visibly upset, she gathered her belongings and walked out of the house. Based on her resolve, she did not return to work in that home again.

Magnitude of Faith. The bold actions of Lucille McQueen demonstrated magnitude of faith. Her husband was unable to work following the stroke that had left him paralyzed on his left side. Her income supported their household's needs. Her unfaltering faith trusted that God would provide, as Scripture assures: "And my God will meet all your needs according to the riches of his glory in Christ Jesus" (Philippians 4:19). By the grace of God, she found work to care for her family.

The courage to stand up for her conviction and to use her voice inspired many who knew her. My grandmother often appeared fearless in stature in her recollection of 2 Timothy 1:7: "For the Spirit God gave us does not make us timid, but gives us power, love and self-discipline." Of course, she had memorized the King James Version, and when she felt the structural resistance of oppression, she could not and would not hold her peace. She was not afraid to share her opinions in an impactful way.

While my grandmother did not have opportunities to be educated, she did not allow a mere man to stand in the path to block her children from being educated. Her journey emulated how Scripture says to approach life: "For we live by faith, not by sight" (2 Corinthians 5:7). Ensuring that her sons had access to learn and embrace education was what she wanted for her children, even though she was not afforded such advantages.

On a warm autumn morning, when the bus arrived to pick up her sons, my grandmother made sure they were well dressed. And she led the way for them to enter the bus.

Grandmother helped them to reach a goal that her foremothers only dreamed about. Years later, as she witnessed her sons' graduations, she stood with an indescribable joy and smile of admiration.

Katherleen McQueen Haney

In the face of myriad societal challenges and trauma, my maternal grandmother raised strong sons and daughters. My mom,

Leaving a Legacy

the youngest of her three daughters, was born in 1934 and passed away at eighty-seven. Her older sisters had married and left home.

As an adult, to help support her parents, Mom worked as a cook in a local restaurant. By supporting her family, she witnessed the positive impact of serving others and caring for those who were struggling.

My mother met my father, Samuel Haney Sr. when she was twenty-six. They were married on the porch of her parents' home and had six children. They continued to live near my grandparents to help care for them.

Inspiring the Community. Guided by the wisdom of my grandmother, my mother used her voice to shape the values of her children and countless others in the community. My mother took her role as a homemaker seriously and taught family members stories about the challenges of being in the South. "Occupy the space that you are in," she often taught us. Her guidance was intended to inspire us to use our positions to advocate and identify ways to improve others' lives. She often reminded us not to hesitate to help someone when there is an opportunity to do so.

My mother's words were inspired. "From everyone who has been given much, much will be demanded; and from the one who has been entrusted with much, much more will be asked" (Luke 12:48).

Though my mother did not attend college, she insisted on that for her children. As my siblings and I were preparing to graduate from high school, she refused to condone any other path. We all earned advanced degrees and serve in education and human service fields.

Using Her Voice. Armed with compassion, my mother also knew the importance of using her voice to guide me and my siblings as our identities and values formed. At the age of fifty, my father was killed in a job-related accident. After his funeral, my mother gathered all of us in her bedroom. Acknowledging our wounded hearts, she prayed and told us we would not give up, because God would see us through life. While we knew she was hurting, she was a stellar role model of grace, fortitude, and resilience.

As we grew older, she shared how she would cry when we would leave home for school. When life became challenging for us, my mom would listen carefully to our stories and empathize when she heard the tremor in our voices and saw our tears.

My mother's compassionate responses would often counsel us to keep the faith and pray. She would also tell us to not give up and to "cover the ground you stand on." Those words were intentionally shared for us to remove negative thoughts associated with the situation. Her words urged us to remember we were capable of exceeding expectations if we would not back down in the face of adversity. Although Mother passed away a few years before this writing, there are present moments when I can hear clearly her admonishments to us: *"Speak up!"* and *"Be bold in the face of fear."* The strength of her stance, the tone of her voice, the grip of her hand—all created a social-action legacy. For many, the legacy of this grandmother and mother impacted their destinies and set the course for individuals, like myself, to pursue their purposes.

The legacy of this grandmother and mother calls us to participate in social action, to use our voices, and to act when faced with injustices. There were times when life became challenging and difficulties prevailed. In those dark moments, my grandmother and mother became models of how to look for the light in the lessons, and to gain strength to march on to build a lasting legacy ourselves. Their fervent prayers, intrinsic motivation, inspiring faith, and graceful wit have made their journeys impactful and remarkable.

Leaving a Legacy for the Next Generation

We intentionally lifted specific elements from the lives of our foremothers, our African American grandmothers and mothers who modeled spiritual, educational, and social-action behaviors that were pivotal to their legacies. From our lens, understanding these foundational pillars of the African and African American experiences is necessary to leaving a legacy for the next generation. Try to personalize and add to these suggestions for developing and leaving a legacy for the next generation:

- Talk to your family about the importance of leaving a legacy for future generations.
- Discuss the values that are vital to your legacy: your Christian faith, love of family, supportive relationships, and education and successes. Why are these important to pass on to the next generation?
- Provide true family stories that reflect your values and can be passed from generation to generation.
- Have family gatherings periodically that include food, fun, and fellowship with each other.
- Share family history and true stories at family gatherings.
- Emphasize the experiences that reflect Christlike values and bring success that is pleasing to the Lord.

Today we stand on the shoulders of our foremothers, grandmothers, and mothers. They are our champions. Where would we be as a people without this rich heritage? We are delighted that their outlook was forward facing for positive and hopeful outcomes that we can share with others. Leaving a legacy means these foundational pillars will continue to influence future generations.

Notes

Introduction

1. Marc Schulz and Robert Waldinger, "An 85-Year Harvard Study Found the No. 1 Thing That Makes Us Happy in Life: It Helps Us 'Live Longer,'" *CNBC*, February 10, 2023, https://www.cnbc.com/2023/02/10/85–year-harvard-study-found-the-secret-to-a-long-happy-and-successful-life.html.

1. Good Morning! The Shape of Things to Come

1. Amanda Gorman, "The Hill We Climb," in *The Hill We Climb: An Inaugural Poem for the Country* (New York: Viking Books, 2021), 5.
2. Maya Angelou, "On the Pulse of Morning," in *On the Pulse of Morning* (New York: Penguin Random House, 1993).
3. Baptist Joint Committee for Religious Liberty (BJC), "She Had the Dream: The Freedom Faith of Prathia Hall," *Medium*, March 15, 2021, https://bjconthehill.medium.com/she-had-the-dream-the-freedom-faith-of-prathia-hall-a629d0394830.
4. Gregory A. Smith, "About Three-in-Ten U.S. Adults Are Now Religiously Unaffiliated," Pew Research Center, December 14, 2021, https://www.pewresearch.org/religion/2021/12/14/about-three-in-ten-u-s-adults-are-now-religiously-unaffiliated/.
5. Kiana Cox, "Nine-in-Ten Black 'Nones' Believe in God,

but Fewer Pray or Attend Services," Pew Research Center, March 17, 2021, https://www.pewresearch.org/short-reads/2021/03/17/nine-in-ten-black-nones-believe-in-god-but-fewer-pray-or-attend-services/.
   6. Delores S. Williams, *Sisters in the Wilderness: The Challenge of Womanist God-Talk* (Ossining, NY: Orbis Books, 1993), xvii.
   7. "Dr. Mary McLeod Bethune," *Volusia Stories*, accessed November 13, 2024, https://www.volusia.org/residents/history/volusia-stories/dr-mary-mcleod-bethune.stml.

2. She Came to Slay
   1. Angela Tate and Romya-Jenevieve Jerry, "Harriet Tubman: Life, Liberty and Legacy," National Museum of African American History and Culture, March 4, 2022, https://nmaahc.si.edu/explore/stories/harriet-tubman.
   2. Shirley Spencer June, "Women of Color in the Bible and Church History," in *Women to Women: Perspectives of Fifteen African-American Christian Women*, ed. Norvella Carter and Matthew Parker (New York: HarperCollins, 1996), 19–30.
   3. Darlene Clark Hine, ed., *Black Women in America*, 2nd ed., 2 vols. (Oxford: Oxford University Press, 2005).
   4. "Kimberlé Crenshaw Delivers an Exceptional Jing Lyman Lecture," Stanford University, February 13, 2017, https://gender.stanford.edu/news/kimberle-crenshaw-delivers-exceptional-jing-lyman-lecture.
   5. Arlisha R. Norwood, "Ida B. Wells-Barnett," National Women's History Museum, 2017, https://www.womenshistory.org/education-resources/biographies/ida-b-wells-barnett.
   6. Beverly Johnson-Miller, "Mary McLeod Bethune," Biola University, accessed September 19, 2024, https://www.biola.edu/talbot/ce20/database/mary-mcleod-bethune.
   7. Reginald Culpepper, "Eva Roberta Coles-Boone," HBCUConnect.com, https://hbcuconnect.com/content/25990/eva-roberta-coles-boone.
   8. Cassandra Waggoner, "Fannie Jackson Coppin

(1837-1913)," BlackPast, November 20, 2007, https://www.blackpast.org/african-american-history/coppin-fannie-jackson-1837-1913/.

9. Thabiti Asukile, "Drusilla Dunjee Houston (1876–1941)," BlackPast, February 12, 2007, https://www.blackpast.org/african-american-history/houston-drusilla-dunjee-1876-1941/.

10. DC Historic Preservation Office, "Civil Rights Tour: Education—Nannie Helen Burroughs," DC Historic Sites, accessed September 19, 2024, https://historicsites.dcpreservation.org/items/show/920.

11. *Oxford English Dictionary*, "game-changer," accessed October 2, 2024, https://www.oed.com/dictionary/game-changer_n.

12. William Dwight McKissic Sr., *Beyond Roots: In Search of Blacks in the Bible* (Woodbury, NJ: Renaissance Productions, 1990), 42, 45.

13. Walter Arthur McCray, *The Black Presence in the Bible: Discovering the Black and African Identity of Biblical Persons and Nations* (Chicago: Black Light Fellowship, 1990), 126–27.

14. June, "Women of Color," 19–30.

15. Herbert Lockyer, "Alphabetical Exposition of Named Bible Women," in *All the Women of the Bible: The Life and Times of All the Women of the Bible* (Grand Rapids, MI: Zondervan, 1988).

16. Charles B. Copher, *Black Biblical Studies: An Anthology of Charles B. Copher: Biblical and Theological Issues on the Black Presence in the Bible* (Chicago: Black Light Fellowship, 1993), 134.

3. Foreign Body

1. S. Grabe, L. M. Ward, and J. S. Hyde, "The Role of the Media in Body Image Concerns among Women: A Meta-Analysis of Experimental and Correlational Studies," *Psychological Bulletin* (2008): 460.

2. "Body Image," Office on Women's Health, February 17,

2021, https://www.womenshealth.gov/mental-health/body-image-and-mental-health/body-image.
3. Beth A. Abramovitz and Leann L. Birch, "Five-Year-Old Girls' Ideas about Dieting Are Predicted by Their Mothers' Dieting," *Journal of the Academy of Nutrition and Dietetics* (October 2000): 1157–63, https://www.jandonline.org/article/S0002-8223(00)00339-4/abstract.
4. Grabe, Ward, and Hyde, "The Role of the Media," 460–76.
5. Lucia Prinzi, "Hair Facts: 56 Hair Color Statistics Including Genetics," All Things Hair, September 16, 2022, https://www.allthingshair.com/en-us/hair-color/hair-color-statistics/.
6. "Garnier Releases Study Unveiling New Hair Color Habits of Women During Quarantine," PR Newswire, January 12, 2021, https://www.prnewswire.com/news-releases/garnier-releases-study-unveiling-new-hair-color-habits-of-women-during-quarantine-301205754.html.

4. Girl, You Are Not a Black Superwoman

1. Andrew Dyce, "Wonder Woman: Rebirth Begins Diana's Real Origin Story," Screen Rant, June 9, 2016, https://screenrant.com/wonder-woman-rebirth-origin/.
2. Erykah Badu, vocalist, "Bag Lady," by Erykah Badu and Isaac Hayes, Spotify, track 12 on *Mama's Gun*, Motown Records, 2000.
3. Kendra Cherry, MSEd, "What Is a Schema in Psychology? How We Use Shortcuts to Organize and Interpret Information," Verywell Mind, updated March 13, 2024, https://www.verywellmind.com/what-is-a-schema-2795873.
4. J. S. Knighton et al., "Superwoman Schema: A Context for Understanding Psychological Distress among Middle-Class African American Women Who Perceive Racial Microaggressions," *Ethnicity & Health* 27, no. 4 (September 15, 2020): 946–62, https://doi.org/10.1080/13557858.2020.1818695.
5. Deirdre Cooper Owens, *Medical Bondage: Race, Gender,*

and the Origins of American Gynecology (Athens: University of Georgia Press, 2017), 11, 47–48.
6. "Therapist Demographics and Statistics in the US," *Zippia*, accessed September 20, 2024, https://www.zippia.com/therapist-jobs/demographics/.
7. R. R. Cabral and T. B. Smith, "Racial/Ethnic Matching of Clients and Therapists in Mental Health Services: A Meta-Analytic Review of Preferences, Perceptions, and Outcomes," *Journal of Counseling Psychology* 58, no. 4 (October 2011): 537–54, https://doi.org/10.1037/a0025266.
8. Badu, "Bag Lady."
9. Gungor, "Please Be My Strength," track 9 on *Beautiful Things*, Relevant Studios, 2010, YouTube, https://www.youtube.com/watch?v=5VI0pkRBPZw.
10. Tasha Cobbs Leonard, "You Know My Name," featuring Jimi Cravity, track 7 on *Heart. Passion. Pursuit.* Capitol Christian Music Group, Inc., 2017, YouTube, https://www.youtube.com/watch?v=t7owFiihXgg.
11. Jonathan McReynolds, "Overrated," track 4 on *My Truth*, MNRK Records LP, 2023, YouTube, https://www.youtube.com/watch?v=kElI6P4PnOU.
12. PJ Morton, "Lil' Too Heavy," track 9 on *Watch the Sun*, Fly Nerd Music (SESAC), Sony Music Publishing, 2022, YouTube, https://www.youtube.com/watch?v=OvBJU31VeuI.
13. PJ Morton and JoJo, "My Peace," featuring Mr. TalkBox, track 5 on *Watch the Sun*, Fly Nerd Music (SESAC), Sony Music Publishing, 2022, YouTube, https://www.youtube.com/watch?v=SurdkFO8X3k.
14. Naomi Raine, "Find My Peace," track 2 on *Back to Eden Pt. II*, The Bridge Collective, 2020, YouTube, https://www.youtube.com/watch?v=9RmtULuRSSM.
15. Naomi Raine, "Not Ready," track 5 on *Journey*, TRIBL Records, 2022, YouTube, https://www.youtube.com/watch?v=9AYiKiKtSoM.
16. Brian Courtney Wilson, "Fear Is Not Welcome," track 6

on *Still*, Motown Gospel, 2020, YouTube, https://www
.youtube.com/watch?v=euMgUotevog.

5. **How Single Women Thrive**
    1. Diane Proctor Reeder, *Listen: A Symphony of Faith* (Detroit: Written Images, 2013). Material owned by author and used by permission.
    2. Adrian Rogers, "How to Guard Your Heart," Bible Study Tools, updated February 17, 2023, https://www.biblestudytools.com/bible-study/topical-studies/how-to-guard-your-heart.html.
    3. Surbhi Sharma and Anurag Kumar, "Child Sexual Abuse in African American Society: A Study of Maya Angelou's Lived Trauma," *International Journal of Health Sciences* 6, no. 3 (June 2022): 8951–57, https://www.neliti.com/publications/431066/child-sexual-abuse-in-african-american-society-a-study-of-maya-angelous-lived-tr.
    4. "Why Are Older People Happier?," Association for Psychological Science, January 5, 2012, https://www.psychologicalscience.org/news/releases/better-research-is-needed-to-understand-why-elders-are-happier.html.

7. **Engaging Your Faith as African American Mothers**
    1. Brooke Auxier et al., "Parents' Attitudes—and Experiences—Related to Digital Technology," Pew Research Center, July 28, 2020, https://www.pewresearch.org/internet/2020/07/28/parents-attitudes-and-experiences-related-to-digital-technology/.
    2. Yaebin Kim, "Young Children in the Digital Age," University of Nevada, Reno, 2013, https://extension.unr.edu/publication.aspx?PubID=2600.
    3. Daniel J. Siegel and Tina Payne Bryson, *The Power of Showing Up: How Parental Presence Shapes Who Our Kids Become and How Their Brains Get Wired* (New York: Random House Publishing Group, 2020), 23.
    4. Pip Wilson and Ian Long, *Blob Bullying* (Abingdon, UK: Taylor & Francis, 2022), 74–75.
    5. "10 Questions to Ask Kids about Their Day at School,"

Scholastic Parents, April 14, 2021, https://www.scholastic.com/parents/school-success/10-questions-to-ask-your-child-about-his-day-school.html.

8. Mothers Loving a Different Kind of Brilliance

1. "Developmental Pediatricians/Psychologists," Caring Minds Psychological & Cognitive Wellness Centre, accessed September 26, 2024, https://www.aboutmyclinic.com/caringminds/terms/Developmental-Pediatricians-Psychologists/4016.

9. When the Ties That Bind Get Tested, Torn, and Transformed

1. Hui Lui, Debra Umberson, and Minle Xu, "Widowhood and Mortality: Gender, Race/Ethnicity, and the Role of Economic Resources," *Annals of Epidemiology* 45 (May 2020): 69–75, https://doi.org/10.1016/j.annepidem.2020.02.006; Valerie Schweizer, "Marriage to Divorce Ratio in the U.S.: Demographic Variation, 2018," *Family Profiles*, no. 27 (2019): https://www.bgsu.edu/ncfmr/resources/data/family-profiles/schweizer-marriage-divorce-ratio-demo-variation-fp-19-27.html.

10. Navigating the Digital World

1. Simon Kemp, "Digital 2023: The United States of America," DataReportal, February 9, 2023, https://datareportal.com/reports/digital-2023-united-states-of-america.
2. Kemp, "Digital 2023."
3. Kemp, "Digital 2023."
4. Emily A. Vogels, "Teens and Cyberbullying 2022," Pew Research Center, December 15, 2022, https://www.pewresearch.org/internet/2022/12/15/teens-and-cyberbullying-2022/.
5. Vogels, "Teens and Cyberbullying 2022."
6. Vogels, "Teens and Cyberbullying 2022."
7. Sherri Gordon, "The Real-Life Effects of Cyberbullying on Children and Teens," Parents, updated September 19,

2024, https://www.parents.com/what-are-the-effects-of-cyberbullying-460558.
8. "Federal Laws," Stopbullying.gov, updated October 6, 2021, https://www.stopbullying.gov/resources/laws/federal.
9. "Facts about Bullying," Stopbullying.gov, updated September 9, 2021, https://www.stopbullying.gov/resources/facts#_Laws.
10. "Sextortion: It's More Common Than You Think," ICE, updated August 22, 2023, https://www.ice.gov/features/sextortion.
11. "FBI and Partners Issue National Public Safety Alert on Sextortion Schemes," United States Attorney's Office, January 19, 2023, https://www.justice.gov/usao-sdin/pr/fbi-and-partners-issue-national-public-safety-alert-sextortion-schemes.
12. "New Surgeon General Advisory Raises Alarm about the Devastating Impact of the Epidemic of Loneliness and Isolation in the United States," US Department of Health and Human Services, May 3, 2023, https://www.hhs.gov/about/news/2023/05/03/new-surgeon-general-advisory-raises-alarm-about-devastating-impact-epidemic-loneliness-isolation-united-states.html.
13. Margaret Osborne, "An 'Epidemic' of Loneliness Threatens Health of Americans, Surgeon General Says," *Smithsonian*, May 10, 2023, https://www.smithsonianmag.com/smart-news/an-epidemic-of-loneliness-threatenes-health-of-americans-surgeon-general-says-180982142/.
14. Hwajin Yang et al., "Effects of Social Media and Smartphone Use on Body Esteem in Female Adolescents: Testing a Cognitive and Affective Model," *Children* 7, no. 9 (September 21, 2020): 148, https://doi.org/10.3390/children7090148.

11. Home and Career

1. This list offered here is partially inspired by "Work-Life Balance: Why It Matters to Black Professionals," OBSIDI,

July 11, 2022, https://obsidi.com/work-life-balance-why-it-matters-to-black-professionals/.
2. "Work-Life Balance: Tips for You and Your Family," Raisingchildren.net.au, updated June 6, 2024, https://raisingchildren.net.au/grown-ups/work-child-care/worklife-balance/work-life-balance.
3. Amy Gill, "How to Set Family Goals: 5 Best Tips and Tricks," SplashLearn, February 20, 2023, https://www.splashlearn.com/blog/how-to-set-family-goals-and-build-a-happy-family/.

12. Generational Wealth

1. "Mary Ellen Pleasant," National Park Service, accessed September 27, 2024, https://www.nps.gov/people/mary-ellen-pleasant.htm.
2. Farrell Evans, "How Neighborhoods Used Restrictive Housing Covenants to Block Nonwhite Families," History, December 15, 2022, https://www.history.com/news/racially-restrictive-housing-covenants.
3. Kedra Newsom Reeves et al., "Racial Equity in Banking Starts with Busting the Myths," Boston Consulting Group, February 2, 2021, https://www.bcg.com/publications/2021/unbanked-and-underbanked-households-breaking-down-the-myths-towards-racial-equity-in-banking.
4. "Financial Terms Glossary," Consumer Financial Protection Bureau, accessed September 27, 2024, https://www.consumerfinance.gov/consumer-tools/educator-tools/youth-financial-education/glossary/.
5. "Financial Terms Glossary."
6. "Financial Terms Glossary."
7. "Financial Terms Glossary."
8. Annamaria Lusardi and Nan J. Morrison, "Financial Literacy Transforms Students' Lives. Here's Where to Start," *Education Week*, July 25, 2019, https://www.edweek.org/teaching-learning/opinion-financial-literacy-transforms-students-lives-heres-where-to-start/2019/07.
9. Liz Knueven, "The Barriers Black Families Face in Building Generational Wealth," CNBC, updated May 26,

2023, https://www.cnbc.com/select/3-barriers-to-building
-generational-wealth-for-black-families/.
10. Knueven, "Barriers Black Families Face."
11. Knueven, "Barriers Black Families Face."
12. John Egan, "Survey Exposes Gaps in Black Ownership of Life Insurance," *Forbes Advisor*, November 2, 2020, https://www.forbes.com/advisor/life-insurance/black-ownership/.
13. "5 Ways to Fund Your Startup," Merrill, accessed September 27, 2024, https://www.ml.com/articles/how-to-fund-a-startup.html.
14. William Darity Jr. et al., "What We Get Wrong about Closing the Racial Wealth Gap," Samuel Dubois Cook Center on Social Equity at Duke University, April 1, 2018, https://socialequity.duke.edu/research-duke/what-we-get-wrong-about-closing-the-racial-wealth-gap/.

13. The Church

1. Quoted in Gail Collins, "The Women behind the Men," *New York Times*, September 22, 2007, https://www.nytimes.com/2007/09/22/opinion/22collins.html.
2. Meghan Weaver, "'Freedom!': Black Women Speak at the March on Washington for Jobs and Freedom," Martin Luther King Jr. Research and Education Institute, accessed September 27, 2024, https://kinginstitute.stanford.edu/freedom-black-women-speak-march-washington-jobs-and-freedom.
3. Anna Arnold Hedgeman, *The Gift of Chaos: Decades of American Discontent* (Oxford: Oxford University Press, 1977), 86.
4. Beth Allison Barr, *The Making of Biblical Womanhood: How the Subjugation of Women Became Gospel Truth* (Grand Rapids, MI: Brazos, 2021), 140.
5. "The Fontenelle Family, 1967," Gordon Parks Foundation, accessed October 7, 2024, https://www.gordonparksfoundation.org/gordon-parks/photography-archive/the-fontenelle-family-1967.
6. *Family Portrait*, directed by Patricia Riggen (London: PR Films, 2004), DVD.

7. Gordon Parks, "A Harlem Family," *Life*, March 8, 1968, 48.
8. *Family Portrait*.
9. John Edwin Mason and Jesse Newman, "Gordon Parks's Harlem Family Revisited," *Lens*, March 5, 2013, https://archive.nytimes.com/lens.blogs.nytimes.com/2013/03/05/gordon-parks-harlem-family-revisited/.
10. Rodney Stark, "The Truth about the Catholic Church and Slavery," *Christianity Today*, July 1, 2003, https://www.christianitytoday.com/ct/2003/julyweb-only/truth-about-catholic-church-slavery.html; Rick Boyd, "Many in Slave Sale Cited by Georgetown Toiled in Southern Md," *Southern Maryland News*, September 30, 2016, https://www.somdnews.com/enterprise/spotlight/many-in-slave-sale-cited-by-georgetown-toiled-in-southern/article_410468dc-f7f7-5b7a-b961-493468ca7d2a.html.
11. *The Color of Compromise Video Study: The Truth about the American Church's Complicity in Racism*, presented by Jemar Tisby (Grand Rapids, MI: Zondervan, 2020), DVD.
12. Steven D. Gish, *Desmond Tutu: A Biography* (New York: Bloomsbury Academic, 2004), 101.
13. Etim E. Okon, "Christian Missions and Colonial Rule in Africa: Objective and Contemporary Analysis," *European Scientific Journal* 10, no. 17 (June 2014): 199, https://eujournal.org/index.php/esj/article/view/3557/3397.
14. *Color of Compromise Video Study*.
15. Quoted in Kellie Carter Jackson, *Force and Freedom: Black Abolitionists and the Politics of Violence* (Philadelphia: University of Pennsylvania Press, 2020), 12.

14. Discipling through Love and Relationship

1. Corinna Suk Yin Ho, "Discipleship and Leadership Development through Small Groups by Mentoring and Coaching Practices" (PhD dissertation, Fuller Theological Seminary, 2018), 2–3, https://core.ac.uk/download/pdf/230651259.pdf.

15. My Journey Caring for Parents with Alzheimer's
1. Claire Samuels, "Caregiver Statistics: A Data Portrait of Family Caregiving," A Place for Mom, updated June 15, 2023, https://www.aplaceformom.com/caregiver-resources/articles/caregiver-statistics.
2. William B. Todd, "Potential Pathways for Circadian Dysfunction and Sundowning-Related Behavioral Aggression in Alzheimer's Disease and Related Dementias," *Frontiers in Neuroscience* 14 (September 3, 2020): 2, https://doi.org/10.3389/fnins.2020.00910.
3. Pierre Gérain and Emmanuelle Zech, "Informal Caregiver Burnout? Development of a Theoretical Framework to Understand the Impact of Caregiving," *Frontiers in Psychology* 10 (July 31, 2019): 2, https://doi.org/10.3389/fpsyg.2019.01748.

16. Overcoming Grief
1. Norvella Carter, "All Things?," in *Our Help: Devotions on Struggle, Victory, Legacy* (Grand Rapids, MI: Discovery House, 2018), 39–40.

17. Leaving a Legacy
1. Stephanie Gaines-Bryant, "Women Make Up Majority of Church Congregations, but Small Percent of Leadership," *WTOP News*, April 5, 2021, https://wtop.com/maryland/2021/04/women-make-up-majority-of-church-congregations-but-small-percent-of-leadership/; J. Kline Harrison, Margaret Chadwick, and Maria Scales, "The Relationship between Cross-Cultural Adjustment and the Personality Variables of Self-Efficacy and Self-Monitoring," *International Journal of Intercultural Relations* 20, no. 2 (March 1996): 167–88, https://www.sciencedirect.com/science/article/pii/0147176795000399.
2. Janice E. Hale, *Black Children: Their Roots, Culture, and Learning Styles* (Baltimore, MD: Johns Hopkins University Press, 1982), 14–17.

About the Contributors

ANGELA ABNEY, PhD, is an assistant professor of Elementary Education at Langston University, Langston, Oklahoma. Dr. Abney is the assistant director of Clinical Experience and University Supervisor for Preservice Teachers. She was a public educator for thirty years. She served in campus leadership as a department head and instructional specialist for fifteen years. She also served on the Superintendent's Advisory Board and as a mentor and master teacher for novice teachers. She currently works as an educational consultant specializing in equity audits and parent involvement. Dr. Abney is the mother of three adult daughters and three grandchildren.

MICHELLE BRISCOE, MACL, is a retired educator and current teaching leader for Bible Study Fellowship in Dallas, Texas. She served as a teacher in the Dallas Independent School District for seventeen years. She then served as an administrator at A. W. Brown, a charter school also in Dallas, Texas, for five years. Her professional career has been dedicated to serving and modeling the importance of culturally responsive teaching. She recently earned her master's in Christian leadership from the Dallas Theological Seminary. The pinnacle of her career has been her advocacy for the inclusion of children and youth with disabilities in public school and faith-based settings.

NORVELLA P. CARTER, PhD, is professor emerita of Education and retired endowed chair in Urban Education at Texas A&M

University, in College Station, Texas. She also served as interim chair of the Department of Education at Trinity University in San Antonio, Texas. Dr. Carter earned her doctorate at Loyola University, Chicago. She has numerous awards for her work in urban education and is an author and editor of many publications. Her latest book is an international publication entitled *Intersectionality of Race, Ethnicity, Class, and Gender in Teaching and Teacher Education*. A highlight of Dr. Carter's career was providing expert testimony for a congressional hearing at the Capitol Building, Washington, DC, on educating Black children. This was sponsored by the Children's Caucus and Black Caucus. She is married to William Carter. They have seven children and eighteen grandchildren.

KELLIE CARTER JACKSON is the Michael and Denise Kellen associate professor in the Department of Africana Studies at Wellesley College, Wellesley, Massachusetts. She received her doctorate from Columbia University in New York City. She is author of *Force and Freedom: Black Abolitionists and the Politics of Violence*. Her essays have been featured in *The New York Times*, *Washington Post*, *The Atlantic*, *The Guardian*, *The Los Angeles Times*, *NPR*, and other outlets. She is the host of *You Get a Podcast!* and cohost of *This Day in Esoteric Political History* on Radiotopia. Carter Jackson's newest book is *We Refuse: A Forceful History of Black Resistance* (Basic Books, 2024).

VICTORIA CARTER JONES, PhD, earned her doctorate in educational administration from Texas A&M University, College Station, Texas. Her scholarly work and teaching concentrate on secondary and urban education, leadership in public schools, and culturally responsive administration in higher education. Dr. Carter Jones has published on issues related to teaching African American and Latinx learners, culturally responsive pedagogy, diversity, and social justice. She currently works as an educational consultant specializing in professional development of teachers and administrators in secondary education.

JOYCE M. DINKINS is a writer, author, and editor, and a contributing editor for this book. Joyce Dinkins Publishing LLC owns and directs Publishing in Color (publishingincolor.com) to help increase diversity in Christian publishing. As former executive editor of the *Our Daily Bread* devotional, she became the founding editor of the ministry's VOICES Collection. As the founding editor of David C Cook's *Echoes* curriculum, she earned a master's of curriculum and instruction at Colorado Christian University. A prolific writer and editor, she has contributed hundreds of stories, articles, and books and earned several industry awards. She and her husband, Minister Steven Dinkins, are blessed with three adult children. Throughout their marriage, they have served as leaders in Christian publishing, in Christian education with new church plants, and in local and international missions.

MYRA HANEY-SINGLETON, EdD, is an innovative academic leader with more than twenty-five years of higher education administration experience. She has dedicated much of her professional endeavors to the mission of student affairs by designing programs, building teams, and mentoring with a keen awareness of the challenges that come with recruiting and retaining a diverse academy of learners. Dr. Haney-Singleton prioritizes working with initiatives focused on the empowerment of youth and women. She is active in numerous regional, state, and national organizations. She also enjoys supporting the music ministry of her husband, Dr. Wayne M. Singleton, who is the minister of music of Mother Emanuel AME Church in Charleston, South Carolina.

VICKI HARRIS is the chief people and culture officer and oversees Diversity, Equity, and Inclusion at Our Daily Bread Ministries, a global organization with thirty-eight offices around the world. She earned a dual master's degree in human resources and business administration and received two honorary doctorate degrees in the humanities. Harris trains and develops leaders globally and in her local church and community. She is also the executive leader of Global Women Who Lead, a program designed to train and inspire female leaders to pursue their God-given gifts and talents.

GEORGIA A. HILL pastors Life Church Riverside, an Evangelical Covenant Church based in Detroit, Michigan, that was planted online in 2020 during the global pandemic. Reverend Dr. Hill is an attorney who has taught African American history at Wayne State University and has served as a mentor and instructor at Ecumenical Theological Seminary. She has been a leader and team member on mission trips to Africa, Central America, and the Middle East and has joyfully baptized believers in Liberia and Israel. Her devotions have appeared in several publications. She is a graduate of Harvard University, Howard University Law School, and McCormick Theological Seminary.

CHINA M. JENKINS serves as the dean of Academic Support and Resources and assistant professor of Education at Houston Christian University in Houston, Texas. She earned her PhD in educational human resource development from Texas A&M University in College Station, Texas. In her career in higher education, Dr. Jenkins taught at university and community colleges, directed faculty development centers, and created programming for faculty, administrators, and students nationwide. Dr. Jenkins is a public speaker who trains academics on issues concerning leadership, professional development, and teaching in higher education. She is married to Franklin Jenkins, and they have two sons, Donovan and Trace.

GENALYN L. JERKINS empowers and serves others within the educational, humanitarian, and philanthropic arenas. She earned a doctorate in educational administration and leadership at the University of Houston in Houston, Texas. With more than twenty years of service in the public, collegiate, and private education sectors, Dr. Jerkins served in various capacities, including middle school principal within the public school system and adjunct professor in higher education. Beyond her academic endeavors, she leads the Houston Fund for Social Justice and Economic Equity. She is also the founder of Refresh, a 501(c)(3) organization. With more than fifteen years of experience in the nonprofit sector, she helps to establish nonprofits.

DENEESE L. JONES is professor emerita and vice president for Academic Affairs emerita at Trinity University, San Antonio, Texas. She also served as provost of Drake University, dean of the College of Education and Human Services at Longwood University, and associate dean of the Graduate School at the University of Kentucky. While speaking and publishing extensively on equity pedagogy for literacy instruction, inclusive excellence, and leadership development for forty years, she initiated the first Call Me MISTER program in the state of Virginia. She is married to Stephen Jones, and they have two daughters, three grandsons, and one great-granddaughter.

ALTRICIA LARKE is an instructional coach in Augusta, Georgia, and has been an educator for more than twenty years. Prior to working in the Richmond County School System, she served students and teachers around the greater Houston area, with Fort Bend, Klein, and Spring Independent School Districts. She began her career as a science teacher with Bryan ISD while earning her advanced degrees at Texas A&M University, College Station, Texas. She received her undergraduate degree from South Carolina State University, Orangeburg, South Carolina, where she was initiated into the dynamic sisterhood of Delta Sigma Theta Sorority, Incorporated.

PATRICIA J. LARKE is a retired professor emerita from the Department of Teaching, Learning, and Culture, Texas A&M University, College Station, Texas. She has been a scholar in the field of multicultural education for more than thirty-five years. She also has more than 125 publications, including journal articles, book chapters, monographs, and three coedited books. Her latest coedited book is *Cultivating Achievement, Respect and Empowerment (CARE) for PreK–12 African American Girls: Implications for Access, Equity, and Achievement*. She currently resides in Beech Island, South Carolina, with her husband, Dr. Alvin Larke Jr., retired pastor of Cumberland AME Church in Aiken, South Carolina.

ADRIA E. LUSTER serves as an educator in the Atlanta area. She has dedicated her life to serving at-risk children. Prior to earning her PhD in education, she received specialist, master's, and bachelor's degrees in related fields. Dr. Luster has presented at numerous workshops and conferences to local, national, and televised audiences. As a cancer survivor, she encourages women to focus on self-care practices that promote physical, emotional, and spiritual health. Dr. Luster has also assisted various educational entities, faith-based organizations, and empowerment coaches with developing their professional curricula. In addition, she has authored numerous inspirational publications.

MICHELLE M. OBLETON is principal of Lions Math and Science Christian Academy in Waukegan, Illinois. She has a bachelor of arts degree in religious education from William Tyndale College in Farmington Hills, Michigan, and serves as the executive director of ministries at Waukegan Community Church. Obleton is founder and director of WINGS (Women in Godly Service) Ministries and teaches women's Bible study, preparing women for leadership. In addition, she serves as a national speaker for women's organizations and churches. Her husband, Dr. Winfred Obleton, pastors Waukegan Community Church. They have two adult children and one grandson.

QUINITA OGLETREE is a clinical assistant professor in the School of Education at Texas A&M University, College Station, Texas. Dr. Ogletree has written journal articles and presented internationally and nationally. Her publications focus on urban and multicultural education. She married her college sweetheart, Pastor Johnny D. Ogletree III, senior pastor of First Metropolitan Church in Houston, Texas. They have five daughters.

KARON PARKER's education afforded her the opportunity to teach nine years in private Christian schools and the privilege of homeschooling (until the eighth grade) her own children. Her dedication to ongoing self-improvement and life enrichment fuels her passion to educate young minds and train the next generation. She is married to Matthew Parker, president of the Institute for Black Family Development. They have five adult children.

DIANE PROCTOR REEDER writes primarily on spiritual topics that move readers to think more deeply about their faith. She has served as a writer and an editor for works from Our Daily Bread Publishing's VOICES, Urban Ministries, Parker Books, and numerous authors. She has written plays that imagine the interior lives of biblical women, which have been performed in Michigan, Ohio, and Illinois. Her most recent book is *A Cloud of Women: The Powerful Connection between Black Women and Women of the Bible*, coauthored with Dr. Georgia A. Hill (VOICES from Our Daily Bread Ministries, 2024). Proctor Reeder is founder and owner of Written Images and president of Strategic Partners International, an integrated communications firm. She has a BA in journalism and a master's in public policy from the University of Michigan. She is a proud mother of two and grandmother of four.

SELENA D. TATE is an associate professor and graduate program coordinator at Prairie View A&M University, where she has served since 2017. She earned her doctorate in counselor education and supervision from the University of Akron, specializing in marriage and family counseling. She holds a master's degree in marriage and family therapy from the University of Akron and a bachelor's degree in music therapy from Sam Houston State University. Her research interests include both mental health wellness and family violence. When not working, she enjoys spending time with family, baking, gardening, yoga, watching British murder mysteries, and listening to music and audiobooks.

DEBBYE TURNER BELL is a veterinarian, author, corporate trainer, ordained minister, speaker, wife, mother, and Miss America 1990. She is the author of *Courageous Faith: A Lifelong Pursuit of Faith Over Fear* (VOICES from Our Daily Bread Ministries, 2021). Dr. Turner Bell provides leadership development training as founder and CEO of Debbye Turner Bell Consulting. During her twenty-five-year career in broadcast journalism, Dr. Turner Bell was a staff correspondent for CBS News in New York City and an anchor for a global cable news network. Dr. Turner Bell has served on many national boards, including the National Council on Youth Leadership and the Children's Miracle Network, and on an advisory board at the National Institutes of Health.

DIANA WANDIX-WHITE is assistant professor of Multicultural Education at the University of Houston Clear Lake. She grew up in a loving Christian home that valued family and community. She earned her bachelor of arts in communication studies at Washburn University of Topeka, Kansas, a master of education from Prairie View A&M University, and her PhD in curriculum and instruction, with a focus in urban education, from Texas A&M University. She is the first African American woman to serve on the board of trustees for the College of Biblical Studies. She and her husband have four adult children and four grandchildren.

GWENDOLYN C. WEBB is an associate professor in both the Department of Educational Administration and Human Resource Development and the Department of Teaching, Learning, and Culture at Texas A&M University (TAMU). She is also the associate director of the Educational Leadership Research Center at TAMU. She is the coauthor of a book on African American girls: *Cultivating Achievement, Respect, and Empowerment (CARE) for African American Girls in PreK–12 Settings: Implications for Access, Equity, and Achievement*. She has received service and research awards through the years. A highlight of Dr. Webb's career was receiving the George Bush Excellence Award in Public Service. She has two children and three grandchildren.

KAMALA V. WILLIAMS is a mother, grandmother, and in-home caregiver for her loving parents, James and Claude Stewart. She, along with her late husband and children, provided care for her parents for more than nine years and walked with them through the various stages of Alzheimer's disease. She has worked in ministry at First Metropolitan Church in Houston, Texas, for more than twenty-five years. Dr. Williams is the director of Prairie View A&M University's Northwest Houston Center in Houston, Texas, as well as an adjunct instructor in the College of Education at Texas A&M University in College Station, Texas.

See Us.

Hear Us.

Experience VOICES.

VOICES amplifies the strengths, struggles, and courageous faith of Black image bearers of God.

Podcasts, blogs, books, films, and more ...

Find out more at **experiencevoices.org**

Who do you turn to when you have nothing left to give?

Draw from the perfect source of strength by seeking Scripture and prayer to sustain you. Your faith is ready fuel for the self-care you need as you look after others!

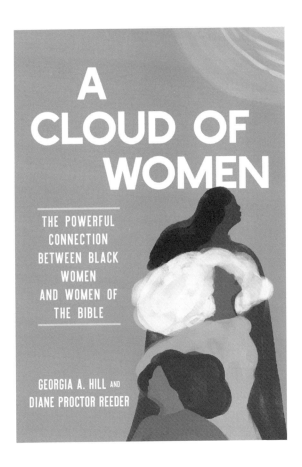

A Cloud of Women elevates dozens of biblical women, pointing out parallels between their life experiences and the lives of contemporary and historical Black women. See God's eternal influence on the lives of these inspiring figures and realize the opportunities for your own service and impact today.

There Is Hope

In this 90-day devotional, you'll encounter unique daily readings with Scripture, godly wisdom, warm guidance, and reminders that even Jesus and His followers cried out to God during depressing times.

How do you deepen your relationship with and understanding of God?

At the source.
Get to know Him through His own Word, the Bible.

Know Him devotes 365 days to revealing the character of God solely through Scripture. These passages, drawn from every book of the Bible, highlight 12 unchanging attributes of our Creator. Whether you're new to the Bible or a longtime reader, you'll gain a deeper awe of God's holiness, transcendence, and glory along with a renewed appreciation for His mercy, justice, and truth.

Buy It Today

Seek and she will find.

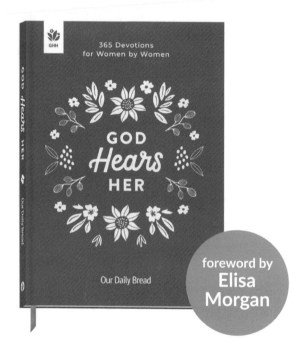

You'll be reminded that you are intimately known and deeply loved by your heavenly Father when you spend time with Him while reading *God Hears Her*. The personal stories, along with Scripture passages and inspirational quotes, reassure you that you are heard, cherished, and enough—no matter what you're going through.

Order today

Spread the Word by Doing One Thing.

- Give a copy of this book as a gift.
- Share the QR code link via your social media.
- Write a review of this book on your blog, favorite bookseller's website, or at ODB.org/store.
- Recommend this book to your church, small group, or book club.

Connect with us. [f] [☉]

Our Daily Bread Publishing
PO Box 3566, Grand Rapids, MI 49501, USA
Email: books@odb.org

Love God. Love Others.
with Our Daily Bread.

Your gift changes lives.

Connect with us.

Our Daily Bread Publishing
PO Box 3566, Grand Rapids, MI 49501, USA
Email: books@odb.org